MARSH CREEK PRESS

Published by Marsh Creek Press, PO Box 700, Pocatello, Idaho 83204 1-208-232-3535.

Distributed by Betterway Books, an imprint of F&W Publications, Inc., 1507 Dana Avenue, Cincinnati, OH 45207. 1-800-289-0963.

ISBN 0-937750-19-0

Illustrator: Craig LaGory
Editor: Carol Cartaino
Production Manager: Tobi Haynes

Excerpts from *How to Have a 48-Hour Day*, copyright © 1996 by Don Aslett. Reprinted by permission.

Excerpts from *The 10 Biggest Lies*, copyright © 1986 by Don Aslett. Reprinted by permission.

Library of Congress Cataloging-in-Publication Data

Aslett, Don, 1935-
   How to handle 1,000 things at once : a fun guide to mastering home & personal management / Don Aslett
        p.   cm.
     ISBN 0-937750-19-0 (pbk.)
   1. Home economics. 2. Time management. I. Title.
   TX147.A78   1997
   640--dc21
                        97-26787
                           CIP

Also by Don Aslett

More help with Personal Management:
How to Have a 48-Hour Day

Help for Packrats:
Clutter's Last Stand
Not for Packrats Only
Clutter Free! Finally & Forever
The Office Clutter Cure

How to Clean:
Is There Life After Housework?
Do I Dust or Vacuum First?
Make Your House Do the Housework
Don Aslett's Clean in a Minute
Who Says It's a Woman's Job to Clean?
500 Terrific Ideas for Cleaning Everything
Pet Clean-Up Made Easy
How Do I Clean the Moosehead?
Don Aslett's Stainbuster's Bible
The Cleaning Encyclopedia

Professional Cleaning Books:
Cleaning Up for a Living
The Professional Cleaner's Personal Handbook
How to Upgrade & Motivate Your Cleaning Crews
Construction Cleanup
Painting Without Fainting

Business Books:
How to be #1 With Your Boss
Everything I Needed to Know About Business
I Learned in the Barnyard
Speak Up!

How to Handle 1,000 Things at Once

Table of Contents

LIFE: The Puzzle of 1,000,000 Pieces

If the real beginning of most brilliant management could be isolated, I wouldn't be surprised if it could be traced back to putting a puzzle together. Here in embryo are the principles of management A-Z.

We see the beautiful picture on that box lid, just like we imagine the finished product of any project or mission we have. Then we pour it all out and there is a big pile of random parts from which we have to pull off the picture or the project. Now it needs to be put together.

First, both in puzzles and in life, we start with some outlines or boundaries—the edges. In life and on the puzzle table these are easy to identify and give us some parameters for the goal at hand. Then we put together the most striking and obvious parts of the picture or the project. We save the vague (the sky and trees and everything else that looks more or less the same) till the last, figuring—rightly—that once the other pieces have been eliminated there will be less to paw through and try to piece together.

During this process, there are, within the puzzle and the project, sudden breakthroughs, losses, arguments, false hopes, and wrong fits. There are the times we almost have it all together and someone messes it up or accidentally upends the table. There are the light areas, the dark areas, the last piece, the lost piece... the times two puzzles get mixed together (talk about a test of management), the times we try to force things to fit, and end up regretting it, and the times we swear a certain piece isn't there and later it turns up in plain sight!

Like so many of our personal management challenges, we often work at puzzles in time fragments. We may concentrate on a section, put it together independently, and only later join it to the big picture.

In personal management and in puzzledom, there are those who help in spurts and those who stick it out (not even going to the bathroom until the tower is all together). Plus, of course, those who criticize and judge and advise, never fitting a piece or turning a hand toward completion.

Then, as the reward of all our work, we finally see a finished puzzle and a finished project... and amazingly, we don't admire it long. We're soon onto the next challenge, because the fun of all this is in the doing!

Introduction

Knowing, having, being, and owning don't mean much in life if you can't "get it all together" so you can enjoy it. That means **managing**, or processing the parade of heavy traffic that marches in and out of our lives, and making those 1,000 everyday things work together—and work together well—for a smooth, happy, and productive living.

Whatever you do, don't let "Big Business," "Top Executives," "Fortune 500," and all those overused power labels bulldoze or bully you. The corporate world doesn't own the word "management." There are plenty of homemakers out there right this minute in ordinary homes who could manage the socks off most of the inhabitants of "mahogany row" in any big office. (They don't need a business degree or a power tie, either.)

"MANAGEMENT," that big, scary word so often suggested as the solution for all that ails us, isn't the exclusive province of business, educational, financial, or political people. Where do we need it more than at home, where 90% of the real goings-on of life are? At home we have all the clear-cut, thoughtfully established tasks and responsibilities businesspeople do every day of our lives (no weekends or holidays off), plus hundreds of competing wildly varied interruptions and mundane demands on us, right at the same time.

At the office or factory, in business, we wear only a couple of hats at most and work within a framework, a neatly established structure. In the real world, at home, where that quality of life we're working so hard for really comes to bear, we wear a hundred hats and work in a free-for-all. Our ordinary everyday activities are where we **really** need to know how to handle and manage things.

Work has rules and boundaries, policies and procedures; it's a carefully controlled comfort zone for "adults only." Home doesn't—it's every man, woman, and child's game.

The biggest management challenges in life are not in the boardroom, but the living room. Yes, at home, where we have to deal with and juggle family and friends, near and far, schoolwork, shopping, cleaning, home maintenance, car maintenance, yard care, finances, health, grooming, community and church activities and service. Even pursuing our own and our children's favorite sports and hobbies, taking a hassle-free vacation, and pet care–it's all management! Management is actually much more important to a grade school kid or a new mother than it is to the biggest businessman.

Self and Home Management is About 90% of the Picture

I need to repeat this again and again because most people think the word management is synonymous with "business"–not so! Most of the management maneuvers that enhance life and make people successful are personal management skills–how they handle themselves and their domestic responsibilities.

It's at home and in personal life where 90% of MANAGEMENT is really needed.

Let me use a little graphic here to underline this.

REAL LIFE MANAGEMENT NEEDS

Here are some (by no means all) of the things a home manager has to be concerned with:

moneymaking work, to make a living
financial matters (handling, managing, and dispersing money)
child care
providing housing, heat, electricity, water, etc.
supplying the household (buying and storing everything needed to keep it running)
maintaining and protecting the things the household members own and use
cleaning and dejunking the house, garage, any other buildings
improvements and repairs to the house and any other buildings
yard care and gardening, if any
maintenance and repair of tools and equipment
planning and scheduling
recordkeeping
the health and fitness of all household members
the spiritual/emotional welfare of all household members
the education of all household members
the feeding/nutrition of all household members
clothing all household members
transporting all household members everywhere they need to go (and maintenance of transport vehicles)
the appearance of all household members
maintenance of the human relationships within the household
the entertainment/recreation for all household members
socializing with others outside the household
things made necessary by holidays and the change of seasons
animal/pet care

At work, the onslaught of needs and must-do's is served up in controllable eight- or maybe ten-hour installments. At home all those demands and schedules, lists, jobs, requirements, needs, wants, problems, complications, and cravings are leaping, barking, groaning, roaring, and begging for us to feed, cuddle, care for, and clean up after them CONTINUALLY... 24 hours a day... And it only gains momentum as the years go on.

Management is the skill of organizing and lining up all this to function in a rhythm of efficiency. Not only for ourselves, but our mates, our children, the Little League, the hospital committee, church group, PTA, art class, ad infinitum.

This book is for the real business of the world, the business of home, self, family, and friends. Managing it well will give you goosebumps of excitement every day... what a thrilling way to live!

You say the "Home Manager of the Year" award seems to always belong to someone else, they seem to have all the secrets and skills to make things click efficiently? That really isn't so, any one of us is a potential master manager.

Here in these pages are the secrets and shortcuts of good, effective management for every one of us, so we can handle 1,000 things at once, or more! And not just be able to cope with multiple people and multiple tasks, but be happy with the results.

All of Those Hats Off...
to the Ladies!

Men, HEAR ME OUT before you sue me for sexual discrimination. In many of the big corporate "time management" seminars I do, I make the statement that I've hired over 100,000 people in my life and have found that women can generally outmanage men about two to one. Many of the Ph.D. and MBA business managers flinch and groan as I then go on to prove that this summary is pretty on target. For most of their lives women usually have more things around home and elsewhere to manage than men, and they have less time to do it in. As a result, from having more to do all the time than they can do—but they have to do it—most evolve to superior managers.

My thanks and awe to the many women of great ability who have taught me and shown me ways to manage, and even sent in some of the ideas used in this book. I've become a better manager in my domestic and my business life because of them. Thanks and keep the shortcuts coming, we'll do another book!

Thanks especially to:

Jeena Nilson, Alison Herron, Susan Waddell, Martha Jacob, Jenny Behymer, Mary Wylie, Martha Chambers, Sue Davis, Sue Ryan, Ruth Bleiberg, Ruth Kirley, Carol Cartaino, Tobi Haynes, Tim Beeler, and the Belfast, Ohio, Craft and Chat Club.

Don Aslett

Meet the Manager: YOU!

ften we feel like a squirrel desperately running the wheel—performing all kinds of tricks and tasks beautifully, but getting and going nowhere. So we say: I'm going to get my ducks in a row... get it together... get organized... get my house in order... get my life in order... When we think this, we are thinking... MANAGEMENT.

Management is the process of handling, organizing, controlling, regulating, governing, accomplishing all of the duties/jobs/events of life. It's not only what we have to do to handle our daily and "tomorrow" objectives and problems, but "next week," "next month," "next year" and the rest of our lives, too. Every single one of us has to do this—you and me and every third grader, truck driver, coach, mother of eight (or one), cook, cab driver, farmer, college student, teacher, salesperson, and janitor!

Managing is just navigating ourselves and others through all of life's situations and challenges to our end goal. It's the art of handling 50 or 100 or 1,000 things at once, and having them all turn out well, the way **you** wanted them. We all have plans and dreams and needs and assignments and jobs. Managing is how we make them mesh efficiently and satisfactorily.

Not a single one of us—no matter what our age, sex, race, creed, color, or status—is exempt from MANAGEMENT. Everyone has to manage. It isn't something you get into business to do, or get a job to do. It isn't a profession or a position, it's just a big part of everyone's everyday living. We start managing (our parents) when we're about two months old and go on from there. We manage the food on our plate, our vacations, a family, a project—everything.

What if you had all the hundreds of parts for the perfect motor laying out on the garage floor and just shoveled them under the hood, and tried to start the car? It would never run. Likewise management isn't just a question of the elements present. It's the elements fit together for a purpose, assembling things in proper order to run smoothly.

Even driving a car, for example. We look forward to it from the time we first touch a steering wheel as a tot. Finally on our list of things to do it appears: learn to drive. Like lots of things we launch into, it looks simple, as if putting together starting, steering, and stopping would be no big deal. But after our first excursion, we get out of the car shaky and sweaty, and every dog in the neighborhood has run for cover. There are black tire marks on the pavement and two wounded stop signs in our wake—and everyone watching out of the rest home windows is on the edge of their seats. We've found out driving is a little more than starting, steering, and stopping. It's a few extras like 175 rules of the road, reading signs, watching others, regulating your speed, handling distractions, knowing your way, coping with bad roads and breakdowns, weather, and about 300 other possibilities including the very real likelihood of accidents, even death, once your hands are on the wheel. We have the desire and ability to drive, but all of this is overwhelming. "How can drivers whiz around confidently and flawlessly with no accidents or violations for the past thirty years?" The answer is management.

Good game players are managers, too, right there on the chessboard, Monopoly board, poker table or puzzle table. The ability to remember things, keep them in or-der, consider their relationships with each other, take advantage of timing, track down the missing parts, find a fit, etc., is all part of management. As kids we played bingo and thought that us-ing two or three cards at once was hot stuff. A while ago I visited with an expert adult bingo player who regularly uses 5-10 cards at a time, noting that she'd in-creased my respect for such management. "Are you kidding?" she said. "I know a woman down at the senior center who uses 50 cards at a time, **without beans!** She doesn't cover the numbers as they're called, just keeps track of them in her mind and does it errorlessly. In fact, one old greedy fellow down there has played 100 cards at a time." Just one more little demonstration of what we all could do in our life's dealings if we "set our minds to it!"

The more we do (the wider a swath we cut in life) the more we will get or have to manage, to organize and set up some order and means of accomplish-ment. Our ability to take it all in and control it is management. We might as well face it. If we want to live well we have to manage well.

Good management is almost spiri-tual when you think about it, because it's the single biggest influence on the quality of our life.

Management, in brief:

The ability to handle and effectively control the traffic of your life.

- *Use your time, emotions, and money well.*
- *Keep a lot going at once.*
- *Move along what you want moved along.*
- *Do more things well in less time.*

Meet the pilot: You

Piloting is what a good manager does. You may never have seen your-self as a pilot, but what you direct (in this case, your life), you pilot. You decide what you fly, when, and how. It's all up to you—how high, low, fast, slow, and how level you fly, who you take with you, how long you're up, when you leave, when you return, where you take off, where you land, and where you go! You navigate and you steer, and up in the air there are many more directions to worry about than just right, left, or straight ahead. You decide to fly around storms or through them, or to land and take a hike. In short: You govern the goings-on in your life, it's your responsibility.

The key to your success as a manager is right here. Realizing and accepting that *you* determine your every direction and duty. As managers our biggest failure is confusing ourselves with one of the passengers, thinking we can just select a seat and cruise through life. Being the pilot is much more committed and complicated than merely sitting back with a bag of peanuts. Most people are content to let someone else fly them through life. That's fine, but if you want to reach **your** destination, **your** goals, **your** wants and wishes, then **you** are the pilot, you have no choice in the matter. If you can't accept that, then you'll never be a manager, because **to manage is to pilot**.

The day we understand this and take the wheel of our home and life or the project, ball team, our relationships, possessions—anything we need to care for and manage, the day we take control of it, start answering for the direction, speed, and all repairs, we'll at last begin to manage.

You are the only one who can manage your own life. Don't wait for someone to come along and solve all your problems and tell you how to make your life a nonstop flawless production. It will never happen. You'll get a few helps, but remember, there's a lot of difference between **help** and **do!**

Dispelling some old myths about management

So many people are terrified of the word "management," almost afraid to be a manager because the aura of the word is so intimidating! A great deal of hot air surrounds the subject of "management," seemingly placing the mastery of good management out of the reach of we ordinary people—teens, seniors, or anywhere in the middle. Such as:

1. Good management is dependent on education or degrees.

College degrees are no assurance of good management, even if the degree is in management. Some people (regardless of their education or IQ) can barely manage three or five happenings at once, while others can

handle 2,000 things masterfully without even breaking out in a sweat.

Knowing more doesn't automatically result in handling things better. If you were raised by a one-armed grandmother who got everything done, you'll probably be way ahead of an MBA. For years I've watched people file in and out of expensive management seminars and courses, showing little or no improvement afterward. Knowledge doesn't manage, nor degrees nor certificates of merit. Lack of direction or ambition, poor decision making and timing don't disappear with the accumulation of knowledge. Educational status has little to do with our management ability—in fact we're often better off not having our good sense altered by the theories of the classroom.

Management is a strange animal, it seems to have little to do with education, less with vocation, but a lot to do with imagination. And we all have quite an imagination!

2. "I have to be mean, hard, and tough to be a good manager."

So wrong! The soft and gentle people are always the best managers. They get things done by cultivating and coaxing and motivating instead of giving orders. Sure management responsibilities mean you take some heat and flak and that you aren't in a position to please all the people all the time. But good managers can easily make people like them better, not less. You can become even more popular by making things run right.

3. "If I had more money, things would run smoother."

Wrong again. Extra money generally means greater inefficiency in running things because we too often try to buy things done instead of working them done. More money gives you more opportunity to make bad judgments. Wealth can give you flexibility, but don't confuse it with ability.

4. "A lot of good management is just plain luck."

Not so! Luck is almost nonexistent in the good manager's mind and vocabulary. In the good manager dictionary, luck is defined: Planning and endurance!

5. And finally... "If I stay in the battle of life long enough, fighting, trying, hoping, praying, 'it' (good management and success) will surely come..."

This is the slickest of all illusions when it comes to management, because it's at least half true. Yes, we do pick up some mighty good management maneuvers by absorption, just hanging in and around. Mere exposure may mean some good management qualities rub off—or are forced—on us.

But counting on chance to learn management or to get through life is too much of a gamble for me. Don't we all like advancement better than dead center? Controlling things better than being controlled? The things we let happen never come out as well as the things we make happen.

How well we manage is kind of like how well we play the piano. We can use one finger and hunt and peck one key at a time to produce some sort of recognizable result and get by. We can use one hand and get some harmony and double tones. Or we can put all ten fingers to the keyboard and smoothly and effort- lessly turn out some real music, pleasing ourselves and everyone around us.

That's managing. And you can do it.

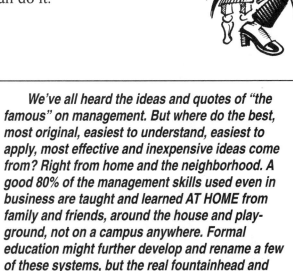

We've all heard the ideas and quotes of "the famous" on management. But where do the best, most original, easiest to understand, easiest to apply, most effective and inexpensive ideas come from? Right from home and the neighborhood. A good 80% of the management skills used even in business are taught and learned AT HOME from family and friends, around the house and play- ground, not on a campus anywhere. Formal education might further develop and rename a few of these systems, but the real fountainhead and finishing school of top management is the home.

So go directly to those "1,000 things handlers" you stand in awe of and watch and ask. (What a source!)

In the type like this in the following pages, I've included a few "how-to-do-its" from some of those many other master home managers out there. Agreeing with them or not is your preroga- tive, but when the people who employ them are able to manage a multitude of home dealings, I stop, look, listen, and list. (I think you'll discover they sound like some of your own ideas, too.)

On Target: YOUR Target

he game was tied, just seconds to go, and the crowd was in a frenzy. It was the big final game of the season, for the championship. The pressure on both teams was incredible. A nervous, over-cautious pass was intercepted and in a desperate scramble, glory be! Craig Young, the fine senior star of the home team, came up with the ball. The crowd leaped to their feet as Young weaved, faked, spun, and darted around, slipped through, over, and under the opposing players who were trying to stop him. With a final whirl and a quick shot, one second before the buzzer, he slammed the ball through the net.

The game was over, but Young's team didn't win. In his finest form he had scored the winning basket all right, but the visitors went home with the trophy. All because of a slight technicality. The basket Young managed and maneuvered the ball into so brilliantly was the other team's basket!

This happens every year in every sport, and in lots of other places: perfect application and technique, but wrong goal. It occurs millions of times a day in all of our personal management, too. We're sincere and busy, but often confused on direction. All chance of good, sound management is reduced—if not eliminated—if you don't know what you want or where you're going. Because you have nothing to manage for or toward. This is the second big secret of management: **direction**, a target.

Most poor management doesn't come from poor management skills or technique, it comes from us not really knowing **what we want** and **where we're going.**

Look around and listen! When most people are asked where they're going and why:

"I'm just going to head out and see what happens."

"Kind of depends on the weather."

"What do you think I ought to do?"

"Well, nowhere particular, just goin' west."

"We're just going to cruise, Dad, drive around."

"I don't know, I'll see what comes up."

It took me years of answering calls and requests from friends and family as to "How do you get so much done, Don?" before I was able figure out why so many people put out so much effort without seeming to really get anywhere. I finally realized that most of my own ability to manage was no brilliance on my part, it came from wise and caring parents who clearly and consistently established direction—always a plain and important target to shoot at.

In my young entire life, from the age of six on, I can't remember one single day where I didn't know what was up, or the next day wasn't planned and outlined. Whether it was a work, play, church, or community project or agenda, my folks always told us exactly what was to be done and why.

Nowadays, when we ask people where they'll be next week or what they're going to do next Sunday, we hear them say, "Oh, I don't know. Get up, read the paper, sit around, wait to see what happens, we might visit…" etc. In my deepest brain cell I can't even imagine that. How can you run your life if you don't know where you're going? If you haven't decided what you **want** to do and be for your eighty or so years on this earth, then there isn't much point in knowing how to manage. If you don't know where you're going, you don't know what to pack or prepare, or where to push or pull. You just have to sit out in the stream of life and let it sweep you where it's going. If there's no purpose or target, there's no reason to manage. On the local school board once we held a trial for some high school kids who stole a parking lot "bumper." I was intrigued, what would anyone want with such a thing? When asked why they swiped that ugly 200-pound hunk of concrete, the answer was: "**they had no idea**." They were out stealing and the bumper was the only thing around, so they stole it. You can't even manage good, smart thievery if you don't know what you want!

"General direction" isn't enough, because it, too, is difficult if not impossible, to manage. It's like someone after a "good job" or "the good life." You ask them for a specific and they can't give you an answer. You can't always get exactly what you want, but you have to **know** what you want.

Playing basketball as a kid, I was a reasonably good shooter, but seemed to level off in high school somewhere below maximum efficiency. One day the coach took me aside and pointed out that instead of shooting in the general direction of the basket, or at the basket as a whole, I should aim for the exact pinpoint center. You wouldn't believe how much difference that made–a giant improvement! If you want to make a direct hit on a goal or project, don't just aim at the whole target. Know where the core or center is and zero in on that!

You may not always get what you're after, but if you have direction you'll seldom be in doubt… and it's doubt that undermines management.

So many people don't plan or pursue anything. They just enter and circle around in life's arena (home, business, community, etc.), waiting for the telephone to ring or the mail to come, someone to give them an order, a job, a solution, or a goal!

Consider a family of six I knew, taking a trip to Hawaii. Hooray! Wow! At Last! They all wanted to go! Why? Well, some of them weren't really sure, but they wanted to go. They heard it was wonderful–and it was HAWAII!! Not knowing or questioning what made it wonderful, they just bought the word "wonderful" as the reason. The twelve-year-old and eight-year-old in the family checked out a book and got some brochures and read up on the islands, studied maps, and for a month before made a mental and physical list of what they wanted to do and see. As the time drew near all were equally excited. The parents and two older children waited for the day and just "headed over to Hawaii" to see what would happen. The two youngsters by now had a list of thirty things to do and see and packed the gear they needed to do it. It was great to get there, but guess who enjoyed it the most? Yes, the two little managers. After a couple of days in paradise, believe it or not, just sitting, eating, and looking got old and **boring**. The parents and older children complained

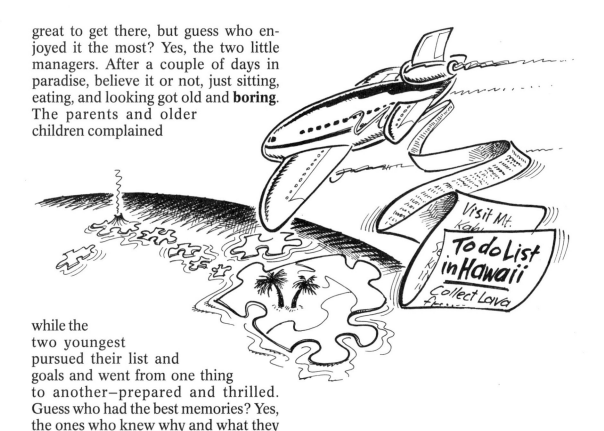

while the two youngest pursued their list and goals and went from one thing to another—prepared and thrilled. Guess who had the best memories? Yes, the ones who knew why and what they were going for.

You can't plan for the unknown

Good management is planning and preparing for the expected. That alone is tough enough in these busy and fast-moving days, especially when the unexpected also comes along. But planning for the unknown is a real life loser—lots of work and few rewards.

It's hard to start if you don't know where you are going—
It's hard to keep going, if you don't know where you are going—
It's impossible to know if you got there or not, if you don't know where you are going.

Direction is more important than "time management"

Beating, fighting, racing, and outwitting the clock or calendar isn't management. Knowing and seriously pursuing what you want is the real source of personal management. The biggest reason so many people fail at it, is that they don't know their direction or purpose in life or are unwilling to pursue what they do know. So instead, they labor to organize whatever comes at them.

It is that simple. Management doesn't depend on or really have much to do with time. Everything is YOU—what you really want, where you're going, and just how bad you want it.

Direction will help you overcome

We're all great managers when things are going our way, right on schedule! But if the flight is delayed on the runway for two hours and we miss our connection or the wedding, "it" doesn't arrive in the mail, something expensive on the car breaks right before or during the trip, we have a fire or flood, or someone "totally trustworthy" breaks their word–these are true tests of management. That straight shot at things we imagine and plan for seldom comes to pass without detours and unscheduled surprises of all kinds.

If, however, we know where we're going and why, a whole stack of well-organized opposition will just be steppingstones on the way.

Make sure your direction is YOUR direction

Millions of people are just in the sheep shed of life, coming and going, baaaing and battling life as it is dealt to them, going not where they decide, but where they are told by parents, teachers, job security, advertisements, or whatever. Deciding where you are going and why is something **you** have to do. You must either take control or be controlled. People will find your direction for you, if you don't find it yourself!

I would dare say that over half of our home direction is chosen for us, not by us as it should be. This is why we find ourselves thrashing unhappily through lots of things we don't enjoy, or even want to do.

For example, when we decide to build or buy our dream house is a pretty special and important time in our life. We should build or buy a certain place or structure because it contains or embodies the things that really matter to us, that will enhance and edify our life. We start out strong in the direction of what we want, and too often end up, because of money, codes, community pressure, and availability, taking what is there. We surrender our direction and commitment, and with it goes most of our love and energy.

We all have hobbies, arts or crafts or other part-time pastimes that mean a lot to us, we really enjoy them. That is a direction and a good one. Yet, when it comes time to make provision for them (getting a house or land with a separate shop, full basement, or a big back yard for the kids or the dogs) we run into a few obstacles and then cave in and forget it.

Stick to your guns, even if it takes a little longer or costs a little more, or gets some criticism. Only you know your direction–honor it and stay with it and sound management will come naturally.

"Why" is more important than "how"

We've all seen some master managers out there.

Parents who are run ragged by two kids, run into parents of ten who function in total order and harmony and take in a couple of extra juveniles and a homeless teenager or two just to keep in practice. Grandparents of eight who go into orbit at Christmas meet peers with thirty-five grandchildren (and these grandfolks are skipping and humming and not wealthy either) and every one of those kids have a card and a gift coming.

Too often we ask HOW they do this, when that is not the big secret of doing 100 or 1,000 things at once. It is WHY they are doing it. You decide on the why and then the how grows out of it.

Most of us go about this backwards. When we come up with something we want to do, we immediately concentrate on the most apparent question: How do I do this, and then begin the famous logical process of planning and "organization." But doing 1,000 things isn't a matter of logic–it's direction and purpose. If you will first establish a strong **why** you want to do something, much of the organization and management will just happen.

Consider how many people start up a business knowing little or nothing, but they have a strong want and need to do it. Two weeks later they know how, and the how happened because the why made it happen. Look at the big doers and master managers: few are all that talented or super intelligent, but look at their why. **That's** their secret, what fuels their ability!

Having things lined up that **you really want to do** (for a good or bad reason–either works) is the primary source of those big numbers. So:

1. *Have dreams and plans.*
2. *Zero in on the ones that mean the most.*
3. *Make sure the reasons you want to do them are real and concrete (wishy-washy things like "ought to" or "need to" won't work).*
4. *Jump in and get started.*
5. *Keep at it, don't give up those dreams.*

The secret is direction, or desire. If you really **want** to, you can do 10 or 100 or 1,000 things at the same time, many of them without even thinking about it. We humans all have a built-in ability expansion band that is marvelous to behold.

Tackling the "To-Do's"

aven't we all felt like the mosquito in the nudist camp? ...just don't know where to start. We do finally gather up all of our old and present targets and commitments, but all the while, new and tempting (and maybe even more important) things to do keep popping up. Suddenly we realize just how much we have to do, how much is expected of us, and we want to do it all!

In fact, sometimes our lives get like that junk drawer in the kitchen—we know there are lots of good things in there, but it's so crammed full and jumbled we have to dig and paw and hunt to come up with our objective. The only solution after a while is to dump the drawer out and separate and organize it all so we can see, find, and choose.

About 99% of us use the same method—affectionately called "the list"—to handle the piles of things to do in our lives.

Our lists are about as personal and sacred to us as our sex lives, our thoughts and dreams, and our relationship with the Deity. Whether they're ragged scraps of paper or several-page printouts of projects and duties—when and how we make them, what's on them, and how we use them, is as unique to us as our fingerprints. And we often depend on those lists almost as much as our lungs!

Attempting to tell you what and why to list for your life would be like ordering a meal for you, choosing your vocation, or picking your spouse, so that's not my purpose here. But since our lists

are the map or memory jogger we use to organize, prioritize, and order things in our life, a quick examination of their use might be in order.

Lots of us make a list, a good list of things to do: have-to's, should-do's, want-to's, and requests from others, with a couple of bolt or blouse sizes we need mixed in there too. But then it doesn't seem to work very well for us. After "listwatching" myself and many other managers for years, at home, work, and in the community, I've arrived at some conclusions you may find helpful:

1. The first purpose of a list is to capture.

Capturing, recording, is the first purpose of a list—not organizing and managing. The thing you never want to fail to do with a list is use it to capture all the big, medium, even tiny things you hear, see, feel, find, think up, or just pick up somewhere. If you just try to hold them in your mind they'll slip and drift away, but once they're on paper they're yours. So when something sparks your interest, comes to your attention, needs to be done, suddenly occurs to you, or looks like an answer to your wants or needs—write it down, no matter how roughly or crudely. Don't worry about order, style, or penmanship. Just get it! You can enter and record it on your "fancy lists" later if you want to, but get it NOW so you can relax.

You can divide your list into columns or categories, whatever you like. I just list my to-do's in a long line, my main goal being to capture and keep all my notes, ideas, and to-do's so I won't lose or forget any.

"Lists are an absolute must for any family. Lists of groceries, chores, what to do on trips to town, etc. I have a little notebook I carry around with daily chores and responsibilities on it, and a large calendar on the wall with dates and times of commitments, for everyone in the house."

"I operate off lists all the time and I couldn't function without them. I have lists for home, for my job, for church, and for the kids. If I go off to do a bunch of errands I always make a list for it.

If I get a few minutes at the end of the day or waiting at the doctor's office or whatever I update and consolidate and scratch things off my list."

2. Keep your list with you everywhere—even in bed!

Yes, and in church, while driving, working, playing, on vacation, at social or athletic events (whether you're competing or watching), at meals, etc. No, I'm not crazy, and neither will you be. This is kind of like carrying your canteen across the desert, so when it rains

or you stumble across a waterhole, you have the tools to capture what you need. Your best and most brilliant thoughts and plans will usually come to you while you're engrossed in something else, not when you're just sitting somewhere "listing." If your list is with you, you can get those inspirations and ideas while they're fresh.

If your list is in a big notebook or something that looks awkward in the steam bath or dancing the rumba, then a plain old notepad and pencil will do—as long as you transfer your jottings to your real list SOON.

"One of the best inventions of this century are those little post-em pads. They should be kept near your bed, favorite chair, the mirror where you spend the most time, by the front door, and yes, even next to the toilet. So many times I'll have a great thought, and by the time I find a pad and pencil, like a vapor, it's gone."

"I have a pen with a velcro strip on it, that goes onto a spot of velcro attached to the gearshift console of my car for easy access in case of emergency!"

3. The satellite list.

Sometimes it makes sense to just make a short list to fit the occasion rather than hauling along the whole notebook with your lifetime list. I sometimes transfer a few things off my big list to a satellite list and just use the satellite list for the day, making and doing everything on it and then throwing it away. It's kind of an offshoot of the main list, more direct and easier to use.

I wouldn't even bother to enter some of this satellite stuff onto your main list. A sub-list on a Post-it note or the back of an envelope will do. Just the six things you're going to do in town, or the four things you need to do before you go.

4. The order things are written on your list doesn't necessarily mean the order you do them in.

So many seminars, books, and articles focus on the pointing finger called "priorities." YOU MUST PRIORITIZE are usually the first words out of the mouth of such authorities. We must make a list of the first most important, second most important, etc., tasks we have to do, prioritizing our day. Then do the items in order, not moving on to the next until the one before it is done.

This is management suicide because need and priority can change two minutes after a list is made—when a child starts throwing up, you get a call from a long-lost classmate who's just in town for another hour, or a nice offer comes in on the phone.

Whether or not you've made an official schedule of completion, order is a fickle and changing thing and if you cannot or will not change with it, you'll be an inefficient slave to your list.

5. Don't just record everything you want to do on your list, include enough detail to do it or where to find the information to get it done.

For example, if one item is to make a call, put the phone number right on the list, if another item is to get new blinds,

put the measurements on the list. (The entire three pages of specifications for your new house addition, however, don't belong on the list.)

6. Focus on the A's and fit in the B's and C's.

On every list some items are definite "have-to's" like the photography session at 11 o'clock, doctor appointment at 3:30, meeting at 6:30. But a big part of any list is things like (on my list) get a haircut, call Mother, send for a catalog, order more toilet earrings, prepare talk for next Fourth of July. They have built-in flexibility, so you don't really have to sweat it. Zero in on the have-to's on your list and then just treat all the other things on there as tag-on or optional things. Do them, work them in, if you can, but don't lose any sleep over it if you can't.

The easiest way to accomplish B, C, and D priority things is slip them in around or tag them onto an A objective. Leave a few minutes early for the photo studio, for example, and on the way there or back knock off the "B" that's easiest, already on that side of

town, or something you just happen to be in the mood to do.

When I woke up last Monday morning, for example, my list (I use legal pads) had 51 things to do—most of them not today or this week necessarily, just to do. By the end of the week I still had twenty things left on the list to carry over to the next week (like dig out the spring, pick up some 2 x 4's, recheck the log house, order Valentine's Day flowers, put a decoy duck on the pond for the grandkids, get four gallons of Olympic Oxford Paint...). I did, however, do **30 extra things** that week that never made it to the list, those things just pop up and are fitted in as life goes on.

My big "have-to's" included a eulogy for Uncle June, two youth conference talks, three radio phone interviews, and a ribbon cutting at the new Scout park. During the week, I just tagged onto and around the big objectives on the list, coming and going, to, from, and during the have-to's. The barber shop was full every time I passed it, I wasn't driving anything fit to haul lumber, and decoys don't die waiting, so I just let those lesser listees slide. This week when I do them, fit them in around other priorities, it'll take about thirty minutes total for all of them, and little gas and effort. Had I insisted on doing them, and stuck to the order of a list, they would and could have taken three or four hours worth of special trips and stops out of the way.

Good home managers anchor their lists and schedules in the musts and #1 objectives and just work-in the others, fitting them in as possible when they most smoothly fit the routine. If they don't fit, **carry them over**. I have six items like name the puppy, draw up plans for new gate, reread the VCR programming instructions, tune up the tractor, and make extra house keys for guests, that have been on my list for six months and it doesn't worry me. One of these days I'll find the right niches and they will be done, but to stop and ponder for half a day till I found the perfect name for a pooch before moving on would kill incentive as well as time.

7. Fit the list to your feelings.

Stay aware of your mood—heavy, light, tired, alert—and look for things to fit how you feel. Some of us like the mean stuff first or the ugly last. I don't know about you, but when I don't feel like doing something I don't do it well and I don't enjoy it either. I know sometimes we do have to do the "NOWs" and unplea-sants, but not always. We usually have at least some degree of choice.

Fit order and priority to your feelings and you'll do much better than if you try to make yourself rigidly follow the order on any written list.

8. Moving things to the long-term list.

I happen to think that those big, costly, imaginative, or speculative things you'd like to do someday—maybe, if, and when—are worth keeping track of, but not worth the anxiety of carrying around and copying and recopying for five years on your daily lists. So put them on a backlog or long-term list.

Having a backlog is like going on a vacation where there is more to do than eat and sightsee and lay on the beach. It's knowing that if you want to there are forty-five other hikes, tours, and activities you can take part in. It's a comforting feeling, having a big dream list tucked away somewhere. More often than we imagine the situation changes or the funds or the means or whatever will suddenly pop up. So then in the normal course of cruising through life we can quickly and efficiently reach in there, grab that "to-do" and do it in stride, right along with all the urgent and demanding chores of keeping up every day and week.

A big backlog gives you a feeling of being worth something. Anyone who can think up all this to do must be pretty smart and have high expectations!

9. What about the "tired of transferring" stuff?

You recorded it, it had a nice ring to it, you felt it was important right then, and added it to your list of "to-do's." Then when most of the things are scratched off the old list, there are still one or two or more things that you dread, can't afford, or haven't gotten to

yet, so you transfer them to the new list... but how many times?

Some things just aren't worth doing if you wait too long, or after you think about them a while. They get outdated or you lose interest. Don't worry about this, because your list is just practicing the old evolutional concept of "survival of the fittest." A list isn't a blueprint of your future or a life sentence, it's a harbor, a calm place to park things until you want or need them. Just because something is parked in your harbor or lot doesn't mean you have to sail or drive it... you can sink it!

Let the moldy things go. "To-do's" don't always age well, so snip them off the list when you lose the need or interest—no harm done!

Even though it's a sound idea, a solid request (and has been a priority on your list for a long time) you never seem to get to it... for some reason. In cases like this there is a simple little word that will give you the answer and the solution.

Hold that "to-do" up in hand or mind and ask yourself "why?" Then give a firm and honest answer. Most of us will even do things we hate or dread, if the why is there. If for all that fighting and putting it off you cannot give yourself a practical, financial, moral or whatever reason why you should do it, then maybe you should find a way to de-list it. The last fifteen on a list of 1,015 things to do might have some merit, but not enough to crowd you or weigh on your mind and agenda for no good reason. Just because you decided to do it once, or wanted to do it for years, doesn't mean it's still worth doing.

11. And last... Keep your old lists.

Yes, you heard right, date them and keep them, you can even paste them on 8 1/2" x 11" paper and put them in a binder or notebook. You'll have a record, or at least the outline and nucleus of your life's story! One of the best personal journals you can keep, all done for you right as you go along.

The list is a fine, fine tool of management, but enough about lists and recording systems. Let's look at some of the applications of what's on there now!

Prioritize

As I mentioned earlier, we are often told to PRIORITIZE, assign a priority to everything and then stick with it. This is a great idea and a worthy goal, but almost impossible unless you happen to be master of the universe, with complete control over the weather, germs, kids' bladders, spills, the economy, and the impulses and emotions of others. It's not hard to line people up by height, some priorities can be assigned by sight and sheer arithmetic, but in home management, prioritizing gets pretty elusive at times. Sure, we can line up all our duties and

projects and chores and appointments in some kind of order of importance, but stopping a sudden fight in the family has priority over picking out a new refrigerator, our original #1 objective. Or if we're on our way to deliver some fresh-baked bread to a neighbor, seeing a gate swinging open and about to tear itself off the hinges suddenly reprioritizes everything. Even if we just stand still all day, nothing stays static! And neither do priorities.

What if you have your priorities all picked out and you hear that five-pound trout are hitting down at Henry's Fork, your sister has a free ticket for you to Hawaii next week, someone has stolen your car, or the pussy willows are perfect for picking (and won't be on Friday when your list assignments are finished). Do you walk past all of that with your prepicked list items? I wouldn't say that was wise or fun at all.

One of the biggest frustrations of management is trying to set and stick to an order of priorities when right in the middle of things something else springs up, more urgent than what you're doing right now, or what you have scheduled for the day. Some people call jumping off one important

thing to another being "sidetracked." Not necessarily so, you basically make priorities up as you go along. People think interrupting a schedule is wrong. It's irritating and sometimes exasperating, but not wrong, because if you're making good time toward Yellowstone Park and some kid suddenly has to go, your good time isn't your priority any more. You either face that fact, or potty cleanup will force another new priority on you.

I weigh the potential for damage and time loss when I'm reprioritizing. What will be damaged or depreciate the least if it waits? No matter how solidly I'm scheduled, when something comes along that can hurt anything or anyone, or steal long or short range time and resources from me, it gets immediate attention.

When a conflict of importance comes up, I worry about the living (person, animal, or plant that needs attention NOW) before the inanimate.

If I have to let something go, I let self-involved, self-controlled things go first and do the things that involve other people. This way I don't have to call and re-call and rearrange with others to re-group and re-schedule. When something is being done for and with me alone, I can ditch it without "permission" for anything else on my agenda, and pick it back up again when I'm ready.

All is going well, right on schedule, and your rhythm of doing is about even with your need for output... and then suddenly something new, surprising, and unscheduled is dumped on you! If you can't cope with this you'll never cope with life. You can be efficient and tack the unforeseen on the bottom of the list, put it in line and do it after or later. But the truly effective people quickly evaluate the need and place it first, middle, or last and do it according to when it needs done.

Too much to do?

Why does everyone worry about having too much to do? When you think about it, it's the greatest of all blessings in life, being busy, and over busy is even better! The more fronts we have to work on, the more options we have to stay fresh and enthused and progressive. It even forces a little creativity (which we can all use more of) out of us. Notice it's the people with little or nothing to do who are bored, depressed, and discouraged, not the overloaded.

If you suddenly have 2,000 things to do after you get the 1,000 going, then great. The busier you can get the better off you will be, for the only way you can get lots done is to have lots to do. You'll hear ten thousand times in your life, "Ask a busy person." Why is that? They are the ones who've learned how to get things done, and can double, triple, and quadruple their intake of tasks… and enjoy it.

You can and should have a lot going. There can never be too much of anything that's productive and changing lives to the good. Having a lot to do helps you figure out how to do things faster and better, and best of all it gives you selectivity. You can pick the best and let the rest wash, or wait until you're good and ready to do them.

Schedules

Most people don't think they can operate without being scheduled. Over and over from audiences, I get the question "How do I schedule my housework, how often should I clean?" That's kind of like asking, how often should I gas my car? How often and when depends on how empty (or dirty) things get.

The same house could need to be cleaned twice a day or once a month, depending on the furnishings, season, location, and the number of occupants and their ages and inclinations. All of life is like the house. Living by a **standard** makes more sense than a schedule. A standard says "keep the house reasonably clean," where a schedule says "clean the house once a week."

Let a schedule prepare, not program you!

Schedules: What necessary, valuable tools for organizing our lives… until they start managing our lives! Schedules are to time, as budgets are to money—regulators, and both have their drawbacks. Scheduling is done to allow "room" to complete a job or task. The problem we're up against here is the difficulty of accurately estimating the cost of something or the time it will take, the cooperation of weather, traffic, etc. Nothing kills inspiration and incentive as surely as having too much or not enough time available to accomplish a task. Case in point: Unskilled managers (most of us) appraise a project (be it packing for a trip, preparing a garden, organizing a community or club assignment, sewing a dress, or painting a room) and allow time for it, often even setting a *deadline*! Then we fit and pace ourselves and our energy and resources

to the time allotted. **Always** there is either too much or not enough. The former ends up wasting time and making us inefficient, the latter overworks both our nerves and our body—often those around us, too. What if you set aside a whole day for a project but finish it in three hours? Then you can do something else—**what**? Most of us will waste the rest of the day, like we do the rest of the money if we come in under budget on something.

Budgeting or setting aside time, space, and resources to do something shifts control from you to it. You end up adjusting your effort to, and filling the allotment allowed, instead of what was really needed. You'll generally make the task come true to the estimate.

Even if you do outline a particular project for a certain time period, always look ahead and have a big backlog of "anytime to-do's" handy, too. You'll stay in control and double your production.

Keep GO more important than SHOW

We've all met people who seem squared away, in control, and on top of everything—yet they get next to nothing done in a day. Because they spend their time keeping track, not making tracks. The systems they've adopted to "get all their jobs and assignments organized" require more time and energy than the actual duties themselves. Some have elaborate card files to find the file to find the item, or a date file to keep track of dates and times. They label cans of beans already labeled and on the bean shelf, and keep a written inventory of minor or visually obvious things. Instead of just counting the remaining they card and record it.

Forms and formality are needed and impressive in a bureaucracy or at work where you have to look important, educated, and busy (and cover your rear), but at home, who's watching? "Done" is all that matters. Cut the classification systems—work done will testify to and reward itself.

Calendars

"What day is today?"

How many times a year do we ask that? At least 359! And right when we are asking it we have at least a dozen places recording the date around the house (datebooks, watches, clocks, computers, the newspaper and TV, as well as all those calendars we have crammed in a drawer somewhere).

Yet we will be signing things, writing checks, making appointments and decisions, mulling over dates, scheduling things and always asking aloud, "What day is this?"

Two key parts of management are knowing where you are, and when you are going to act, and a calendar is designed just for this. Calendars are terrific tools for charting and keeping track of our 1,000 things at once. They keep us aware of what's coming up, where we need to be at a glance. So here is some calendar coaching you might consider:

1. All good calendars have at least a dual use
   A. They are "my calendar"—a way of keeping track of and organizing our own personal things to do and remember.
   B. They are also "our calendar"—they perform the same service for ALL members of the household.
2. For this reason, especially, calendars need to be posted in public, not hidden away somewhere.
3. After almost forty years of home and business management, I finally learned to just keep ONE CALENDAR. When I had one at home that my wife and I scheduled our family outings on and one at the office for me and another at the office for my secretary—talk about a mess. Now I have **one central calendar**. Like many of you, I do carry a portable or pocket calendar with me, too, to help organize trips and errands. But that central calendar back home is THE calendar, and any new dates or important

notes I pick up on my travels are entered on the household calendar the minute I get home.

4. There are more important things about a calendar than nice pictures or attractive type. You need to be able to write on it—and the more space in those squares the better! It's nice to have room to record not just the time or the date but where the place you're going is and how long it's open, or when the party starts and how to get there. Writing these things down here right away is much better than saving and shuffling around little pieces of paper and then tearing apart the house two weeks from now looking for them.

5. Right beside the phone is an excellent place for the calendar, so you can enter invitations and other data right off the wire. Tethering a pen or pencil right by your calendar will assure that you and others always CAN record when you need to.

6. Tend that calendar religiously—keep making those notes and entries as new dates and occasions and things to remember come up. If the doctor says he'll need to see you again in six months, flip ahead on your calendar and make note of it. If those booster shots are needed once a year, don't be caught unawares. Page ahead and pencil in a reminder to yourself. Write in important birthdays and other dates a year ahead, then mark in reminders to yourself a week or so before so you can get the card or gift off on time. Many people like to add quick notes and impressions about surprises that crop up (and the things they did expect to happen, too), so their calendar serves as a mini diary or journal.

7. Hang onto your old calendars and file them. They, too, are a thumbnail family or personal history, and can yield hard facts you suddenly need, too, such as how old the puppies are now (when they were born) and when the accident was.

"The school gives out a calendar showing all the days off from school and early dismissals, and school fundraisers, etc., and this is the main family calendar we all post things on and add to."

"I like a LARGE calendar or dry erase board posted in a prominent place so all can put their occasions and appointments on it."

"My daughter has two children, and both she and her husband work. The boys are in school, and the whole family is involved in many activities of all kinds. They keep a large calendar on the fridge, and each person is obligated to write his/her schedules in, doctors' and vet appointments, school activities, are all listed here too—as soon as someone knows of a commitment, they put it on the calendar, the day and time."

My own favorite "portable organizer"

Ever notice how we all eye each other's "day planners" or portable organizers? We all have different sizes and shapes, with different things sticking out the side. (Unless we all went to the same seminar, and then we'd all have the same big purple plastic ringbinder that would strain a pack mule.)

We're all a little suspicious, if not critical, of the other person's pocket organizer. I've seen hundreds of them, and once eight people sitting around me on an airplane all had theirs out, listing things or looking them over. None were exactly the same. I personally think this is good! Tailoring your planner, adopting and adapting it to you, is the most important thing here. People are fascinated with the simplicity of mine and are always asking to look at it. It's kind of homespun, but it fits me, and it works to organize all of my affairs–home life, business, hobbies, church assignments, and all the rest.

My "organizer" is a leather folder (shaped like an old-time outhouse) with carrying handles.

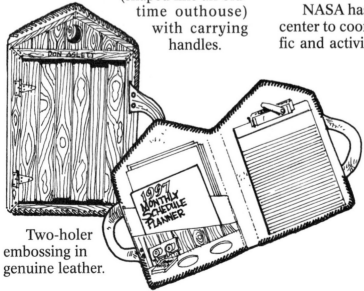

Two-holer embossing in genuine leather.

Opened up on my lap or desk it has only three parts:

In the first pocket on the left are all the letters, articles, and the like I carry with me to work on. In spare or slack moments I process everything in here until it is ready for its final resting place.

The pocket below this contains a standard 7" x 9" $1.99 calendar. I make notes in the squares of the calendar both before and after, so I have a total record in the end of my comings and goings and the result.

To the back of the calendar, I've added a little directory with the phone numbers and addresses (birthdays, too) of all the key people and contacts in my life.

On the right side, I have my old faithful yellow legal pad with not just my list, but room for notes and writings.

I carry this with me everywhere, and there are no zippers to fumble with, ring binder holes to tear, or sections to shuffle in and out of. Simple.

Create a control center

NASA has a control center, a nerve center to coordinate and direct all traffic and activity. Why not do the same in a house? We rarely, if ever see a house (and that includes the newest and best designed) that actually designates an area to monitor, store, and distribute the paraphernalia of daily functions in a home–keys, mail, papers, lost and found, grocery lists, freshly arrived photos, messages, etc. Most of this is stuck on the refrigerator, stacked on the counter, crammed in a drawer, or piled somewhere else in the kitchen or the hall. Who knows how many family fights and schedule foul-ups have been produced by this approach?

The best place for a control center, the place it's usually needed most, is in or near the kitchen. A center right in the kitchen itself can get a little cluttered at times, so you might want to locate it inside the pantry or mud room. Other parts of the house can benefit from a control center, too—as I explain in Chapter Three of *Make Your House Do the Housework* (see page 215).

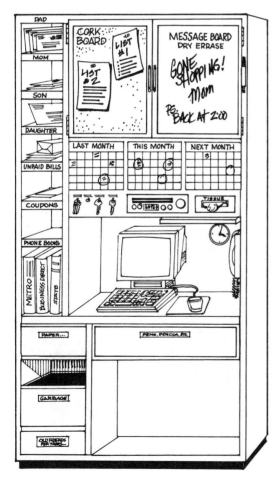

Beware of the great time stretchers in our head

"You've got your work cut out for you."

"It will take all night."

"We'll never get done."

"It took nine hours last time!"

We all have this automatic timing estimator in our brains that too often gives us a perverted projection of how long "it's going to take." Your neighbor painted his kitchen last month, it took him four days. Yours is bigger so you figure you have a five-day job ahead of you. It scares you to death so you never start, you just agonize over it for months, eliminating other important to-do's to make room. When you finally do it, it takes **less than a day**.

Preparing too big for a little fight is poor management. Most projects take half the time of the mental mountain we've made them into. We've all put off things for months (and years) and when we finally did them, realized that we'd spent more time transferring and carrying the project from list to list than it actually took to do. Every item you put off puts you a notch farther out of control. Often one call, one letter, one meeting, an hour can erase or accomplish something that's driven you buggy forever.

The bottom line is: it won't hurt as much or take as long as you imagine. That goes for those overdue gifts, letters, and acts of kindness, too—they will **all go quicker** than you think. So don't let those imaginary time stretches put you off or stand in your way.

The ten things most often put off which generally end up not as bad as we imagined:

1. Going to the dentist
2. Quitting or changing an unhappy job situation
3. Breaking off a love affair/relationship
4. Changing clients/customers
5. Paying that bill/getting the loan
6. Returning a call we really don't want to return
7. Letting the owner know that we ripped off a fender
8. Getting an annual physical
9. Making a visit to our family/the needy
10. Cleaning and painting

Don't keep putting off that trip to the zoo, either

This mental magnification of things takes place with our fun, family, and recreational plans, too. I'm sure you've been through an experience where in reality the effort required for a big result was so little and yet we put it off or never did it and so missed the result, lost all the benefit. We all need to be reminded of this, maybe every morning before we start getting our 1,000 things lined up for the day.

I remember once when a company party/dutch oven dinner was to be held out at our ranch. We made arrangements six months prior and I made a quick list of what would be included. (Isn't that always easy in the mind?)

For the children, I conceived a treasure hunt and so put it on the announcement, and the longer I waited to set it up, the larger the project loomed in my mind. The party was a month, a week, and finally three days away and by then we were right in the middle of the annual company meeting and buried. One hundred of our people from all over the U.S. were en route by now and my thoughts were, "Oh well, one

little missing item won't hurt... I'm busy... this event is really focused on the adults, anyway... the parents probably won't want the kids getting their clothes dirty..." (You well know the excuses we use to wiggle out.) But then there is always "your word." What you promise (publicly or privately), if you have any character at all, you have to honor.

Not wanting to face the final consequence of some little seven-year-old asking, "Mr. Aslett, where is the treasure hunt?" I woke up guiltily at 5:30 a.m. the very day of the dinner, tried to think of something else to distract the kids, and finally decided "I will!" I wrote up seven little two-line verses on a paper sack and ran through the ranch yard taping and burying clues. I tossed some dollar bills, candy, lapel pins, toilet key chains, toy trucks, and other prizes into a fishing tackle box and set up the treasure hunt in a total time of 34 minutes.

Between two pine trees
    west of the old cabin log
Is a treasure map, so dig like a dog.
Find a place where newspapers arrive
    and another map to keep the hunt alive.
Now there's a big hill with a flag on top
    10 paces East, you'll find a can of pop.
Go to the North of a big willow tree
    look up, look up, what do you see?
Cats and horses, pigs and sheep
    and a deer horn with a secret
    for the treasure leap.
There's other clues in the tree house floor,
    and over by the spring...
    need I say any more?
Now find the trail below the wood wagon
    under the bushes a treasure is braggin'.
You found it at last, divide it up fair
    all treasure hunters get their share!

The kids, of course, had all been waiting eagerly for the event. They went crazy running and reading and deciphering and digging and dividing the treasure. Several parents came up afterward and said, "Boy were my kids looking forward to the treasure hunt...." I sagged in relief and kicked myself for the 400 times I've dodged something like this. How often we magnify things in our mind and how quick and easy doing things is, once you say, "I will!"

"It's nearly too late to get my girls a playhouse. I can't call them when they're in college and say, 'Okay, got a playhouse, come home between quarters and play!'"

"One thing I do with my list is mark things as a MUST if I know I would otherwise put them off indefinitely. (For example: 'Go diving with the kids on Monday no matter what!')"

Remember, it isn't all chores and duties, no matter how well done. The end purpose of the 1,000 things is to give you 1,000 thrills!

Can I really do 1,000 things... ALL AT THE SAME TIME?

Most of us, once launched into the demands of life and family, find out there are 1,000 things to do, to be sure, but remain skeptical that we can really have them all "in the air" at the same time. We know our brain and imagination can process multiples like magic, but we aren't convinced our paws can keep up.

You can stop wondering about this right now, because doing 1,000 things (more or less) hinges on the principle that **you don't need to watch a garden grow**. No one would even consider planting carrots and then standing out there beside the row for two or three months until they're finished growing, and then digging them up before moving on. They sprout and grow while we are doing other things. The same is true of ordering something by mail. We never drop the order in the mailbox and then sit down and wait, motionless, for the package to arrive. Or when we're baking, once something is in the oven, we don't have to sit in front of the oven window and watch and wait. And do we ever stop life to watch paint dry? When you're writing a book, you start, but don't give up everything else until it's done–you can be writing (getting ideas and searching for the right word) while gardening, ordering (waiting your turn on that 800 line), baking, painting, etc. Focus is somehow always thought of as a singular. Not so, you can focus on five hundred things–you can worry about the kid or the job while drawing a picture, conversing, exercising, increasing the value of your property, impressing your spouse, saving money, helping a neighbor, eating a cookie, singing, listening to music, planning the day or evening, learning a new skill, fantasizing, teaching, controlling your temper, praying, or fixing the sink faucet. There are eighteen different important actions that can easily go on at the same time as something else. To give just one more example here, consider all the things you can do while traveling (see page 141). Just because you plop in a seat to get from point A to point B, doesn't preclude 100 other things from going on... at the same time... does it? Don't think you're doomed to doing

nity, time and available resources were about the same, there was still a **huge** spread in results. There had to be a king-pin somewhere that good management pivots on! I listed and analyzed for years looking for this magic, to improve myself and teach others in my family and those who worked for and with me in the community and on the job.

The answer finally hit me, and it's so obvious it's easy to overlook. The principle is as simple as piggybacking!

only one thing—you are capable of doing dozens and dozens… at the same time.

The simple secret called piggybacking

It has intrigued me why some people seem to handle 1,000 things with no visible effort, while others are always struggling to "keep up." They seem to have to fight to get anything done, and are forever on the edge of "frantic" instead of in a quiet flow. Some women sail through life smoothly with eleven kids; others are over their head with one. At restaurants I've observed equally hard workers day after day: one handles ten tables, another can barely cope with four—yet their work speed appears to be the same!

Because management is made up of a million habits learned from birth and often ingrained for life, I found it difficult to shake down the basic difference here. Even where willingness, opportu-

A lesser manager will concentrate on specific chores or objectives like–Monday is floor-mopping day, Wednesday is garden-planting day, Friday is Christmas tree day. In other words, earmark a day or time for each important duty they wish to accomplish. "What's wrong with that?" many will ask. It sounds logical, like good sense scheduling, like smart budgeting instead of helter-skelter handling of the floods of "to do's" coming at us daily.

But this is like needing food and going into the woods prepared to get mushrooms—allowing enough time for mushroom gathering and taking only the mushroom bag, looking only for mushrooms, and going home with them. A real manager wouldn't budget for mushrooms, that would be his focus, but not his limit. He'd prepare to find food and carry the means to do so with him and make his trip all-encompassing, not a single-objective trip. During the **same** trip, using the same amount of time, he'd find wild berries and fruit, honeycombs, fish, fowl, and even food he can buy or get free from other hunters or travelers. An Alaskan "bush lady" I know really hit the nail on the head here:

"When I lived in town (a New Jersey suburb), I thought and bought in little narrow slots, kind of a lazy-mind management. I would make a whole trip to town for just a couple of little things. Then I moved deep into the Alaskan bush, where it was about a hundred miles by dogsled or boat to the nearest store. 'Town' wasn't a one- or two-task trip, I had to pack at least fifty things in, really make it count. I managed to assemble a month's necessities in one day, instead of setting aside a day for one or two little things."

This doesn't mean you have to squeeze a mass of chores and duties onto yourself all at once, or put yourself under unreasonable pressure. It simply means **do** have a central focus, job, or task, but prepare for and perform any number of others that fit into the time fragments that fall your way while going after the main objective.

My February and March of 1992, for example, were exhausting just to record on the calendar. I had forty-four straight days of media interviews with three and four personal appearances a day, in addition to drafting six new books, remodeling my home and office, and putting in tens of thousands of travel miles in the course of all this. Most days started at 4:30 a.m. and didn't stop until 10:30 at night. It was exciting and fun, I got lots done, there were lots of personal rewards, and it was profitable. But like all of you (regardless of how much you do get done) I still had a long list of need-to-get-doners

around the house, yard, with the kids, for friends, things to pick up, make, fix, find, etc.

Heading my list was to pour a 150-foot cement sidewalk (usable even by the handicapped) from our home to our garden and grandkid recreation area. This is one of those big jobs you'd like to hire out, but you really need to be there yourself to get the 50,000-pound, nine-cubic-yard truck through your yard and lawn without knocking down the house or smashing the sprinkler system. Pouring cement is no "by the way" job. It's big, heavy, expensive, and requires perfect timing for curing and finishing. It's affected not only by weather—rain, frost, and wind—but bugs, birds, stray dogs, and how hard it is to find help.

My April calendar had two free days, for which there was actually not one single thing on the schedule. So I labeled one of them "cement day" to focus on that job like any good manager would—but I didn't rule out the rest of my life because of it, or plan only for cement. During the two weeks prior to cement day, scores of other needs and "oughts" rolled in. By then I had no more open days, so that was where good management made its move. I tossed those new objectives in with and around what was already going on. Life can't stop because we're pouring cement, doing taxes, having a baby, going on vacation, sick, giving a speech, or anything else. Even death only stops the world for a moment.

I ordered the cement for 1:00 p.m. My son Grant was coming to help, as well as a neighbor whom I'd helped pour concrete a year or so back. Knowing there were lots of final touchups needed on the cement forms and other things that were important for the purpose, I'd used every five- and ten-minute spare time fragment during the week before so I was prepared for cement day.

While my muscle-bound son was there, instead of standing around waiting for the cement truck, we dismantled an old fence and dug up a broken concrete pillar. (Chores I'd been carrying on my list for a whole year.) Before the day was over I'd done two major telephone interviews, drafted a chapter for one of my new books, trimmed all the trees, built a strawberry patch, and answered four fan letters–all in the course of my sidewalk project.

I had a business meeting with my son during the pour and finishing of the concrete, a nice lunch after, met on a new Scout park that evening, and packed for a two-week trip to Washington D.C./San Francisco/Dallas. It was a fairly relaxed day, actually. Had I slotted and saved it solely as "cement day," I'd have missed at least fourteen other tasks that got finished–and I enjoyed. That's piggybacking!

Always have some other ducks lined up ready to shoot. If something is finished early, a good manager never goes into a holding pattern. You know what that is—when weather, traffic, accidents, or any of a dozen other interruptions crop up as we approach the place we're going, so the plane can't complete its task, land. So it flies in circles above the field, using up time, fuel, energy, and patience. Poor managers do that, too, because the destination—the airfield—is all they scheduled and prepared for. Good managers USE holding patterns.

Piggyback or just plain piggy?

You can piggyback through other people, too–catch someone who's already going or coming from somewhere you need to go. With just a few minutes or seconds of extra effort, they can pick up, deliver, or retrieve something for you.

The savings in time, gas, frazzlement, and distraction in just a simple trip to town alone are impressive, never mind the more distant and exotic destinations! People who stay aware of the comings and goings around them can save two and three hours **in one day** by this kind of piggybacking. Here it really helps to make your path public (see page 126)–tell everyone what you're up to, why and when.

The only pitfall of piggybacking on others is getting apathetic about it, coming to expect it.

It's so handy to have someone willing to run errands for us, and so presumptuous to think they're just standing by available to leap whenever we say leap. Bosses do this way too much to their staff, and men to their mates. The attitude I call "Fetch, female!" is wrong–an insult! None of us should do this to anyone, even if we do hold some kind of power position or age advan-

tage over them. Inconsiderate assigning is just plain **piggy**.

Piggybacking is a great and honorable practice between equals. Use it as such (which means take your turn at fitting in favors when it's due). I do this for people all the time, even employees of mine, and I'm glad to. It feels good.

And be not just grateful but generous with gas money, tips, cookies, or other little rewards.

The multiple track system

It's Saturday morning, the day you were going to relax and breeze through a couple of final projects before Sunday. But new babies in the family and the flu used up the last three days—**totally!** All the things you were going to do in those three days are facing you this morning, along with the usual Saturday stuff. Including picking up paint for the garage door, preparing a lesson to teach at Sunday school, your promise to visit a friend in a retirement village, and that TV special about Alaskan grizzly country you're determined to see (the VCR is broken, too). Your poodle needs a little affection, you're four months behind in that expensive magazine you subscribed to, plus you have your Saturday morning piano lesson to give and a salesperson coming to give you an estimate on vinyl siding. You also have to make a new flower box and pick up the materials for it at the lumber store. And though it only happens every twenty years or so, you find this morning that the septic tank is full and has to be pumped today without fail. Your spouse and all the kids

old enough to help are out of town on a camping trip and you are left with two little ones under five years old. So you can count on more than a few hours being used up for diapers, dressing and re-dressing toddlers, patching up injuries, and peacemaking. But it all has to be done today—all four days' worth!

There is a way out of this and it's called the multiple track system, a way to do lots of things at once and make them all come out together on time. We all can do this to some degree, so why not do it more?

How?

Get up thirty minutes ahead of even the kids, call the paint store and order the paint mixed, billed, and ready to pick up. Call the lumber store and do the same with the flower box materials, having the lumber cut to size. Call the septic pumper and make an appointment and then schedule the siding salesperson about the same time, so he can be there while you're waiting and watching for the tank truck.

Open the church lesson manual and read the objective for this week's lesson and make five minutes worth of notes and tuck them under your arm.

Hold your poodle during the piano lesson you're giving, and when you need to, hand him to one of the kids sitting by you (the other kid will be out of trouble once the one is occupied). When you're done, take the dog and kids and magazines with you to pick up the flower box materials and the paint which are ready. Call your friend at the village that morning and tell him you are taking him for a ride and take him with you to get the paint and have him read one of the magazines to you on the way. Then park under a tree in the park, and let the kids play while you and your friend finish reading the magazines and talk and outline the church lesson. By now the kids are tired as little lambs and fall asleep on the way home, so roll down the windows and let them sleep in the car while you nail the flower box together and plant some nasturtiums. Put the final touches on your lesson while you paint the garage door (this is some of the best thought time) and when the kids get up, feed them while you all watch the grizzly program. One-hour shows have at least fourteen minutes of commercials, so there's the remaining time to write up your lesson. Now it's five o'clock and you can take the rest of the day off. Oh yes, you had to collect twenty signatures on a petition today, too, but, like your list, you had it with you on your trip around town to the lumber store, paint store, and nursing home. Everyone signed it and it's done, too, right in with the rest of today's chores. So now you won't need the full day you allowed for it.

The above is an exaggerated example of course, but this is multi-track moving and many people do it. Once you learn and use it, it'll become a habit and you'll do it smoothly and naturally.

The only problem you'll have afterward is the time lost explaining to all your jealous friends how you do so much!

"What's my #1 secret for getting 1,000 things done? Doing three or four things at once, such as doing laundry and watching kids while balancing the checkbook and making out bills. Combine activities whenever possible!"

Almost a commandment of management: EXPLORE BEFORE!!!!

This is a simple, but indispensable ingredient of good management at that all-important planning stage. Let me give two quick examples:

Check all the channels. You want to relax and enjoy some TV. If you flipped the set on and hit any old program and watched it, only to find out that your favorite actor's best-ever movie was on another channel at the same time, you'd be furious with yourself. In less than a minute you could have churned through the channels, all 25 of them, then watched the one you really wanted.

Read the whole menu. If you are hungry, pick up the menu and order the first three things you see, or "the special," you'll eat all right. But not long into your meal you'll see stuff served to your neighbors that you crave and savor. Take 35 seconds to scan the whole menu—then order.

When you are doing or planning something, always explore—list and consider—**all** the alternatives. Much mismanagement is the result of people (smart people, too) launching out before they know all the options. When you have only one or two courses of action you are restricted in approach and outcome. When you have ten options or alternatives, you can often choose a better course. In other words, instead of taking the first offer, go on till you get five. It might turn out that first one was the best, but you'll eliminate wondering or regretting forever after.

Good managers always start by quickly exploring and listing all the possibilities. And then (after reading the whole menu, checking all the channels, gathering more offers and choices) they do the task at hand faster, better, cheaper, and with more peace of mind.

YOU... the prime resource of all good management

Good management is, bottom line, choosing and using the best means available to cure or contend with a matter at hand. We call these **options.** The more options you can come up with from which to choose a course of action, the better manager you will be. Poor managers generally panic and take the first one at hand, or do nothing until something comes along, both of which spell trouble and more trials. But there

are ALWAYS all kinds of options for handling what is about you. When you are convinced of that (and make the effort to discover them), I promise you a 30% instant increase in your management ability and popularity.

For example, you've got a wedding. I mean a big-time wedding where your best friend ever is getting married. He's relied on you for most of the arrangements, bringing the ring, coordinating things with the best man and bridesmaids, hosting the reception, everything! You've done it well so far (despite tons of pressure and some near misses), everything has gone fine—even brilliantly. The wedding is this afternoon. You have the cake in your station wagon, the gifts, rings, the bouquet, the key to the church, and twenty other critical things. The wedding is forty miles away, and to allow for traffic, possible blowouts, etc., you leave two hours early.

Then it happens... you stop to get gas and ice for the punch at a convenience store and lock the keys in the car. Meanwhile, traffic has gotten steadily worse and a tanker of taco sauce has tipped over on the interstate, backing up traffic for an hour. You're still twenty miles away.

Two channels communicate with you—PANIC OR OPTION. You are calm and see an option: you can break the window if you have to. Surely a 700-person wedding is worth a window... you can also find a wrecker to tow the car there, make a call... As you consider the options your spouse is pounding "Oh no" panic on you. As you check with others at hand (always an important resource) it happens to be your lucky day... the clerk in the conve-

nience store is a retired car thief and assures you he can open your car in minutes, and he does. He proudly opens even the back door. And then while your spouse is going back for the ice and you are chatting and tipping the attendant, a big ugly dog leaps unnoticed into the back of the car and buries its head in the wedding cake, removing two tiers of it. Now it's really hit the fan... you are running late, the cake is demolished, could anything else go wrong? Yes, your wife chooses this moment to confess that she left the key to the church on the counter at home. Well... this story goes on and gets worse. It's a true story and believe it or not the wedding went off without a hitch, simply because with every setback, came more options. Maybe not pleasant, but options. Good managers who keep cool and keep choosing the best option can swing any situation around.

Look at the options at their disposal here, for instance (use your imagination):

There were two of them—and phones.

They had started early, so there was still time to spare.

The cake was replaceable/repairable (the caterer met them at the church with two new tiers).

Weddings always run late (it adds romance) and a friend who lives close to the church had another set of keys.

There were back street (non-interstate) ways to get there, too.

The dog's owner was a policeman, who, in his embarrassment, was happy to offer a fast way to cover those last twenty miles.

I want to show you how good you really are...

...so I'll give you this little management quiz for practice... it will be fun. See how many options you can come up with for each situation. Don't try to reach a decision, just quickly list all the available options (even if they include run, cry, lie, or start over).

- *A situation requires a good loving mood and you are in a rotten mood.*
- *You are already overloaded with jobs, and another "have to" was just dumped on you.*
- *You're totally out of money, your credit cards are at the limit, and you need to make a "life and death" purchase.*
- *Your foothold on a relationship you've fought for and worked for years just fell through.*
- *Your most trusted friend has just done you really dirty.*
- *You're deeply involved in something and all of a sudden you realize "this is taking longer than I thought... there's no more time."*
- *You're the main feature on center stage today, all eyes are on you... and you woke up feeling sick–really sick.*
- *You've been put in charge and no one is respecting or accepting you... no one!*
- *Someone scheduled to do something you really need (babysit, give you a ride somewhere, etc.) doesn't show.*
- *You have a week's worth of work to do and only two days to do it in...*

There are probably fifty or maybe even a hundred options for each one of these. Very few of these would seem like problems at all if you suddenly had all the options right there in front of you. On the home front you have a lot more options on everything than you do at work or in business. Best of all, it is YOU who can go bananas thinking up the options. I've cornered sheep and I've cornered foxes... I've caught the sheep and never the foxes. The sheep lunge and run in the first open direction; the fox's brain goes like a calculator, processing probably 200 possibilities to pick his best survival option. If that one fails, he goes down the list to number 199, and so on.

I can't give you all the options for all of these, and neither can anyone else, because only you have your brain, your values, and your database. But I will give you the principles and the ammo to come up with and use all the options you need to make you a superb manager.

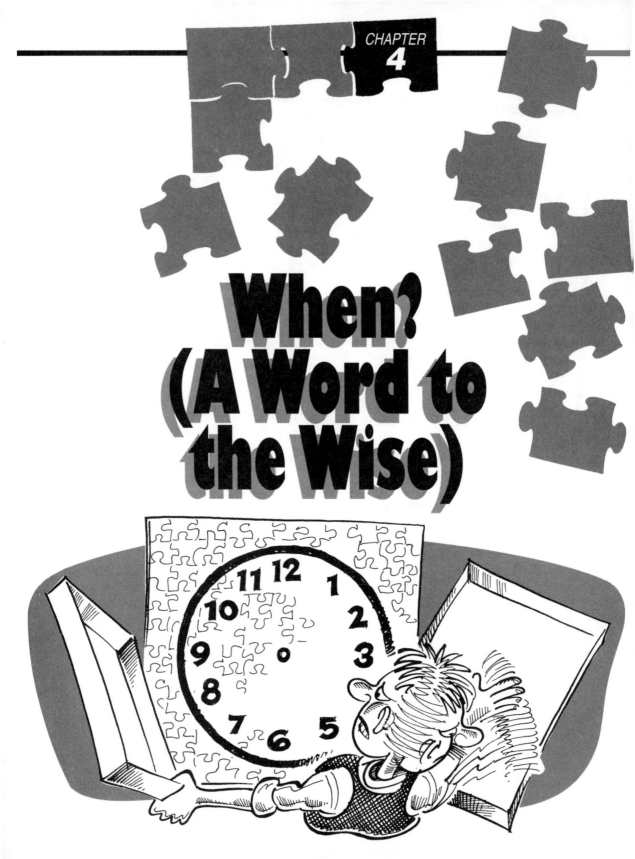

When?
(A Word to
the Wise)

When we get into the self-improvement arena, the first thing everyone wants is the big secret, the one-word solution.

In real estate it's "LOCATION"
In war it's "CHARGE"
In want it's "PLEASE"
In marriage it's "LOVE"
In athletics it's "SCORE"

So what is it in management? Is there really a single word that above all others sums it up? Yes, and that word is "WHEN."

How the "what's," "where's," "who's," and "why's" are lined up and applied is important, but all of the above (even if done perfectly) will be nullified, worthless if our "when" is wrong! **Doing** is so important, **how** we do it is crucial, but **WHEN** is everything.

There's a time to get ready and a time to do, a time to speak and a time to shut up, a time to cook the food and a time to serve it, a time to pick up and a time to return things, to stop, to go, to save, to spend....

You can, of course, do any of these things anytime, but if it happens to be the **wrong** time, you may be worse off than if you hadn't done them at all.

GOOD TIMING–a #1 skill of star managers

Don't we all know smart, talented, sincere, hardworking people who constantly struggle to get things operating well, but never do? They obey every management principle they learned in school or the seminar, except timing–

who teaches timing? It really can't be taught! You have to figure it out to fit your life, workload, speed, circumstances, and schedule, and if you can't master timing, you're going to be a thrasher.

WHEN determines how well and efficiently you operate as a manager on the homefront or anywhere. All great people know this. When you look at the Lindberghs, the Lincolns, successful mothers, generals, and actors, they all seem to use "when" wisely.

Wayne Gretzky, the world's greatest hockey player, said when he was asked for the secret of his successes, "I skate where the puck is going to be." So it is with us in everyday life. If we wait until we're called and the job is there waiting, we're too late. We generally already know what's going to happen, we just need to be there before it happens.

Don't confuse "time spent" with "timing."

Good timing is doing it NOW!

We don't have to be wizards to figure out what kind of management we get from people doing things...

...*"one of these days..."*
...*"when I get around to it"*
...*"when I get time"*
...*"the first chance I get"*

Or the ugliest word in the world of management...

LATER!

The inability to manage any aspect of our personal affairs can be summed up in that fifteen-letter word PROCRASTINATION. So much has been written, said, and preached about this word, I won't add to the misery of the many who have well earned this label (or think they have). Let's not make a national hang-up out of it. It's not a disease or a curse or an addiction–it's just a simple matter of when, **timing**. You either do things at the right time, when you're still in control, or when others force, beat, beg, or shame them out of you.

"Later" always takes you out of the running for the fresh and new because all your time and attention is being consumed catching up!

Procrastination can be cured with this one word–**NOW!** You just need to get tired of eating dust, being behind, and decide to be one of the ones out in front making the dust. All you have to do is exactly what you've done up to now, or will do later, only do it sooner. Good timing costs nothing, and takes less training, time, and money than "later."

You don't have to change anything to overcome procrastination except the way you read and heed the clock and calendar. Just switch today to the NOW Doctrine–decide to operate current. Simply doing things as you go along cuts tons of scheduling time. Move "someday" to "today" and watch that backlog shrink.

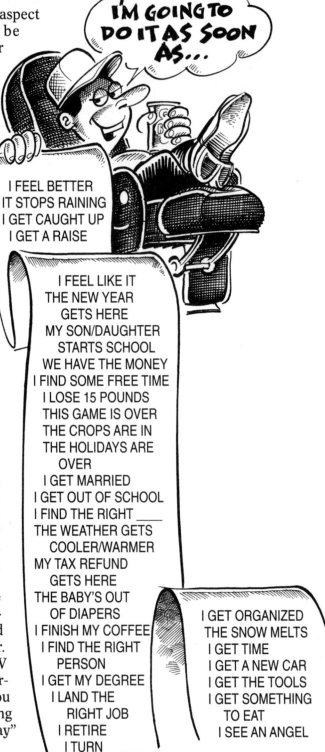

I'M GOING TO DO IT AS SOON AS...

I FEEL BETTER
IT STOPS RAINING
I GET CAUGHT UP
I GET A RAISE

I FEEL LIKE IT
THE NEW YEAR
  GETS HERE
MY SON/DAUGHTER
  STARTS SCHOOL
WE HAVE THE MONEY
I FIND SOME FREE TIME
I LOSE 15 POUNDS
THIS GAME IS OVER
THE CROPS ARE IN
THE HOLIDAYS ARE
  OVER
I GET MARRIED
I GET OUT OF SCHOOL
I FIND THE RIGHT ____
THE WEATHER GETS
  COOLER/WARMER
MY TAX REFUND
  GETS HERE
THE BABY'S OUT
  OF DIAPERS
I FINISH MY COFFEE
I FIND THE RIGHT
  PERSON
I GET MY DEGREE
I LAND THE
  RIGHT JOB
I RETIRE
I TURN ____

I GET ORGANIZED
THE SNOW MELTS
I GET TIME
I GET A NEW CAR
I GET THE TOOLS
I GET SOMETHING
  TO EAT
I SEE AN ANGEL

One of the best arguments for doing it now is explained in a booklet of mine called *The Ten Biggest Lies*. What was one of those lies?

LIE NUMBER 7

I'LL HAVE MORE TIME LATER ON...

You've laughed at people only a few years older than you who have to stop and think a moment to answer the question: "How old are you?" It's not senility, and you aren't being put on... TIME has begun to pass by so fast, they've become so busy, so buried, so burdened with responsibilities that they honestly have lost track of what year of life they're in. This is guaranteed to happen to you, too, starting right now. The adult world of less and less time is upon you. Up to now, people have regulated, scheduled, and paced your life for you, and up until now, you've always had lots of time to wait, waste, and ding around in, a seemingly endless resource of time. In the morning, watch out, because your available time is going to erode away. You'll soon have more friends, more demands, a new family. Opportunities for job growth, and church and community service will begin to weave in and crowd your life. These are good, positive things, exactly what you're living for, but what about all those other dreams of things you wanted to do "someday"? There is no "someday" in time. You have more time now, today, than you ever will, so devour it! Materialize your dreams, your "gonna's," today!

Anything you want or plan to do, like: learn to sing or write

poetry, travel, condition your body, right a wrong, visit or call someone, do it TODAY, in your youth—get with it! There will be less or NO time later, and even LESS by retirement.

Don't kill any more time in excess sleep, idle activities, TV, playing around and hanging around and cruising aimlessly. Don't just go for it... RUN for it!

"Late" is always bad timing

It doesn't do any good to plan ahead if what you plan is implemented at a bad time (especially late).

It isn't long remembered **if** you showed up or not, but **when** you showed. Visiting people in the hospital or at a time of need, for example, is good timing–visiting them after it's over takes the same time, effort, and gift, but isn't nearly as appreciated.

Lateness has a destructive effect, too. It shrieks out to all the people you interact with in your life:

"YOU WEREN'T THERE, YOU DIDN'T CARE."

Late is always bad timing–a real manager doesn't even have the word "late" in his/her vocabulary. **No** management skills can compensate for late or behind.

Real managers don't set clocks ahead, they work to be on time. They plan and prepare for things, and practice the famous "Lombardi time," which was fifteen minutes early for practice, ready to go. Being "on time" isn't smart, it's just acceptable. It may meet the schedule, but because the majority of people are late or on time, it's a crowded time and place to be. "Before" is when you get the best selection, when things are enjoyable and relaxing. "After" means leftovers and cleanup. Anytime you're late, you've locked yourself into the "survivor" mode. Ninety percent of the things left behind or forgotten on trips, in motels, busses, or taxis are the result of leaving in a rush... behind. "Behinders" do more patching than pacing!

"On time" is sitting there waiting for your ship to come in. Early means swimming out to meet it.

"Later" is the sire of that system we call crisis management: waiting until you're in need or something is due, then going all out to meet the deadline. I have friends who do a job and could get paid immediately afterward if they'd simply tally up the bill and present it. But they wait thirty to sixty days (double the billing time), and then suddenly the electric company is going to shut off their power or their kids need something big. **Bang!** They're in a crisis and take the day off to collect the bills and straighten things up. Rushing to the client, standing there with big sorrowful eyes, then running the check to the bank. Lots of times the client's gone, not at their beck and call when they need them and then they're in big trouble. They waste a couple of days every month doing this. Waiting always costs you and it irritates people, causing them to forget the positive impact and value of the job you did for them.

Being late is no joking matter. ("Hi, I'm the president of the local 'put it off' club.") People tolerate, but don't like, late people... period. **Late** and **behind** is defensive; **on time**, you're in the game; **early** you're on the offense, where you have all the advantages to score.

To get more done I learned quickly to be early. **Real** early! When I have to appear on a TV show, I get there two hours early, and I'm at the airport an hour to an hour and a half early. Let me give you an example of why:

If your flight leaves at 9:00, and you get to the gate at 8:30, it'll be crowded so that whole half hour will be spent waiting in line to be checked in, to have your baggage checked, etc.

If you get to the gate at 8:00, one hour early, you'll be checked in in five minutes, and gain 25 minutes of good usable time. Early birds double the usable time, no waiting, no stress, no emergency.

Timing is taking three seconds to put the lid on NOW

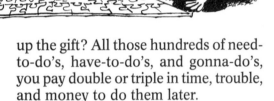

I've seen paint jobs double in time and agony after a single three-second error: the failure to pick up the paint lid and put it back on the can when the job's finished. The painter was in such a hurry to get the job done that she didn't have time. Well, when the paint spills on the carpet and your four-year-old steps on the lid, cleaning up and going for more paint takes longer than the original job!

How much time have all of us spent finding a phone number or address that someone carefully gave to us? Yet right then we were too busy or distracted to write it down. We didn't have fifteen seconds to record it and now everyone is waiting for it. We spend a half hour looking for it before we end up calling to try and get it again!

Most of the time, in anything,

LATER TAKES LONGER!

It takes twice the time to be late. Remember when you waited to pull the weeds, take something to the cleaner, fix the sink drain, mail the taxes, check that rattle under the hood, get that sore checked out, call for reservations, pick up the gift? All those hundreds of need-to-do's, have-to-do's, and gonna-do's, you pay double or triple in time, trouble, and money to do them later.

Timing is fixing it before it breaks

The exhaust pipe on my farm tractor was getting loose and flopping around. I knew it wouldn't heal itself, but I watched it carefully as it got looser and looser, waiting (like for three months) for a handy time to tighten it.

One day, while I was assaulting the morning glories in high gear, the pipe fell off, and before I could stop, I ran over it and crushed it. Because I failed to do five minutes of early prevention, my timing error cost me $75 for a new pipe, as well as two hours wasted ordering, picking up, and installing the parts. Plus I was irritated and distracted for weeks by my stupidity. (All from poor timing!)

Ever notice that we always have or get the time and money to fix or patch up, pay penalties and interest for something we put off or neglected, but we never have a fraction of that time or money beforehand to do it **on time?**

Good timing isn't always "convenient"

Here is a place where we really have to lean on our natural tendencies. We always like to do things when it feels good or "it's convenient." Convenient is a killer word for management–kind as it may be to us, it's equally unkind to our efficiency. Take the repair of a roof for instance. It's leaking a little, we know it needs to be fixed, yet right now it isn't convenient. We want to wait until we're ready (even though **it's** ready now). Now the job is smearing on about $5 worth of tar and it'll take fifteen minutes, which we just can't spare right now. Soon it's a $50 stain on the sheet rock of the ceiling, and by the time we finally get to it, it's a $500 beam warp problem.

How many times every day is it not quite convenient right that moment to unplug or pick up something–it would have only taken about a second at that "inconvenient" time and now it'll take hours to restore the damage that's been done. It's the old "closing the gate" parable all over again. Our hands are full as we go through a gate or door (house or car) so we don't shut it as we should. Then a dog or skunk or the wind or rain takes advantage of the open door and we have a real mess on our hands. The

REAL inconvenience is repairing the consequences of convenience!

We lived by that on the farm where I grew up. Sure it wasn't "convenient" to plow in the bitter cold, round up cattle in the scorching desert, or play in the tournament or milk the cows with a smashed hand, but you did it anyway and were always glad you did. The setbacks, agony, and problems that mount up as we wait for a convenient time to do something can do us in.

Forget convenience as a time slot for accomplishment. Convenience is great when you can have it, but it's a luxury, a bonus. "I'll take care of that at my earliest convenience" is a death sentence to whatever you need done. Good managers seldom wait for convenience. They manufacture it.

Get the bad news fresh!

The sergeant lined up his tired soldiers after eight days on the march: "I have some good news and some bad news," he said. "The good news, the good news!" they chanted. "Okay, the good news is we get to change our underwear." "Hooray!" came the chorus from the ranks. The bad news? "The bad news is, with each other."

Bad news makes us groan mentally as well as physically, we really don't want to hear it. It's only natural to want to dodge it. But with all we have going on in our lives at any given time, we're sure to get some. So we'd better just count it in as part of the package of life, because if we put it off and ignore it, we pay **dearly**. There's a time and place for bad news: right away, early, now! That gives us our best chance with it, the biggest break. Later, bad news becomes a sinkhole or a crater. Tomorrow just adds sorrow. Acting on, or delivering bad news is about the most critical timing in management. Just think of all the opportunities to complicate bad news when:

You don't open the bill or letter and face it...
You don't go to the dentist when...
You avoid going to the doctor to find out what's wrong...
You don't want to check out that crack...
You hear a bad noise under the hood and ignore it...
You don't return that phone call from the IRS...
Or you don't answer the phone after you've stood up someone...
You spent all the money, and don't tell your spouse...
You don't report the accident...
You can't bring yourself to tell him/her you've started seeing someone else...

All of these, and just about any of the unpleasant situations that pop up in our lives only get worse from waiting to face them. Waiting for the right time to hear or tell is agony, a waste of time and only gives those wrong impressions and unreasonable fears a longer play and makes them harder to remove.

When the wolf is at the door, using the back or side door to avoid facing him isn't going to make him go away. You don't please people or yourself putting off bad news–face it while it's fresh! It will only be half as bad, and you can correct things much more quickly and get on to the good news.

So don't wait until morning or later for the bad news. Find out where you are and what's going on as quickly as possible. Putting off facing and knowing about something that needs you to fix it (be it a fight, a fence, a financial matter, a fumbler on the committee, or a frightening health report) only builds anxiety and pressure and eats up emotions much better used in dealing with the event. You have to find out to work it out. Just as with cancer, the quicker the catch, the smaller the problem area and the quicker the cure.

Timing is picking the right job for the time

Timing is choosing, from the huge menu of "things to do" we all have at any moment in time, the job that best fits our flow and energy level. For example, when your mind is most alert and concentration most precise, do your thinking, your creative work. Do the doggy, flunky work in your doggy, flunky times. I never let low-fuel jobs burn any of my high-fuel time. I save so-so stuff (mail, magazines, routine chores) for so-so times, and do the forward-looking and ambitious stuff when I'm feeling fresh and frisky.

Good timing requires access

Good timing requires a little word called **access**. You might arrive and find the room you have reserved for something, but if you can't get in it when you need to, it doesn't do you much good. If you don't have a key, a camera, a pencil, a pass, a badge, a code, or a card, when you really need it, it may not accomplish much to be there. Management is making things happen, making things work; and even if you have the time right, if you don't have access, or entry, you can't get much done. I've seen plenty of people arrive ready and willing to work, with perfect timing, but they forgot some tool or proof of authority they needed to be *able* to work.

Be sure you have access.

Just what does this mean down home? Ever tried to find a hammer or a Band-Aid, **right now** when you need it? But you can't? Ever tried to get your cash out of some unwieldy investment account when you needed it… now? Ever need something that you own but it's stored away somewhere, and you have to go find it to get it? Ever been too hot or cold but can't reach or read the fancy new temperature control unit in the house? Ever been in the midst of cooking something good, and lacked one ingredient that is buried somewhere in your cupboards? Or not had a phone when and where you need it the most? All of this is simple accessibility, a real secret of management.

You need access to all your resources, not just to have or own them, or know where you can get them. So start right now and gather and line up the things, people, and projects you most often interact with, and if there are any delays, obstacles, or struggles to get to them, then change it. One little change of an account, a number, a place, a location will bless your life 2,000 times a year. No more fighting and waiting for "it"–that is good home management. So hang it right where you need it, carry it on you, enlarge the type, transfer it, anything that leads to easier access is legal.

P.S. If you thought I'd missed the cleaning end of things, think of this. When cleaning gear is accessible, right where cleaning usually needs to be done, you and the other members of your household will get to it quicker and be able to do it five times faster.

The advantage of "the perfect" time

When I was very young, I realized my dad was running 350 acres of land well, while most of our neighbors ran 80. They worked just as hard and long as Dad and had as much or more experience, but bottom line, at harvest time, they had far less in the haymow and the grain bin.

Not until years later did I find out **why** Dad could outmanage them three to one. It was all timing. For example, when the ground was prepared and planted, both the bean seed and all kinds of awful weed seeds had the same start. The beans came up first, nice and plump and proud, but the weeds (millions and millions of them, with the potential to be ten times as big and tough) were right behind. And now they were coming along faster than the beans–a critical moment had been reached. Now it was time to cultivate, and cultivator shanks armed with "bull tongues" were pulled past both sides of

46

the beans. This was a process called hilling, which buried both the bottom of the bean stems and the entire little weeds, suffocating them. If hilling was done right, hardly a weed would survive. Ultimately this saved not only lost, choked-out crops, but thousands of dollars of hand weeding and plugging damage to combines, and billions of new weed seeds to worry about next year.

There was a "perfect time" to cultivate, not only the right day and the right tools in the right adjustment, but the right time of day. In the morning and before noon, the beans leaves were up high and allowed their stems to show and be surrounded by soil. In the hot afternoon, the leaves drooped and the dirt would fall on them and hurt the plant. The low-hanging leaves would also cushion and protect the weeds, which in a few days would grow into non-cultivable giants.

Dad was always ready. He captured and used the prime cultivating time while the neighbors were coffeeing and fixing and adjusting their machinery. That tiny bit of timing had a tremendous influence by the year's end.

Inside the home, the same principle applies as in the field (and not just in the physical organization of things, either). Take for example the question of how and when we present those lessons of life conduct we all want to instill in our children. My mother was a master at it. She knew precisely when to seize a moment of disagreement, discouragement, or disappointment to teach a truth or principle that would stick with you forever.

I remember the hottest Idaho day in my young life—I was thirteen, and I'd been lollygagging, griping, and groaning out in the garden, making my mother force me to pull every weed. She waited until I'd reached a complete standstill, and then sat down and told me about a soldier she'd met while in the hospital once. He'd lost both legs and arms in a land mine explosion and this grown man sat there in his bed one day and wept for the opportunity to work in a garden, among the plants and flowers again. That really stunned me— I remember feeling so sad for that soldier and so lucky I could work, that I vowed that moment, regardless of how I felt, I would never be lazy again for the rest of my life. (And the rest of those rows were cleared of weeds mighty quick.)

Likewise, my mother could have just given the old "don't drink or smoke" lecture to her kids anytime, but she was smarter than that. She always waited for "the moment," the best frame for something, before she laid it on us. I had a bad stomach virus once and was sick, vomiting, dizzy, nauseous to my very toe tips, looking forward to death as a release. As I was leaning over the toilet in agony I remember Mom putting her hand on my forehead and saying, "Donald, remember, this is exactly how you feel after you drink alcohol." My brain cells quickly organized a "no way will I ever drink, then" commitment, and I've never had a twinge of desire for any form of booze since. All because of the masterful timing of a good mother!

Good timing is being ready

I must have been eleven when that big day came for my first Boy Scout Board of Review. It was more awesome than a Senate hearing and did I ever know my material. Man! I knew it backward, forward, and sideways. So I stood there confidently with only slight shakes as that row of uniformed leaders tested me. "Scout Motto?" one asked. "Be repaired." I snapped back, and everyone broke into laughter, I knew I had it right—why the laugh? Finally composing himself with a kindly smile, the Scout executive said, "Son, that is **prepared**, not **repaired**."

Almost fifty years later now, I've come to realize there isn't actually much difference between being prepared and repaired. Both are a condition of being ready when the time for action has come.

Don't be like the person lost in the wilds who waits until they hear or see the search party to start making a signal fire. The plane is overhead and he's still searching for firewood. Be ready, be repaired.

Homemakers, business managers, ballplayers, surveyors—everyone on every continent—will struggle to master and memorize the latest management techniques and philosophies, concepts and theories, formulas and ratios. But all of them clumped together and applied on their very best day can't hold a candle to the power of simple preparation. Getting and being ready takes no talent, little time, little money and always gives big results. No drug on the market can alleviate anxiety like simple preparation.

Just thirty seconds of preparation can save a lot of money and strain.

Everyone locks keys in the car, or locks themselves out of the house, for example. We'll make this mistake ten or twenty times in a lifetime. A little metal hide-a-key box is a cheap, easy way to solve the problem and prevent the hassle. Without it, getting back into the car or house the long, hard, cat-burglar way (if you even can) will tear something up and strain your back, along with everyone's nerves. You can choose the locksmith route for fifty bucks, but whatever you do will take phone calls and maybe hours to solve the problem. All for the failure to spend a few cents and a few seconds to prepare.

Or consider my loaded typewriter trick. Before I leave my office on the second floor of our home, I always load my typewriter (roll in a fresh, clean sheet of paper), so that when I return I can sit down and begin typing immediately. I have to do it anyway, now or later. If I do it now, I'm prepared so that if an idea or concept hits me while I'm on the phone or at my desk or even outside, I can rush right in and type it. It's on the page; I have it. If the machine isn't ready, by the time I fumble for the paper and load it, I may forget the idea or just how I wanted to say it. I could lose an article concept worth several hundred dollars, or spend several hours trying to come up with that original clever idea again.

My dad was always successful on hunts. Even when no one else in the entire group got game, Dad did. For years I'd hear all my uncles and the neighbors joking and telling him, "Duane, you are the luckiest hunter." You might be lucky to stumble on a big elk or pheasant once or twice in a lifetime, but **every time**, every year? Nope. It's preparation.

The hunt for antelope in our part of the country is only a couple of days a year—no weeks or months of open season—so you have to make it count.

Many compensate for the short time by getting more and more sophisticated equipment, faster four-wheelers and bigger guns (a tendency of many managers when they're trying to get more done). Dad and Mom just drove out to the area late in the afternoon of the day before, and Dad, unarmed, just walked around for three to four hours. He read antelope sign, listened and looked and sniffed things out, and came back knowing where to go to get game. He was up the next morning with the sun, and in forty-five minutes or so, bagged a trophy antelope. The meat was good, and the kill was clean. About the time Dad was cleaning and dressing his big buck, the other hunters showed up. Giant clouds of dust rose up as jeeps and trailers and bikes, horses and trailers and campers pulled in, horns blaring and flags waving. Soon there were beered-up people screaming and shooting and wild-eyed antelopes darting in every direction, trying to get out of the way of these crazy humans (most of them did get away, too).

DANG! THIS IS PUZZLING... I CAN'T TELL WHETHER HE'S COMING OR GOING.

Management could almost be defined as simply **being ready ahead**.

The ratio is about ten to one–for every ounce of preparation you'll save ten times that at least in wasted motion and lost time.

We're so caught up today in the idea of DOING that we forget more time is (or should be) spent getting ourselves ready for things than in the actual doing. Just clock yourself on the next undertaking–you're going to add on a new room, have a baby, move your aged mother in with the family, hold the family reunion at your place this year, or have serious surgery. Where is most of the time, and the most important time spent here? In planning and managing all of this in advance to bring it to pass smoothly and enjoyably. Think through and work out all the details–not just the physical and financial preparations, but the social and emotional angles, too. That ready time unquestionably controls the quality of the event at hand.

Play yourself a mental movie

As for **how to ready**, the best way to do it is:

Simply play a mental movie of the project, journey, or undertaking before you start, to see what happens along the way, and how it turns out. Engineers call this making your mistakes on paper, and it costs only a tiny bit of time and no money. We all have an imagination, so let's put it to good use here.

As soon as an objective has been set (a trip, talk, meal, game, party, that long-awaited improvement, whatever), run off a reel in your mind of what's going to happen and how you'll do it. The script will be written by instinct in seconds, and presto! You'll have a good start on what you need to gather or prepare to pull it off.

Many of us do this already at least in part, but we tend to focus on the high points and the rewards. In this particular "short" you want to include every crossroads and detour, pothole and pit stop. I always have a pencil in hand during my mental movies and a "ready" checklist completed by the end of my "show." The rest is just mechanics.

PICNICS—Amazing, how after ten days of planning, $100 worth of food, and transportation in a $25,000 van, a $1.99 can of bug repellent can make or break the event.

Prepare far ahead

You don't just want to be prepared, but **far... far ahead**. If there's a single identifying mark of a good manager, it's always being ready a long way ahead of whatever you're after or in charge of.

Many managers at home and work get praises and even raises for handling problems, but the best managers seldom have problems. They have breakdowns, fires and floods, family upheavals, quittings and sudden unexpected losses—or they have all the problems that other managers sometimes have. The only difference is that it doesn't take a good manager all that time and trouble and cost to correct them, basically because of being ahead.

Let's take two people, about equal in all qualities except timeliness. Both Hank and Harriet are assigned a PTA committee report due in three months, a charting of the safety problems and violations at school crossings in their part of the school district. Both Hank and Harriet know they can round up what they need in that time. So Hank carefully charts it on his Day-Timer, scheduling it a few days before it's due. (A logical thing to do.) Harriet gets back home, spends twenty minutes making three calls, starts a file, and has the project going now. A week later, as she assimilates the information she has already, she discovers that some people she needs to hear from are on vacation, some information has to be gathered at the state capital, and the folders she needs to present the report are out of stock at the local stationery store. None of these pose Harriet a problem because she has the time. After a few five-minute calls now and an hour and a half assembling the report later, Harriet places it in her drawer ready for the next PTA meeting (two months early).

When Hank reaches the appointed day in his Day-Timer–the report soon due–he picks up the phone. The person he needs is on vacation and some information must be researched in person at the state capital. The local stationery stores are out of the folders he needs and it will take a week to get the exact kind he and Harriet were told to use.

Hank, shifting into "smart manager's" gear now (he didn't get an MBA for nothing), tells his wife to drop everything (lots of important daily work gets put off), and they both dive into the project. He spends a half day on the phone and finally input from only three more people is needed. He lines them all up just in time, for the day before the report is due. He finds a neighbor willing to take a day off from work and go the state capital, dig out the information, and fax it to him. Brilliant! Now he calls the three more people still needed. His wife, meanwhile, has run down a company who has some of the folders in stock. She drives seventy miles round trip and gets them. Hank is elated. What an organizer he is. Hank and his wife stay up until 3:30 a.m. the night before, getting everything together except what they need from the capital. The next morning the fax arrives and ends Hank's anxiety, and he and his wife type, photocopy, and collate like mad till 2:00 p.m. (the meeting is at 3:00).

Hank and Harriet walk into the meeting with the reports, both well done. Harry spent $250 cash getting his, cutting himself, his wife, and the neighbor out of several productive days on other projects, and added a lot of stress to his life. For the same job, Harriet spent half a day and $8. Any onlooker might judge them both good managers. But Hank didn't manage, he reacted to a problem he created himself by waiting too long. Harriet used EARLY.

Consider, too, that whole group of thrashers out there who show up every April 15th. On the 14th and 15th they are alive and around but generally useless for anything but interrupting and irritating everyone (including their accountant, who always counsels them to spend a few minutes each week over the whole course of the year and save the two days at the deadline date). Last April 15th might as well have been a holiday for me. Every friend and associate I called on (except the good managers) had blotted the day out and were on tax time overload–bending over calculators and rushing around with handfuls of papers and priority mail envelopes. If you are in this group you are a poor manager. And you aren't giving yourself a chance to look things over in an unhysterical moment to make any necessary adjustments and catch mistakes, or find out before the last minute that you need to come up with more funds.

We all have returns, forms, trips, projects, talks, and proposals that are due a long time from now. Doing them now, even a year early (if you're sure they have to be done) will take you a fraction of the time than if you run into obstacles doing them later. No sweat! Why work yourself into a lather or work until midnight? If you're working ahead and you hit a snag, you can just make an adjustment and wait until the problem irons out and then get on with what you're doing.

The One Day at a Time doctrine
(Don't believe it!)

How often do we hear someone summing up our whole problem by telling us to live "one day at a time"? We may go to sleep at night and wake up the next day to a new morning, but life is an unbroken span of time, divided for convenience by the clock and the calendar and other counting and keeping track of systems. Our days are prepared for and nurtured years, even decades ahead—not from first thing in the morning on. Everything in our lives laps over and overlaps from birth to death, and if those days you are planning to live one at a time aren't prepared, stored up, and educated for, you'll end up a victim of the day, not the director of it.

Do it ahead!

When you get the juice out of the freezer the night before, mixing it in the morning is a five-second job–not five minutes of chiseling that frozen hunk into dissolvement, splashing and slopping all over and using six tools you'll have to wash afterward.

A good manager never packs for a picnic on the day of the picnic. She has most of the delicacies ready to go days or at least the night before and puts them all together on the last day. She makes the potato salad an hour before the picnic so it'll be fresh and good and won't spoil, but digs the potatoes (or buys them) days before and boils them the day before.

Here are just a few of the things you can do ahead, early, to save time and stress and be ready to roll:

- ❐ Laying clothes out and ironing them ahead (so you find the stain or moth hole now)
- ❐ Getting everyone's dress clothes assembled for that big event tomorrow
- ❐ Beautifying yourself ahead (so you aren't trimming cuticles and bangs, and searching for bracelets ten minutes before you have to leave)
- ❐ Packing your suitcase
- ❐ Preparing for the big outing or camping trip
- ❐ Assembling all your gear and tackle for the big fishing or hunting trip
- ❐ Preparing meals
- ❐ Making the time-consuming part of the recipe ahead
- ❐ Finding every paper and document you need for that important meeting
- ❐ Cleaning the house the day before the company is due
- ❐ Getting ready for the party
- ❐ Making lunch for school, work, or going fishing
- ❐ Getting everything (tools and materials) together that will be needed for that home repair or improvement, craft project or sewing project
- ❐ Getting everything ready for pet or livestock feeding
- ❐ Buying greeting cards and gifts (birthday, Christmas, Valentine's Day, etc.)
- ❐ Making sure the car/lawn mower is full of gas/oil
- ❐ Making sure anything that needs to be sharp is sharpened
- ❐ Making those cookies or that casserole you're supposed to bring along with you
- ❐ Having the water pistol handy to shoot the pooping pup

Some things to EXPECT about good home management

How often, when an experience comes, have we found that it didn't feel, look, taste, or work like we had expected? Let's look at some of the "surprise" or unexpected sides of good home management:

It's a three-member team!

Good management calls for three very important ingredients all working together: your head, heart, and hands! No one of these alone or even a combination of just two of them will get things done the way you want them. You have to apply all three. The best thinking and even loving with a hands-off attitude won't cut it. The most skilled hands and willing, determined heart won't do it either, without brains. And even smart and proven doers will fail when their heart isn't in something. If you haven't managed to hook these three members of your being together, now is the time if you intend to manage anything well.

More ticks of the clock than snaps of the finger!

Even good management takes time. Just because it's sure to take less time if we do things more efficiently, we too often think it takes **no** time—only the pushing of a button for an instant play or replay. Wrong! Good management takes any time spent worth more to you, but it doesn't eliminate the need to take time with anything. Progress and accomplishment always take time and patience.

It isn't as painless as it appears

Sometimes we watch a good manager breeze through a day, with all their duties, and it looks effortless. When we watch a thirty-year veteran of the trapeze going through his routine up near the peak of a circus tent it looks easy, too. It takes a lot of experience as well as muscles and mental energy to soar like that. So don't expect management to be a cinch or an instant success. Like anything else, it takes work and practice. And there may be some stretch marks and some temporary pain and discomfort. Just adjust your mental meter to: "It isn't always going to be easy."

Good management, on the other hand, **rewards** you for your efforts, whereas lots of other hard work ends up unappreciated or in vain. Masterful management isn't a way out of work, it's a way to make your work really count!

Every Manager Needs a Crystal Ball

f you don't happen to be one of those gifted prognosticators with a trick knee, sensitive sinuses, or milling herd of livestock who "know" the weather or whatever **before** it happens, don't despair. You have amazingly reliable management predictors right in and around you, much more accurate and useful than any aching joint. And they can do a very fine job of forecasting the future.

Just what are these forewarners we can use for fore-armers?

Believe history

Haven't we all reflected back on our lives to what it was that taught us the most about management? Listening to people say, "Boy, I'll never do THAT again," is what's done it for me!

I know we're all independent, creative, even stubborn enough at times to have to "figure it out on our own," make it work ourselves. It's the "do it my way" mentality. But why re-invent the wheel or re-invent management processes and principles when much of it, most of it in fact, has been done before and tested over and over and what works and what doesn't is right out there in plain view? We watch twelve people wreck their bicycles trying to jump the canal, and note that all twenty who went on the bridge a block away, crossed safe and sound. We should be smart enough to know we will manage better using the bridge.

We can all learn great management principles from observation and other people's accounts of things that **didn't work**. When we hear that arguing with a skunk doesn't work, we don't want to tangle with one, so most of us manage to keep that out of our life.

Yes, we can pay the time and cost on many things to learn personally what just won't work, but better management practice is to believe history. Years ago I began collecting a list of what didn't work even for sharp people. I love this list; it really has saved me some sad steps in life. I think you'll find it helpful, too.

There are a few exceptions here (a few of these do work once in a while), but as a whole, I think you'll agree that history has it… these don't work. Eliminating the "don't works" out of your life is a great way to build good management right in.

two-hour courses in anything
telling a kid "later"
working out rent in exchange
washing windows with vinegar
all-purpose stain removers
lending to relatives
hiring relatives
blind dates
cheap paint sprayers
setting watches ahead
predicting the weather or traffic
overdraft accounts
county fair gizmos
making bargains with God
drugs
colored bathroom fixtures
lending things you don't want damaged
lending books to anyone
hoping the cat/dog won't get pregnant again
setting the paint lid/hose nozzle somewhere
   "just for now"

ignoring surface preparation instructions
not taking the "drying time" seriously
filling the bathtub while you're busy with
    something else
assuming that someone else will shut the gate
waiting for too-small shoes to "stretch out"
hoping a leak will go away
assuming you'll have more time to get gas the
    next time you use the car
waiting for someone to discover you
hoping the baby will leave the kitten alone
dating more than two people at once
junky scissors
trips to town in which "you aren't going to buy
    anything"
planting very old seeds
announcing that you don't intend to get
    involved
"Wet Paint" signs
"No Trespassing" signs
"No Hunting" signs
"Keep Off the Grass" signs
"Do Not Disturb" signs
signs that say "Don't Pick the Flowers"
cutesy file labels
putting your shoes on before your pants
trying to slip on your shoes without undoing
    the laces
taking the kids to town without making a
    bathroom run
razor shaving dry
"fishing lure retrievers," patent pending or
    otherwise
sending fragile things without padding
transporting anything without padding
paint edgers
masking tape
cheap sprinklers

buying things "to refinish someday"
putting only one clothespin on the bedspread
asking someone not to tell anyone what you're
    about to tell them
taking the turkey out of the freezer the same
    day you intend to cook it
taking the animal home without putting it in a
    box or carrier
not changing your clothes before painting
cleaning the paintbrushes "later"
leaving your good clothes on after you get
    home
the "glug and guess" method of liquid mea-
    surement
doing without a drop cloth
counting on your memory to remember all
    those important birthdays
resetting the date of something you're really
    not committed to
not bothering to make a copy of something
    important
wearing a big-brimmed hat with nothing to
    hold it on
wearing anything white on a bus or subway
guessing how long it will take to cook soft-
    boiled eggs
planting things too close together
letting a tiny child play with anything good or
    valuable of yours
handing specs to someone else and expecting
    to get what you've been dreaming of
expecting a product to sell itself
walking to the mailbox in your socks
sex without pregnancy, disease, or heartbreak

asking everyone to smile for the picture

asking the babysitter not to use the phone

adding a little extra anything to "make it work better"

stacking just one more on top

carrying a cup or bucket that's too full

bill consolidation loans

Japanese beetle traps

waiting for the phone to ring

starting a diet three days before the class reunion

starting an exercise program one week before the big skiing trip

surgery for obesity

head cold cures

repairs on plastic toys

giving gifts ahead

giving an inheritance ahead

moving the refrigerator/piano yourself because you're in a hurry

telling people not to scratch it

wearing new boots on a long hike

wearing anything that is too small for you

picking a mate, a puppy, or employees by their looks

expecting favors in return

the "general idea of what's in there" method of checkbook balancing

asking mothers not to worry

asking teenagers to keep in touch

raising the heat so something will get done faster

figuring it out/totaling it up "later"

asking people to turn off lights they aren't using

telling yourself you'll remember what's in that unmarked bottle

leaving the car unlocked because you're only going to be gone a few minutes

eating just one (potato chip, etc.)

doing it "just once" (cheating, etc.)

free ballpoints

giving unsolicited advice

things that say "Press here to open"

paying for help in advance

forcing yourself to go with your second choice

getting someone else to make your apologies for you

postponing irksome but necessary small detail tasks

buying or agreeing to anything to get a free gift

telling people something is funny before you tell it to them

getting your hair restyled the day before the big event

assuming you'll remember where the buried water line is without making a map

keeping the pie you made for the church fair in the refrigerator

training cats not to get on the table

talking people into things

telling the babysitter not to let junior nap more than a half hour

having "a good idea" of where the place is

eating tacos while driving

sleeping for "just five minutes more"

leaving yourself no leeway (in a trip or schedule)

promises to do something "one of these days"

telling someone else to declutter

telling someone else to lose weight

telling someone to stop smoking

trying to talk the doctor into giving you a prescription without seeing you

serving something exotic and expecting everyone to eat it

putting anything sharp or breakable in your pocket

setting anything on top of the car when you're getting ready to depart

miniature vacuums

hangers that are supposed to hold ten pairs of pants

cutesy answering machine messages

plastic tops that are supposed to keep the fizz in the rest of your can of pop

desk organizers

assuming that "they" know you want or need it done

making someone love you

specifying "No calls, please"

shoe racks

setting out garbage bags with bones or meat scraps in them

plastic laundry baskets

55-mph speed limits

cat harnesses

holding your tummy in

addresses from old directories

walking off to do something leaving the iron on

furniture set too close to the swing of a door, or to the traffic pattern

telling people to wear safety glasses

putting a glass bottle of anything in your suitcase

working when you can't really see what you're doing

one-coat paint

rinseless stripper

no-fault divorce

swearing

monitorless examinations

telling the plumber/electrician that he can come whenever he gets around to it

asking for something cooked "rare" without **emphasizing** it

letting anyone know where your Hide-a-Key is

operating on empty

putting classified ads in the paper over major holidays

telling the cashier she doesn't have to individually wrap those tumblers you just bought

freezing the leftovers of things you didn't really like

Head off those surprises!

Surprises are for little kids, to add some spice and excitement to their lives, some extra little rewards (all the while being steered and sanctioned from the sidelines by a wise adult). But we adults, ourselves, don't need any surprises around home because excitement in this case translates to anxiety. Good or bad surprises will throw us off course, break our rhythms, and interrupt the finest schedule so fast and well that we're always amazed. One of the surest paths to disaster is not knowing where you are, in anything from your checkbook balance to the condition of your teeth, and because of this you suddenly get a surprise.

Surprises are generally negative—something breaks, aches, and takes us in a direction we can't afford in either time or money. We may think we'd rather not know about it, but if we shut ourselves off from a potential problem and wait for it to go sour (and surprise us) it will, with ten times the damage and delay when it does hit.

We should all adopt the practice of doing a little self-audit of all our goings-on, a quick check on things, a short daily, weekly, or whatever review, a few minutes of asking and charting just where am I with...

1. *my marriage*   6. *my education*
2. *my children*   7. *my job/employer*
3. *my health*   8. *my parents, etc.*
4. *my finances*   9. *my neighbors, etc.*
5. *my spirituality*

Don't lie to yourself, this little appraisal is one of the best management tools around.

Pay attention to predictability

A young woman unloading her car had a back seat full of stuff to carry into a building. To take fullest advantage of the trip, she piled one last ceramic bowl in a precarious position atop an armload. As she started up the steps the beautiful bowl rolled off and smashed on the concrete, and out came that old "after the fall" remark: **"I just knew that would happen."**

Have you ever stopped to consider that at least three quarters of the time foulups are predictable? It's a knack for preventing problems, not how brilliantly we deal with them after they've happened, that makes us real managers.

How many times when we get the car stuck, miss a flight, get an "F", cut a finger, the cake falls, we're sick after an eating binge, someone doesn't return a call, or our spouse leaves home, do we utter that famous phrase, **"I knew this would happen."** The last pitch I ever threw in organized baseball (my senior year in college) I had three balls and no strikes on a good Montana State hitter. The bases were loaded with no outs, so I needed a strike and decided to chuck it right down the pipe. I did and he hit it 80 feet over the wall in center field. I just knew before I threw that ball, he was going to hit it, and he did.

Isn't it incredible how many times we say to ourselves, as we sit slumped or stumped over a problem or disaster, "I knew darn good and well this was going to happen"? We're always point-

ing out how animals can't reason and we can. Why do we so often find ourselves in predicaments if we're so smart? Because we don't listen to reason—**our own**. No one is better than us at assessing the perils, potential threats, and problems in our own lives. We know what we can do and how the people and things around us will react. We can fairly well predict what will happen if we do thus-and-so—when it comes to ourselves, we're first-rate fortune tellers. Now the way to make ourselves at least twice as effective in life is to start believing and following our own instincts. Sure, we can foretell what should happen. That's great, but if we don't heed the warnings we won't avoid the hassles.

So pay attention to your "predictions" and plug them into your planning.

We've all personally experienced the unfortunate consequences of the follies on the following list, but somehow we didn't let it sink in. Read the list over slowly and this time REMEMBER to avoid these little oversights that can cause big bad (frustrating, time consuming, expensive) consequences.

CAUSES OF FOUL-UPS

Didn't check ahead, or get advance information about something we intended to do/the place we wanted to go

Didn't notify ahead

Didn't pay attention

Didn't look at/read the label

Didn't read the instructions

Didn't read the fine print/ALL of the instructions

Didn't read the recipe through ahead of time (to find out what ingredients are supposed to be at room temperature when you start, or that a three-hour chilling time is called for somewhere in the middle)

Didn't anticipate everything we were going to need

Didn't tell them what we wanted

Didn't give clear or **complete** instructions (i.e. told our helper to get a gallon of Sherwin-Williams' best semigloss paint in the color called Hubbard Squash, but assumed they knew we meant *latex*)

Forgot that the person we were giving our instructions to doesn't know everything we know (asked a friend to drop a cat off "at the vet" and neglected to inform them that we changed vets about six months ago)

Failed to **demonstrate** how to do it, rather than just tell someone how

Didn't make note of the size or model #

Picked the wrong person to do it

Didn't check with someone who'd done it before

Failed to say when something would start or end

Didn't look at the map

Worked from outdated information

Were too distracted or in too much of a hurry when we did it

Failed to finish the job or waited too long to finish it

Overestimated our skill or ability

Underestimated the difficulty or expense of something, or how long it would take

Tried to judge from a tiny sample

Didn't look at what was actually in there

Didn't mark or label it

Made untested substitutions

Didn't confirm the appointment

Didn't think it all the way through (allowed for how long it would take to get to the airport, but not for parking, riding the shuttle, checking our luggage, finding the gate, and running to the bathroom)

Didn't put that important agreement on paper

Tried to fake it

Didn't think about how we were going to get it home/in or out of the building

Didn't realize how big it (dog, tree, bush, bread dough, pasta) was going to be when it reached full size

Learn from your mistakes

Somewhere, sometime, we've all heard (after getting right back into the same problem): "The first time it happens, it's an accident, the second time you do it, it's your fault, the third time you really deserve it!"

None of us have the time or resources to be constantly re-making our mistakes. We might not have known the neighbor's dog bites and suffer a surprise attack, but now we know. Getting bit again the next day and the next is pretty dumb, yet we all do things like this all the time. We need to cook eggs, so we rummage for the cleanest, least used pan, and the reason it is cleanest and least used is because it always burns the eggs and yet we use it again. The last time we used the Flareback pen in our drawer it leaked and ruined the document, but we pick it up knowing and remembering it ruined the paper and use it again. We get stuck driving up the Leavitt's lane and spend hours digging and pulling the car out, and yet on the very next delivery we hesitate at the end of the muddy road and go for it again, only to get stuck again. For years now, we've been buying those disappointing Easter egg dyeing kits, some of the colors are too light and some too dark, the wire dipper isn't strong enough to hold the eggs, and the appliqués run when you try to use them. Each time we cuss and criticize them, yet the very next year we buy another. We're traveling and we're hungry and all that's available at this hour is limp hot dogs loaded with mustard, relish, and onion to disguise their lack of taste. Every time we eat them our digestive system self-destructs and sends messages to our brain and backside that we'll suffer for every bite. Yet we cave in and carry out a bagful. And this one, gadfrey, why do we do it? Our cupboard shelves (even the tallest ones) are twelve inches high and yet the super family size box of Cheerios is fourteen inches high and we have to lay it down to get it in, which means those miniature donuts will dribble out and roll all over. We snarl and slap the box in disgust every time, and yet the next time we're in the store, to save 30¢ we grab the giant size again, so we can gripe and fight and clean again. The mosquitoes bit the blood out of us during the last four camping trips at Pebble Creek—made everyone miserable and almost

caused a divorce—but we sit right down and plan another trip there. Likewise, how often have we seen a movie that really rubs us raw, upsets us terribly, gives us bad thoughts and dreams for a month. And when it comes on again, sure enough, we sit down and watch it again.

We're amazing, aren't we! Even after education and full knowledge of the outcome, we do it again… and again. If we all pooled our lists of "stupid repeats" it would be thicker than the unabridged dictionary. A biography of mismanagement, the perfect formula for wasting time and emotion!

Here's a place we can make a sharp turn from an old habit to save a lot of trouble, money, and energy. Stop the unpleasant reruns and replays right now. Sit down or walk around and review all the things, situations, practices, and people that have bugged you, let you down, and hurt you. Then hang up the list and memorize it—if it broke, bit you, or made you bleed once, it will again! Now just ELIMINATE or stay away from these. It's easy and will pay dividends like you won't believe.

Secrets of Master Managers

on't get jealous or discouraged when you see some superman or woman zipping through their days at high speed, in perfect rhythm. When you find or hear of someone like this, seek them out and watch what they do and how. Don't be afraid to adopt the principles and maneuvers of real managers—follow the leader!

Remember, just getting older doesn't make us better, finding better ways of doing things does. So start tapping your own local wizards today, rather than finding fault or feeling guilty for being in their presence.

Good managers size things up and find a better way

Of all the managers I've seen and worked with in my life, few were in my father's league. He moved mountains at home and at work. At the age of twenty-two he was a grade foreman, constructing many of the roads across the country we drive on today. Then he raised a big family and farmed for the next thirty years. In 1965, Dad developed some land out on the Kimmia, Idaho desert. He dug a 600-foot-deep well for irrigation, and then because there was still a water shortage, he couldn't farm that new land yet that summer. One of my uncles, who owned a construction company, was aware of this and called Dad and offered him a job as foreman for the summer on a road outside of Twin Falls, Idaho. Not being one to sit around, Dad took the job. He wasn't scheduled to start until April 15, but Dad and Mom moved over there two weeks early. Then Dad went out and just walked the road site for a few days, looking and sighting with his hand-held transits, making notes, and talking with all the farmers whose land the road would pass through and by.

Bids for construction work of this type are written in terms of so much per yard of material moved from point A to point B, and all the bidders had asked a goodly amount for this fairly ambitious job. The company had allowed a month for moving the first mile of dirt. It would be tough, but possible if they pushed and all went well. Dad had it all done and cleaned up and graded in two weeks, not only saving the company a ton of money, but bathing them and the state road inspectors in amazement.

Most of the time when construction companies move in to build a road, land for the highway is gotten by forcing landowners to sell right-of-way (the state will even condemn the part in question, if necessary). In spite of this, not only was Dad's job a success, but the people along the route baked bread for and threw confetti on the road builders.

How did he accomplish all of this? All he did was figure out a better way to go about it. There was no magic here, only an approach that contained all the ingredients of good management: planning, public relations, a little charity and consideration, and EARLY. He looked, he asked, got suggestions and advice, and planned **before** the equipment and labor pulled in.

Above all, he didn't limit his options to the way it was usually done. After he thought it over, Dad visited the farmers and talked horses and cows for a while, then said, "You know those lower two fields over there don't have the best drainage. If you raised the level over there and put a little dike right here, you could make one nice attractive tillable field out of it."

"Boy, that would be perfect," the farmer said, "I've thought about it, too. But the cost of moving about 200,000 yards of dirt in and around there would be prohibitive."

"Well, I tell you what, George, if you'll take down the fence and put a culvert across that gate ditch, I'll not only supply you the 200,000 yards of material free, but I'll smooth it to grade."

The farmers were overwhelmed, and of course, agreeable. Which meant that when the big dirt carriers picked up a load of material from a cut, instead of having to haul it several miles down the road, a fifteen-minute round trip with a mighty big piece of machinery, they only had to move it 400 feet.

Dad made several arrangements like this along the way, and they all added up to saving money and time, as well as improving the environment and numerous lives.

We can get these same kinds of results by always stopping to THINK and see if there is a better way.

Don't underestimate the "UN"

You say you planned well and followed through even better, but things still didn't come out like they should have? Everything took longer than you thought, and seemed somehow behind and disorganized? Yet you did follow the plan, got everything ready, and got it all done, just right. Maybe that's the problem, you stopped there. You did the "before"–the preparation–exquisitely, you did the "during" even more brilliantly, but left out a big, big part of every project... the aftermath! The undoing.

As the old saying goes, what goes up must come down! What is packed has to be unpacked. What is loaded has to be unloaded. What is wrapped has to be unwrapped. What is unrolled has to be rolled back up. What is decorated for the occasion has to be undecorated after the occasion. What we bought on vacation has to be shoehorned into the house. And even all that winding up you did of yourself and family, to get ready for the vacation, the visitors, or the project, has to be unwound. "UN-ING" anything–the cleaning up and putting back–takes time and equipment and almost as much planning as the original project. Yet seldom do we think about it, or allow the time, emotion, or money for it. These are kind of the "leftovers" of living, and they get little attention and even less credit, so they forever sneak in to uncoordinate the best laid plans of mice and men.

This is one big reason cleaning frustrates so many people. It's never thought of as part of the action, just a wretched or contemptible necessity after the big doings. And worse yet, **after** is generally when we are out of energy, time, and resources. We used it all for the playing or the project, and there's none left now for the gathering up, the recovery, the unharnessing, or the return after the event. Tell me truthfully now, on how many lists of things to do have you seen any allowance at the bottom

or the end of the list for UNING? Maybe 5% of the time.

Consider our hunting and fishing planning, for example. It's all getting ready, getting there and getting the game. Then planning stops and the dirty coolers, littered boat and car, snarled reels, and smelly fish end up an afterthought. What has to be done with a dead deer, all 100-200 pounds of it hanging out in the garage, is a big item! And totally unplanned for and no time allowed for it, and now we need to get right back to work! Or that parade float for the organization or drill team you're in charge of. Unbelievable all the help, planning, and enthusiasm that went into the building and using and displaying of it. But now the party's over, and there the big ugly thing sits, pieces of crepe paper blowing off into the street. The job of UNING can be almost monumental at times.

Our failure to allow for the dismantling of things—whether sports or pleasure pastimes or undertakings of sheer necessity, ends up casting a negative cloud over the spirit and memory of the event. We're uptight because there's no time for the undoing and irritated because it caught us by surprise.

So, here's a new wrinkle for your home management program. Have three sections in your thinking and on your planning lists for anything from now on: **1. the preparation and getting ready; 2. the doing and enjoying; and 3. the UNDOING** (you can enjoy that too, once it's planned). Most "to-do's" need an "un-do."

This will also help you practice more wisdom up front, like when you decide to paint your windows for Christmas and spray fake snow over everything and drive nails and hang lights and pine branches everywhere to wow the neighbors. Knowing you'll need to UN all of this will make you think twice about how much you do and how you do it. If more people took this approach to not only projects, but the way they ate and drank... well, isn't UNING about like a hangover from the big bash? Incorporating the UN into your thinking will make you twice the manager you are now.

Overbook

One big lesson in life management I've learned is—**OVERBOOK!**

Send out more invitations than you have room to seat! Collect more samples or ideas than you intend to use, plant more seed than you want flowers/crops.

Estimating our own needs can be tricky enough at times, and at home there are usually others: family, friends, neighbors, associates, etc., to be taken care of and taken into account. The secret of dealing successfully with this is to **always overbook**. You can never be 100% sure how much or many of anything you'll need, from party napkins to push pins, so if I expect 50 people I allow and prepare for 60!

Leftovers are easier to deal with, physically and emotionally, than "leftunders." Whether it's Halloween candy, box lunches, camera film, paint, nails, or clothes on vacation, taking or buying a little **more** than you think you'll need (or others told you to bring) is good management. People praise my Scouting leadership because I always seem to manage to have things come out "exactly as planned." Actually they don't. There never is a time when anything we count up, schedule, or pack for is just as planned. Something is always forgotten or overlooked. So I always overbook and 90% of the time it pays off. The other 10% of the time I'm left holding a couple extra watermelons or a dozen too many donuts–super easy to deal with compared to not having enough! Good cooks all know and allow for this, too, whether it's stew or scrambled eggs they're serving up.

Overbooking is an especially good idea when you're dealing with outside sources. Few people are as enthusiastic about **your** project as you are, so when you ask ten people to bid, suggest, or contribute, you won't get ten contributions, maybe only one or two. I'm continually amazed at how sparsely people respond, **even people you pay!** Send out a letter or questionnaire asking for only three minutes' work, and only five people in one hundred will respond, even if you include a keychain or free book with it. One of the editors of *Family Circle* magazine (circulation of seven million) confided to me that once they showed a handsome sweater on the cover and offered free crocheting instructions to anyone who wrote in–they got only **twenty-five** responses.

There are lots of resources around everywhere, so when you plan and fig-ure, be sure to tap them. But go for more than you need, because they dress down to "slimmer pickins'" than you thought (or as those notices on cereal boxes say, "Some settling may occur in handling").

Move out of victim territory

Ever raked leaves in the wind? Washed windows in the sun? Typed with a sore or broken finger? The best efforts, tools, skills, and even determination don't mean much, do they? We're all subject to the circumstances at hand…. You can't focus while fighting constant interruptions, nonstop noises, etc. It's hard to keep in the swing of things when external forces are swinging at you.

If you're giving a speech outdoors and jackhammers are going, pigeons are pooping on the audience, and wind is distorting the microphone, things just don't work out well, no matter how good and committed you are. Good managers don't stay in victim territory. They move, cut the problem off, switch jobs, come earlier or later, or get help, but they don't just keep fighting a losing battle.

Make a list right now of everything that's abusing you. Surprising how many little things may be blocking or pecking away at our efficiency.

1. Like that worthless (well, irritating) friend or relative who is forever hanging around and consuming your day (or life)—change it.
2. The shift, schedule, or travel involved in your job is destroying or taxing your very core of living—change it.
3. You have a hobby that once was great fun, a genuine pleasure, but now is straining, distorting, taking over your home and life—change it.

4. The bathroom storage situation in your big family is a constant source of fights and squabbles—fix it.

5. You've always parked your car there, but now with every passing week there is more tree sap and pet spray on it, and now someone has scribbled on the windows and snapped off your side view mirror. Find a new place to park!

Try the door

Two repairmen needed to get into a vacant house, so they immediately starting trying the windows, climbing up the balcony, and checking the chimney, looking everywhere for a place to "break in." Another fellow watching the proceedings walked up, dusted off the doorknob, turned it, and walked in.

We make ourselves a lot of extra work by working all the angles and alternatives before we try the direct approach. Management is pursuing the shortest, easiest, most economical, environmentally sound course.

The ultimate magic word here is "ask." Good managers always fit "ask" right in there between "look" and "leap."

Skip and condense

Remember that little section in the back of *Reader's Digest* called the con-densed book section? You could read a whole book in a few hours instead of days, and the briefer version was entirely enjoyable, too. So it is with many of the things we have to plow or labor through—condensation has some real merit. You don't want to miss the World Series this year? The last time I clocked it, the seventh game, one game mind you, with all the before, during, and after trimmings, took a total of 22.3 media hours. My best friend said you could see all that was worth seeing in about fifteen minutes. He had other projects that didn't take full focus so he set the TV nearby and did them. When something worth watching came up (things like that are usually replayed) he'd interrupt his work for a few seconds to watch, and then back to his hands-on business.

Taking all day to do an all-day job is fine, if you have all day. If you don't have it, then manage to do the same amount of work in hours or minutes. When in a hurry, I skip a couple of laces on my boots, miss a shower, meal, or an hour of sleep. You can't steal your own time. When I don't have time to read a letter or article or attend an event, I ask my wife or kids what it said or what happened and get a great condensed version!

Remember what you did when you were forced to squeeze and condense something, and then do it on a regular basis instead of just when you're up against the wall!

Don't mow what doesn't show

Sometimes routine and habit are big hindrances of good management, rather

67

than the advantages we may think they are. Like things that are "scheduled"—vacuum twice a week, clean the windows once a month, polish the furniture weekly, clean the oven three times a year. We all know people who wash walls or shampoo carpets that aren't dirty, just because that's how often they've always done it.

Over in my Hawaii home, when the grass isn't doing much I mow once every month or so. But one of my neighbors there mows every week, month in and month out. There are times you can't even tell where he's mowed, but he mows anyway. I finally convinced my wife to stop ironing the sheets and pillowcases (except for the guest beds!) and the parts of my shirts that didn't show. Meetings are another good example. Club and committee meetings and the like are scheduled and so they're held even if nothing needs to be discussed that week or month. So we fill that hour or so with absolutely nothing of value. Just like mowing short grass.

There are things, too, that we keep on doing by habit after they're no longer necessary, such as canning and preserving like mad, and cooking enough for fourteen, after most or all of the kids have grown and gone on to college. How about setting the table unfailingly with three pieces of silverware, even when only one will be used? Or for that matter, religiously making those "three square meals a day," whether or not everyone is present or actually hungry.

Learn to function more by need than by schedule or habit. It does little good to rock the baby after he is already asleep, eh?

Find the guy with the matches

Something isn't working—be it a financial deal or a piece of furniture, a job or a garden site, a tool or a relationship. You've struggled with it and fought it for years and are still fighting. You dread or despise it and yet you have to face it over and over and over again. Things like this really get old and wear on you.

Fresh battles at least have some adrenaline-stirring excitement. Old refought ones are not just unnecessary, they put lead in our boots and discourage and depress us.

I've seen people with balky cars, biting dogs, hard-to-maintain hairdo's, obnoxious friends, uncomfortable suits, one legged-ladders, etc., who were hassled by them and even hated them, but kept them and lived with them year after year, waiting for them to get better or to go away... someday. They don't, and they use up your time managing the same problem over and over.

So right now, today, deal with what you are tripping over or bumping your head on! When something is wrong, **fix it**. Don't just get a bigger cover or a tighter tourniquet, fix the problem. Don't just put out the fire, find the guy with the matches. Find the cause of the trouble and cut it off, heal it, seal it off, abandon it, leave it behind, or get a new one—but fix it.

Forget stress management, pest management, loss management. The idea is NOT to manage undesirables. Don't manage stress or pests, get rid of them!

Simplify

Whenever we hear this excellent advice, our first thought always is: "Easier said than done."

But simplification is simply having less unimportant things around you. Once you figure out which those are, it's easy. The easiest place to start eliminating is with your junk and clutter (see Chapter 8). As soon as you sort out and dispose of all that unnecessary stuff, you'll discover what a pleasure it is to live with less, and your life will start evolving toward simplicity. Luxury and excess unsimplify a life something awful. Bad habits do, too. Go from there and watch simplicity slip into your life without you even working on it.

Remember the man who asked a sculptor how he made an elephant out of that big hunk of rock? "I just chipped off everything that didn't look like an elephant." Just taking away what doesn't contribute to the cause can go a long way toward creating a management masterpiece.

Just for the fun of it (and eventually, a 50% improvement in your personal management) make a column on your "To Do" list called "Unimportant Things I Am Doing Right Now." At first, you won't think of one, but as the days wear on, they will come to you… that repair job on something you won't be happy with even if it's fixed; that lunch date with someone you've never really liked; that auction you were going to go to when you really don't need anything; a meeting you don't need to attend and they don't need you; a new sport or activity you were taking up just because someone else is…. As soon as you think of things like this, write them down. Once you've made them visible, you have a better chance of weeding them out of your life.

Even if you only find and eliminate one or two "unimportants" a week, the unused time you capture back from them will enable you accomplish some of those genuinely meaningful things you've "been meaning to get to."

Duck, dump, and don't do: *Good management isn't doing everything faster, it's not doing things you don't need to do! That seems too obvious to even say, but it's the biggest secret of smart management.*

You can simplify your lifestyle, too

I was in a supermarket not long ago that was so big it was impossible from one end of the store or the other to even read all the labels on the seemingly endless number of aisles one had to go through to assemble the necessities of life. I could have been in there for hours, but I was in and out fast, mainly for two reasons.

1. **I knew exactly what I came in there for—not to browse, but to buy.**
2. **My lifestyle eliminated seventy percent of the aisles.**

   I don't do exotic sauces or foods so I could skip that aisle.

   I don't have indoor pets so I didn't need that aisle.

   I use simple commercial cleaning products and that eliminated at least two aisles.

   I don't do soda pops and colas and that cut out an aisle.

   I don't do pills, salves, gargles, etc., and that eliminated an aisle.

   I don't drink so I could bypass the booze aisle.

I don't read the tabloids and the gossip sheets and that eliminated an aisle.

I was out of there and back in life while others were wearing themselves out wandering the aisles. Look over your life and see if you might be able to do some aisle-skipping too.

Question both the old and the new

The old generation questions the new ways and the new generation questions the old ways. And I think that's a wise exchange for everyone. In management two big stoppers we often come across are:

"THIS IS THE WAY WE ALWAYS DID IT."

"THIS IS THE WAY IT'S DONE THESE DAYS."

We could label these "old hardhead" or "the lazy way" management, depending on which you happen to be partial to. The fact is, good managers hang somewhere in the middle. Just because it's old doesn't mean it's worn out, and because it is new and untried doesn't mean it's unsafe or not worth considering. I've had plenty of people call me crazy or old-fashioned because I still use a 1969 Olympia manual typewriter for all my books. But doing it the old way like this I still produce more books and articles than most folks around (including many of my fellow writers). The original method, the old rhythm might still have a place, or maybe the new should take its place. A good manager questions both the old and new ways.

Sometimes the old-fashioned is still fashionable because it's withstood a hundred years or more of testing. Products age but principles don't. Think on that the next time you feel compelled to "upgrade."

What about all of that advice out there?

There sure is plenty of it around, isn't there? We can get all the advice we ever dreamed of, some of it free and some of it for a big fee. Because counsel can be a way to short-cut years of study, research, and experience on our own, we should learn to take it where it

is merited. So how do we sort it?
- *Listen to it objectively (don't just buy the passion it's presented in).*
- *Consider the source. (Who is it from? How smart and successful are they in marriage, money, and management matters?)*
- *Think: Does it REALLY apply to your situation?*

- *Apply it on paper and in your mind about four times before implementing it in reality!*

Don't neglect that R & D

The biggest trap in management of any kind is to slide into the habit of tending only the daily onslaught. In other words, using all our resources just to do the chores, to keep up and keep even. It's easy to fall into this. We are working away busily and earnestly and gradually do manage to adjust our routine and schedule to handle calls, fill requests, process the incoming, and fix the broken. But slowly or suddenly we aren't doing anything more. We are changing and washing the clothes, maintaining. But we aren't doing anything for uplift, education, edification.

Now I know there's a lot to be said for maintenance—it's important and we do need to spend a goodly portion of each day and week on it. But we also need to get outside and beyond the regular functions and chores and move and grow and turn over new rocks. At least a small portion of our time needs to go into "R & D" as they call it in business (research and development)— creating and expanding, reaching and

exploring for the new and fresh and better, the improved. It's always taxing and expensive, and often unsafe and criticized (definitely not the course of least resistance). In fact it is the course of most resistance. That's why so many avoid it and so few follow it and why there are so few real managers around.

As merely being on time is late, so is just keeping even with things. If you aren't surging ahead and doing more than caretaking the things at hand, you are breeding discouragement, and actually regressing. No matter how small, do something progressive all the time, even as you wade through all of those daily boring necessities.

Are you rushing to do urgent or important things? There is a difference.

Correct sticking, not stuck

(Only read this if you've ever gotten a vehicle stuck.)

We seem to be making good time on this new shortcut we just got wind of when suddenly we notice our car bogging down, sinking a couple of inches in the mud. Should we stop, go back, or continue? Most of us are determined, so we put the pedal to the metal and go for it. Our car surges a little, then slowly bogs down worse than before. Now we're at least six inches in. The car can barely move in any direction, but we're really mad now—we started this and by gosh we're going to finish it. We back up a little, gun it, and plunge another twenty feet... to a halt. When we push the accelerator this time, the wheels spin and whine and smoke! We get out and discover that the tires are out of sight somewhere down in the mud, the fenders are resting on the road. We're in deep–really stuck!

Now we have several choices: 1) Lay our coat under the tires; 2) Try to excavate; 3) Kick and curse the car; 4) Hike out to get a wrecker.

We could (should) have stopped, turned around, taken another route when we first felt bogged down, first felt that softening shoulder. Now, the longer drive we were trying to avoid when we started out sounds like a pleasure trip. It sure would have beat several hours in the mud and an $80 towing bill to unbury the Buick.

Watch good managers drive, they travel some bad roads, like all of us. But you seldom see them involved in a disastrous dig-out situation–they never let their vehicle get lodged or buried. As soon as they feel slippage or seepage they correct it. **Good managers correct sticking, not stuck.** When that little warning buzzer goes off in your brain, listen to it!

Don't fold up because of one wounded finger

Good management means doing more than one thing at a time, and some of us are doing five or ten things at once, some fifty, some a hundred and fifty, and some 1,000 or more! No matter how many things you're multi-managing, you know that for all of us, some projects go bad, come to a halt, fail, or some disaster befalls them. Just because a wheel falls off something, the engine quits, the cake falls, the part is lost, or you're dealt a bad hand somewhere in your wheeling and dealing, you never want to stop the forward motion of the things that *are* rolling.

I see people hit a snag or a setback, a disappointment in some pursuit, and it's like a mortal wound. They might as well roll over and die–they mope around, stare into space, and cease all energy and effort on the other fronts.

Someone's stock goes down, they lose a client or girlfriend or boyfriend, or their car is totaled, and immediately halt all other activities to dwell on or mourn the misfortunate one–bad news! Don't do it.

You don't close all the other factories because one burns down. You don't quit using your fingers or feet because one is wounded. You don't withdraw from the whole tournament because you made a bad shot or two. You don't quit asking new questions because you don't like the answer you got to one of the old ones.

It's poor, poor management to let a setback in one section or part of life affect or shut down others. I've seen people get a turndown on a project or proposal they were advancing, and quit hobbies, stop eating, dress poorly, disobey the law, get drunk, and drive recklessly. Yet, that project was only one of scores of good, progressive things they were doing and managing. Because one point of your plan takes a shot to the jaw, the knees of another don't have to buckle! Keep your "to-do's" independent of each other!

Hold yer horses

Most of us know that we CAN do all the things on our mile-long "to-do" list, but when they're all there at once, in one big demanding "right now" pile, it's easy to go bonkers instead of going to work on them. It gets to be kind of like a juggler who's doing fine with three or four things in the air and then gets five or six and really sweats. Then a few more go up and he suddenly realizes that things aren't going to be running smoothly for much longer. Something's going to come crashing down!

When I was a youngster, my Grandpa, who could run lots of things simultaneously with real finesse, had a saying we all need to adopt. "Hold yer horses," which meant stop the team and let the horses catch their breath (in this case, while you figure out the right order to do things in, instead of charging and milling around in confusion and fighting the problem that hit you first). I watched a mother walk in her door once after being at the neighbor's for five minutes, and the place was in chaos. The phone was ringing, two kids were biffing it out, another was screaming for its bottle that had rolled out of reach, the chokecherry syrup (stickier than Super Glue) was boiling over on the stove top, another phone started ringing, rock music was blaring from MTV, and the sweater she'd stretched out on a towel to dry was stuffed into the planter. This type of mayhem is where management really pays off—stopping to "hold yer horses" and think a minute before you add your own panic to the already existing mess.

The average mom or dad would probably rush to the phone first, screaming threats along the way. Things would only accelerate while they were distracted on the phone. Next, the parent would come down hard on one or the other of the combatees. However, this particular mother was a master home manager and had things quieted down in fifteen seconds. She smiled, shook her head and hollered over to the two fighting, "Oh, my–that might be Santa on the phone. Henry, would you get it and quick Hank, grab the bottle for Tyler so whoever is calling won't hear him crying." On the way to the stove she snaps off the TV, turns off the pot, quickly mops up the splatters before they have a chance to harden on there, ignores the sweater (damage already done), picks up the frightened baby and carries him to the other phone (which really was Santa's helper). This is management at its finest.

If a bunch of choices or even emergencies hit you between the eyes, don't let it panic you, or at least don't show it. Stop, think, "hold yer horses," and never fight it. Ninety percent of us will fight in a threatening environment or situation. The reverse–cool pursuit–is far better. It will neutralize the chaos, quiet it down, and then you can assemble things in some kind of order before you turn them loose again.

The art of "on hold"

The rest of life doesn't shut down when some problem is peaking. When you have lots of demands on you, learning to put other things on hold while you handle a pop-up (new problem or opportunity) is a real skill. In fact, it's a necessary one in home management. Most mothers get to be experts in this and thus learn to outmanage their spouses. It's actually fun, once you get the knack of it, to keep all the tops spinning at once!

Our home can be like a busy airport, and once in a while too many planes get there at the same time to land... and they can't. Suddenly you have a hungry kid, a surprise guest, a call, an urgent errand, your favorite show is on TV, and the best school clothes are on a "three hours only" sidewalk sale... and there is just one of you. These "all at onces" don't always happen, but when they do, don't panic or fly into a tizzy. Have some "on hold" slots and strategies in your life and use them. Hand your kid to another family member (or the guest), get the frozen strudel out of the freezer, let the answering machine get it, call and convince them the errand can wait tomorrow morning, use your VCR, ask your neighbor who works in town to put those shirts and slacks on layaway.

As for dropping everything else when something really important comes along ("the world will end if I don't get this done... everything else can wait") rarely is this wise or necessary. Even in the midst of the most do-or-die project, real managers still keep the other things in forward motion. They slow them down, but don't stop advancing the other "to-do's" just because the dominant one is pressing. It's easy to lose it all when you focus all on a single pursuit. I've had absolutely insane weeks (because of manuscript schedules or book promotion tours or big contracts underway in my cleaning business) demanding my attention twenty hours a day... barely time for a breath. And there, sitting on my desk, with no time pressure on them, is a pile of fan letters my readers made the effort to write. They take time to answer. They aren't as urgent as the contracts or the national media, however, in between sighs and interruptions, I snatch one or two off the desk and fit them in along with the panic stuff, and glory be... at the end of the month the panic is over AND the letters are all answered.

You can turn some of those "to-do's" down to low, medium, or even warm (even if the cookbook says high), but never turn any of them off, even for a while. Learn to use hold. "Hold" means it's still hot... just a little delay in serving it up, is all. This is a practice of good managers. Just watch them.

Good management means little things, too

Good management is watching and handling the little things, too. A tiny leak seems so unimportant, yet a mere drip from a half-inch water pipe can lose 15,618 gallons of water in a year. That's a nice size swimming pool. Even a 1/32 inch pinhole will mean 75,039 gallons **gone** in a year.

When someone is down, depressed, or struggling and you ask, "What's wrong?" They may name one big sorrow: "My spouse left me," "I'm broke," "Car quit," "I lost my job...." But if we were to probe, we'd find seventy more little insignificant things that all made a contribution to the big breakup, the mangled marriage, or the financial failure. "I only made one bad investment," is seldom true. They made lots of little money mistakes over time that all added up to the big loss.

Sure, "nobody's perfect," but around the house, if too many little things are overlooked or ignored, they will add up—nonnourishing meals, little mishandlings of money, undone repairs or maintenance. One or two won't wound much, but little things—lots of them—do make big things.

Efficiently, or even inefficiently, but steadily tackling those small tasks, demands, and opportunities and conquering them will usually yield big results. Enough little things managed well, in fact, is generally what results in getting "the big break" in life.

I speak at numerous conventions and most have a luncheon or banquet or two for which "tickets" ($15-$45 value) are issued at registration. When it comes time for the tickets to be collected by the caterer—it never fails—many people have misplaced them. There is more confusion, rummaging, rushing around, excusing, and promising than you can imagine over this. For years, I've watched this (even at management seminars!) and the biggest, best, smartest companies have the problem. Then one day at a small Idaho Potato Association conference, I saw the woman in charge of registration grab the three tickets for the next two days' meals and staple them to our name tag which we had to wear always.

This little touch eliminated all loss and confusion. There was not one panic, no stress, and the food line went much faster and smoother! **That's management!**

You must be there to manage

There's one dream of home or any management that you have to let go—just forget it, it'll never happen, it's pure imagination, a crazy hope that will never come about. What is it? "Perpetual motion," or thinking that once something is started, organized, and on its way, it's going to be OKAY from there on.

That would be like rounding up the kids' coats, pants, and gloves, bundling them all up perfectly, and sending them out into the snow to play, thinking "Ah, once out the door they'll take care of themselves for a few hours." Wrong! In ten (or two) minutes they'll be back with frozen tears and fingers, for adjustments, explanations, arbitrations, and reports. Likewise, we can't just get cages, cups, food, and water, and assume that the pets will just live in there happily ever after. It just ain't so. Managing things, at home or anywhere, is like juggling—we have to keep our eye on **all** the balls all the time, not just the one we've got in our hand at the moment. We can't just put the candle on the cake, light it, and assume the birthday party is on and running. We still have to run it, schedule and manage all the activities.

In other words, if we start something, we need to tend it. True, as when

growing a garden or getting a tan, sometimes we do have a big assist from outside sources, but we still have to supervise, watch, adjust, and acknowledge.

Management is making things work, not just organizing them.

Herding the cows or sheep back on the ranch was perfect training for this. Because there were a lot of them and they were all usually either relaxing or ambling along–grazing, munching, and feeding–in that big roomy pasture, it seemed that they were more or less taking care of themselves. But if you weren't there, right with them, or didn't at least have them in view or have a dog to help out with riding herd, they could be in big trouble in just a few minutes. All it would take is for one maverick to leave the herd and wander off, one calf to find one little break in the fence, one wily coyote to come too close, one neighbor's bull to decide he'd like to expand his harem. Trouble on the hoof–if not a stampede!

I'm always amazed how many people look for a pat on the head because they handled a foul-up that happened because they were gone. Somehow it's evolved and is universally accepted that management is getting things going, doing a little fine tuning and then sitting back and watching it all work by itself. Any good manager learns fast that **NOTHING RUNS BY ITSELF.** No matter how fast it's spinning, everything loses momentum and direction if left on its own… that goes for kids, cows, crops, and courses! No matter how good an outline, instructions, and incentives you've left the kids

(the crew, the class, whomever) to "carry on" by themselves, no matter how sincere you all are, it's only a short time until chaos sets in.

Stick by with what you start, whether it's a simmering stew or a basement remodeling. Even if you don't need to sit right beside it the whole time, at least stay in the vicinity.

Sometimes "to do" is "to adapt"

There are times–many, or even most times–when we don't have the means or the resources to do the job at hand… not enough money, not enough space, not enough training, not the right tool. Rich, poor, old, young, educated, and unschooled all find themselves in this situation every day, and this is in fact the real fun of management. Making things work with what you have, when you don't have what you think you need.

The professional managers known as homemakers are artists at this. They can make or bake the best out of odds and ends and scraps. Farmers can, too. During the Second World War, one of our farmer neighbors blew the engine of his '37 Chevy. You couldn't buy or get piston rods then, so he found a time-hardened old hardwood fence post and made a rod (yes out of wood) and it worked. Likewise, I looked at the fantastic carving one day on a chair by an old German craftsman. "What tool did this?" I asked. He showed me a unique tool. "Where did you get it?" I inquired. "I made it," he said.

Yes, we can MAKE THE RESOURCES we need to manage, instead of looking or waiting for the resources to appear. You'll need to make a few rods now and then, too. And they'll work if you make them.

Likewise, our "to-do's" may be round, square, rectangular, or triangular, and they don't always fit into the first slot or hole available. We can find a way to make them fit, or find somewhere they do fit. The old word for this is adaptability, and it's essential to "to-doing."

"I built my kids a merry-go-round (complete with safety guards) from a seized-up truck rear end, a broken trampoline, old tires, a scrounged chain, a ruined garden hose, a jack shaft, muffler clamps, and miscellaneous nuts and bolts."

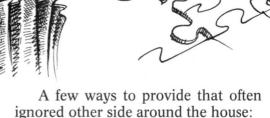

Build the bridge from both sides!

Good management always works from both sides toward the middle. If you want the kids to clean their room, for example, ask, tell, or command them to do it and set a time limit–that's one side. Then provide an avenue of encouragement, either help or a reward or whatever for doing it. That's the other side. Cleaning up after the dog is one-sided management; providing training and prevention is the other side.

A few ways to provide that often ignored other side around the house:

To help see that clothes get hung up–provide the room and the tools

To help achieve good grades–make sure a quiet study place and situation is available

To help everyone eat better–improve the menu and the food budget

To help win games–take them to practice

To help you drive safely–make sure the car is in good repair

To help people be on time–make sure they have alarm clocks and sensible schedules

Do it yourself!

If I were only allowed three words to ever utter again for the rest of my life, those would be the three most powerful ones in the management vocabulary. They're great, impact-filled, productive words: "**Do it yourself!**" It's the power phrase for a happy and productive life, and will beat any other magic words around.

Having to depend on outside sources for results is a thorn in any good manager's side. Programs, groups, organizations, or paid assistance–all of that is great and good, but it never has and never will replace the dignity and efficiency of doing it yourself, with your own hands and brain. Sure, we can't do it all, but we can do much more than we do now.

I've watched people build great kingdoms by picking twenty experts, one in each field, and molding them together. The owner never knows or understands any of their jobs, just depends on his team members and their skills and his ability to manage them. This works somewhat in the simple world of business and sounds ideal, but at home, when you don't know all the ropes yourself, when you leave it all to others, you're in trouble. You can get away with depending almost entirely on other people's talents for a while, but sometime, someday, it will backfire on you and only the ability to "DIY" will enable you to survive.

Everyone seems to want to have things done for them today, instead of being involved in the doing. As if there were something wrong with working on or doing things yourself. We're almost taught now that doing it yourself is dumb, we are all too educated and valuable these days to do mundane chores or ordinary projects, at home or at work.

One day in Detroit, for example, the cab I took from the airport had a blowout, and the driver pulled off the road and said he'd radio for help. Because of the traffic it would be at least an hour before a tire changer could get there. The cabby was only forty years old and 200 pounds of muscle (he could have changed the tire without a jack or a wrench, he was so strong). But he knew how to "manage"–call and get someone else to do the job, that was how he'd learned to do things all his life. He was the driver and radio operator. We all seem to slide into this "radio for help" mentality when a situation has to be dealt with. I told the cabby I didn't have an hour and a half to wait to get to the hotel, I had an interview coming right up so I would change the tire. He stared in disbelief. "Do you know how?" "Everyone knows how to change a tire!" I told him, and had the tire changed in seven minutes "flat" and we were on our way.

There are one-minute, ten-minute, and thirty-minute jobs that need doing constantly and we, trying to get someone else to do them, use hours and even days getting them done.

Be a do-it-yourselfer as much as you can. You can be an expert in many fields, don't believe what the jobologists tell you. **Doing it yourself cuts out more management problems than any other single thing you can do** or course you can pursue. And surprisingly, it's often simpler and faster to do it yourself than coddle, correct, and coerce the same performance out of someone else.

We're always being advised to work with our head instead of our hands. And look what it's doing to us–most of us are overweight, and have to depend, even for yard care or for the simplest sort of carpentry, on someone else.

When you have to call on others to do all your "handwork" I'd get worried. It's expensive, lowers your confidence level, reduces your independence, and puts you at the mercy of others. It cheats you of the chance to develop new skills and abilities, too. Hiring out all your "hands on" needs, even if you can afford it, will eventually make you a poor person.

HELLO EPA? YOU'D BETTER COME OUT HERE! I'M COMING TO A WETLAND & I WANNA MAKE SURE IT'S DONE RIGHT!

Good managers agree: when you can do it faster (and better) than you can instruct it—do it. Teaching children is an exception sometimes.

Make things more convenient

There are a lot of things that can be done around the house to cut cleaning and maintenance and make things more convenient. It doesn't take a big investment, either.

Remember that time spent cleaning and maintaining isn't progressing and paying time, it's just restoration, and restoration only brings us back to where we were. There are hundreds of alterations and adjustments you can make to save you time and effort every single day of your life. And you can take advantage of them even if you're just redecorating, remodeling, or buying a new couch. I'm talking about things like: choosing furniture that's easy to live with, and fixtures that make bathroom and kitchen care easier; floor finishes and coverings that will look great and reduce the time you spend with mop and vacuum; materials and designs for every part of the house that will reduce spills and splashes, and child and pet damage; ingenious ways to camouflage dirt and those inevitable nicks and dings; how to cut down dust and airborne grease and grime, and make trash handling a much less messy operation; improving your storage situation, and finding counter heights that suit **you**; turning the no-man's lands of attic and basement into clean, usable space; and even how to reduce yard upkeep labor!

I can't give all the details here, so check out the book my daughter Laura (an interior decorator) and I wrote called *Make Your House Do the Housework*. You should be able to find it at your local library or bookstore. Or send $15 + $3 shipping for a copy to: Don Aslett, PO Box 700, Pocatello ID 83204.

"I used to keep our food in a pantry, a room next to the kitchen. I'd need to go in there maybe ten times a day, which meant walking back and forth to the pantry, carrying things, opening doors, and then collecting all the little ones that followed me, got caught behind doors, or left on the wrong side. After dejunking (thanks, Don!), I was able to move all of our food to the empty cupboards in the kitchen."

"We used to waste a lot of time looking for them, so we now hang the dogs' leashes and collars right by the door. We groom the

dogs while we're watching TV, so we have a cupboard for pet stuff in the family room."

A two-legged tool

There are all kinds of tools you can borrow from a friend or neighbor to help get your "to-do's" done, but one of the best is another kid to play with your kid, which leaves you free to tackle household projects uninterrupted. Nothing works better; kids keep each other busy and entertained.

Last week, for example, I heard one neighbor ask another (they each have one son), "Can Jeremy come over to play? I've got to get some heavy-duty cleaning done, and Christopher stays out of my way when Jeremy's here."

Do a dress rehearsal

Trying to make anything work smoothly straight off the drawing board is seldom successful. A trial run before the big moment, a test or tryout before you begin, is a wise and rewarding management maneuver (and it sure beats jumping in head first). Just like those Broadway producers do, you need to do a dress rehearsal, with no one in the seats. You need to put all the parts together and see if they fit, plug it in and see if it runs.

This is needed in all we do—a few minutes upfront to get a feel for something before we're in it. Find the faults *before* things fail.

Our harvest time back on the ranch when I was a boy, for instance, always seemed to go smoother than our neighbors'. At the time, I figured it was good luck, but now I understand it was good management. We fixed and greased and shaped up our combines to perfection, 100% ready for the big day, same as all the neighbors did, except Dad always did something they didn't. He took the machines to the field and made a round or two (he called it a shakedown or "working out the bugs"). We always found some flaws—a ditch that needed to be filled, a bolt or belt that needed to be replaced—which he did the day **before** the big day. Then, when threshing started, we threshed. The neighbors found their flaws right in the middle of the big day, so trucks and crews all had to stand around waiting for repairs and parts.

For over a year, I planned a construction project at home that involved lots of concrete and facing rock. I came up with and perfected (all mentally and on paper) an approach and procedure, and had all the materials delivered to the job site. Then remembering Dad's practice, I grabbed a spare hour before a speaking trip, and mixed up a little batch of mortar. I laid a few lava rocks, and guess what, they were heavier in hand than in my head. I also needed thicker rock than I'd imagined on paper, and laying uphill and on the flat each called for different methods and materials. So after that dress rehearsal I ordered (right while I was on my trip) and got the additional things I needed to do the job right. It prevented lots of lost time and frustration on that job when I got back and in the middle of it.

Specifications (yours or experts') are never immune to oversight and mess-ups. Good management is avoiding mess-ups!

No matter what you're doing or planning, you can make your own "test drive" before you head off across the country. Minutes before can save mountains of time after.

1. Good cooks taste before they serve, no

matter how many times before they've made it.

2. Try out new recipes on your family before you make them for company.
3. Always try it out before you buy it.
4. Try it on before you plan to wear it all day.
5. Break it in/learn how to use it before you take it along as essential equipment.
6. If you have spare keys made, make sure they work before counting on them.
7. See if everything fits in the suitcase before the airport shuttle is waiting outside.
8. If you have to borrow someone else's vehicle, be sure to drive it before the big day.
9. If you buy a video camera to record that special occasion, be sure you know how to operate it before the bride starts down the aisle.
10. Try out the party games before the party.
11. Don't assume that anything you've had out/in the shop to be fixed IS fixed 'till you try it out and see.

Don't forget those dress rehearsals—make sure it works or fits and everything's there before the curtain rises.

Handling those "unhandy" happenings

We all experience them, those inevitable "unhandy" happenings:

"The bridge is out"
"The airport is closed"
"It's a blizzard"
"They aren't open today"
"The electricity is off"
"My sitter called in sick"
"I'm out of money"
"I haven't been to bed in twenty-eight hours"
"The computer is down"
"My ride didn't show up"
"The freeway is jammed"

You have a job or two or ten to get done right now and one or all of these unhandy happenings crop up. The market is off, the road is closed, or your appointment was canceled. What do you do? Do it anyway!

Some people will stay up all night hunting for or making a place to sleep and end up with a great place and no sleep. Others make the best of what's available at the moment, lay down on the rug, bench, or concrete, and sleep uncomfortably (but for a full eight hours—stiff is better than sleepless).

When you need nourishment, you've got to eat to live. That's an important principle of management. If the food is cooked and served up with knives and forks, great. If it isn't, then eat it raw with your fingers. Sometimes eating on the run, fighting with a broken sword, playing on a sprained ankle, working while sick, and deicing the car without any gloves is the only way to go!

"Proper" is always nice but because I forgot my tie, forgot a name, wallet, or key, I'm not going to halt my headway. Good management is ad-libbing, winging it, making do, and making it happen anyway.

If the shoe fits, wear it. If the shoe doesn't fit, wearing it anyway, making it fit, wearing your old shoes, or going barefoot is management. Do whatever you need to do to keep walking or running!

Judgment calls

We managers really make use of that "summator" somewhere in our head that appraises, assesses, estimates, adds, subtracts, deducts, and weighs things, and then spits out a conclusion. We might call these "judgment calls," and must make a million of them in a month.

Judgment calls in the shop or office, on the ballfield, and even in an operating room are not too hard because there is usually a flow chart, policy manual, or checklist available, a set of sure guidelines or boundaries of some kind. But at home, not one but one hundred wildly differing situations pop up, and most of them don't come with an instruction booklet and won't wait for a committee meeting or family council. You just call it, and then live with it. Call it wrong, and you and others suffer.

One woman related just one morning's worth of judgment calls to me:

Is Roger really that sick? Should I call the doctor? Which one?

Who should Stevie play with? When? Where?

What size of snow boots should I order for him now? What's the right balance between too big and too quickly outgrown?

What's wrong with the furnace? Should we fix it or keep on fighting it? How much will it cost? Can we afford it?

Does that dog that's been hanging around the back door belong to one of the neighbors? Should I try to find out, or just call the dogcatcher?

Does this salesman have a good product?

Who do I hire for Susie's piano lessons? When should they start?

Should I arrange an alternate babysitter for tonight in case Stella doesn't show?

Now that I've got the fight stopped, who do I punish?

(We could all add at least a hundred more to this list.)

Sure, these are little things, but when you add them all up at the end of the day, they have a profound effect on life and happiness, and **we** decide it all. There is no letup, and no, there isn't any course in Judgment Calls 101.

How on earth do we learn this, the biggie of management on the homefront? And **we do have to learn it**, because if our judgment is poor, then our life is poor-poor-poor. If we don't have some background horse sense or experience, we're in trouble.

What happens at home when one person makes and has made most of the calls all along, and then suddenly due to death, divorce, or disablement of some kind a "do what you think's best, dear" is dumped into a manager role (where they are clearly over their head)?

The solution? Remember all the movies we've seen about a green Easterner being thrust into a western situation to cope and compete, or a country person being set loose in a city? Both

start out doing unbelievably dumb things, are fooled at every turn by everyone. How do they survive? They quickly **find a friend, a master, an intelligence source who "knows the ropes."** Rookies find a veteran they can trust, ask, listen to, and follow. That is the best protection and the fastest way to inherit good judgment.

The key is to pick a good mentor. They are always available, and usually willing—without charge—to tell you the whats, whys, whens, and hows, and even to help or spell you. Here is a big secret of home management. Nice neighbors (nice *wise* neighbors) or that woman with eight kids can help you more with your one or two kids than Oprah or a child management seminar. That old gentleman with an immaculate yard and bountiful garden can transform your potted trees. So take along your questions and visit—ask, listen, and then **follow,** and someday you'll be a judgment call instructor yourself.

What if it's all and only up to you, and there is no help available?

Most value judgments are about 99% hinged on direction, or where you are going. So stop long enough to ask and answer these questions.

"Is this 'road' (decision) taking me where I want to go? If I do this, will I stay on course, and end up where I want to be?"

Worry management

One day a buddy handed me the neatest little polished rock—it was about credit card size and fit nicely in your hand, with a little indentation for your thumb to rub. He called it a worry stone. You could sit there and hold it and worry away with your thumb going like crazy.

Worry management is actually a big part of any managing. Sure, we can't ever eliminate worry, but taking a day—or even an hour—off to do it, nothing but worry, is really the opposite of management. If the seven dwarfs could whistle while they worked, then we should be able to worry while we work. We know that already, somewhere deep inside, but still we stop and fret and stare into space or use good planning or thinking time to worry, worry, worry. Transfer your worrying and save it for down time. Or do it while you're doing something else, something that doesn't call for your full brain power and concentration.

Worry can practically paralyze us, and especially for those long-range or what-if things we have no control over, can't take any steps to prevent anyway, why let ourselves be derailed from the things we need and want to accomplish?

'Tis said in the old proverb, that worry is putting up umbrellas before it rains... hence a waste. Good management is having the umbrellas with you or knowing where they are in case it does rain and then forgetting about the worry and the rain.

The most brilliant and determined mind cannot alter or control the past—only anticipate and prepare for the future. So take a few minutes and arm yourself for whatever might be worrying you—then set it aside and get on with those 1,000 things.

There are always enough worriers watching you anyway, so you don't need to!

What about the worries you CAN do something about?

We all know that little tugging feeling. Something is bothering us, even when everything is going well. Something we said? They said? Something to do? Something undone? Maybe a rash or unkind act on our part? An apology we need to make, a bill we need to pay, an anticipated problem in some area, a fib that may soon catch up with us?

There are hundreds of possible little discomforts, conscious or unconscious "gnawers" like this, and they chip away at our concentration and pull lots of current from our energy package. They cloud clear management vision, gum up our managerial gears, and retard us everywhere we turn. As we carry them around inside they just keep growing larger and climbing to the top of our mental to-do list. Then they sit there polluting and diluting everything we attempt to do. It's like smelly trash—until you dump it, it will smell. When that odor begins to bother you, identify the source, and go take care of it, even if you have to eat crow, or pay extra—the weight isn't worth the wait.

For instance, your dog dug up the neighbors' flower bed and you are waiting for them to come over (you just know they will) and complain about it. Instead of waiting for that someday, go replace those pansies now!

Carry a short, short gnawing list.

The secret management weapon—righteousness

It's unquestionably one of the best principles around for good home or self-management.

Moralistic as it may sound, doing what is right is the kindest, quickest, surest, most longlasting way to solve, handle, and prevent problems. Do what is right and let the consequences follow and you will be on a path that eliminates many persistent management problems. Righteousness means you don't have to deal with, repent of, or repair the damage from dishonesty, immorality, getting even, jealousy, cruelty, etc.—you can use your time and resources to do and advance and grow. (Note I didn't say be religious, I said be righteous.)

SOME KEY GEARS INSIDE THE HEAD OF A GOOD MANAGER

True, there are striking differences between super managers anywhere. They do have their highly individual quirks and oddities. But most of the real winners also have some unmistakable likenesses. Such as:

They spend very little time with recurring problems.

They probably have as many problems as anyone else, however they do something about them (rather than hope or wait for them to go away, or run from them), so they don't have to go back and deal with them again and again.

Good managers fix what is broken, one way or another, so it doesn't come back to haunt them and they don't have to come back to it.

They know the difference between running a tight ship and a slave ship.

They know the difference between demanding and expecting and *inspiring* people to get the chores done or to obey the rules of the road.

They know when to stop and take the rock out of their shoe, and when not to break stride...

and just tolerate the hurt until later. We have a goal and a direction and are going for it, and then along comes a snag. An interruption, a pebble in our boot, a cut finger, a bit of bad news, a change or cancellation that's going to make things a lot tougher than they were. Poor managers will immediately yield to the distraction, focus on it, and stop to relieve the pressure and the hurt. But now they've lost not just time but momentum. Hurts can heal, but times and positions and opportunities don't always come around again.

They don't worry about failure...

or even think about it much. They go for what has to be done and let the chips fall (and gather and sell the chips afterward).

They never get lost in the daily chores and duties.

Good managers work constantly to do the regular, the set, the routine, and the inescapable more efficiently, and squeeze it down to an ever smaller part of our schedule, so we have more time to do new and more forward-looking things. Chores are great for discipline, but freshness and risk are what keep us alive.

They avoid the unnecessary... period.

Life is full of unnecessary things, things that take time and money and space and spirit and really give us back very little. Such as status symbols, for example.

They're always in the middle of what's going on.

On the edge is just an advisory capacity—leave the advising to the second-guessers. In real life, when and where there's lots going on, you need to be in the middle of it. You need to be able to mow better and faster than anyone you hire to do it, and do it yourself once in a while to keep the scent of grass in your sensitivities.

They stay in the game.

Good managers might seem to hop and jump around as much as bad ones, but if you look closer you'll notice they're hopping and jumping in the same direction in the same game, the same activity toward the same purpose. They stick with a project or idea, bad or good, until it works or they discard it, but they don't just start something and leave it. You just can't win in the game of life if you don't stay at the table and keep playing your hand. You leave when you've made a real decision to do so, not because you're uncomfortable for a minute or two, or something is briefly unpleasant.

They're not afraid of "overload."

They work with both hands at once, and will almost always take on more than others do, more than they're asked to do, more even than they at first believe they can do. And most of the time, they'll not only do it, but only be stronger and more respected as a result.

They live by the rule : "Because you're doing 40 things now (and three times as much as any of your neighbors), it doesn't mean you can't do 50 more."

Accomplishment has no limits, limits are established by you only, not the opinions of others, the weather, or the norm. Your mental bridge can carry 250,000 cars and 40,000 tractor-trailers without overloading every day, day after day—as long as they aren't all crossing the river at the same time.

Don't be afraid to play FOLLOW THE GOOD MANAGER LEADER!

Mastering those "Home Matters"

borrowed the title "Home Matters" from the Discovery Channel show on home management I often do with Susan Powell.

Home managers have all kinds of home matters to juggle, tackle, cope with, and come to terms with. How we handle these things, and even more important, our **perspective** on them, makes all the difference.

The phone

The telephone is undoubtedly one of the world's most valuable tools, right behind the fork and the toilet. What a timesaver–what a time waster, too. Everyone in the world now is directly connected to our home any minute they want to tap us–salespeople, freeloaders, poll takers, gossips, cry-babies, idlers, reporters. A phone can and does become a little electronic dictator–we are either running to answer it, waiting for or returning calls, being interrupted by calls, or fretting over the oversized phone bill. Being "phone ruled" is not part of handling 1,000 things at once.

Notice that most master managers don't spend much time on the phone, and don't carry one around with them, either. They get away from the phone when they get serious about doing. I'm sure not anti-phone, but phones do seem to be used more for massaging than messaging.

I've always liked written messages better than calls. A note or letter enables you say only what you want to say in exactly the way you want to say

it. It gives you a clear record, and usually saves several more followup calls after the first one. When you **are** using Mr. Bell's wonder:

1. Keep calls short.
2. Have a list in front of you when you dial (so you can be sure to cover all your key points).
3. Notice, and try to make use of, the times of day and week when personal business phone calls are most effective. It can take forever to get through to many places— doctors' or veterinarians' offices, car repair centers—first thing Monday morning, because everyone is calling in to report the problem they discovered over the weekend. Calling 12-2 will often mean a wasted call (local or long distance) because everyone is out to lunch. If you call about a problem late in the day Friday you run the chance that your problem will be sidelined or stuck onto the wrong message spike by someone whose mind is already on the imminent weekend. Etc.
4. You can also arrange to call people and places when you know you'll get an answering machine, so you can leave a message and get off the phone quickly without seeming rude.
5. If you are extremely busy, don't answer the phone yourself, let someone else do it, and take a message. Or as many people do, let an answering machine monitor things for you. As calls arrive, listen in and either pick up the phone or let the machine take the message.
6. Have a polite one-sentence shutoff ready for solicitors, such as "I work for AT&T," or "I gave at the office." They'll thank you and hang up. (Saying you are only renting will

dispose of those endless vinyl siding and replacement window salespeople.)

7. You can help avoid untimely calls by making calls to friends and family while folding laundry or whatever, to catch up on the news. It still takes time, but at least it's at **your** convenience.

8. Get teenagers and other bigtime phone occupiers their own phone—the best $20 a month you'll ever spend.

"I use a cordless so I can keep moving. If you have a conventional phone, make sure the cord is long enough that you can cook or load the dishwasher while yakking."

"The phone should be turned off, or turn on the answering machine when something important must be done. Don't waste time with salespeople—cut them off quick."

"For quick info, the phone is perfect. I usually make my calls consecutively, and then keep off the phone, unless called.
I also use the phone to 'visit,' thus save the time of making a physical visit."

"If you have a teenager, get call waiting! My daughter signed up for it and now I wouldn't be without it. Now she can clog the phone lines and if someone calls, I'll still know about it."

"I have a phone list by every phone in the house. This is something I do up on my computer. It contains all my most important #'s: businesses, family, friends, kids' friends, church, emergency numbers, all alphabetized by category. I type the names and numbers onto sheets of paper and then cut and paste these into a smaller format (about half an 8 1/2" x 11" page) and

laminate and bind them. The kids all have one in their rooms and I always carry one in my pocketbook. This is a real timesaver–if I need a phone number for any purpose, it's always right there."

Correspondence

Q. "At home and the office I'm buried under letters–there are so many answers and thank-yous to write. How do you manage to keep up?"

A. I can relate to that. I have a huge family and several businesses, plus as an author I get hundreds of fan mail letters and requests for information a week, where courtesy calls for a personal answer. What can I suggest to you?

1. Once you manage to get current, keep current—it's a mental fix that gives you energy.

2. The more clippings, copies, articles, recipes, photos, drawings, seed packets, etc., you can send along to bulk up that envelope, the less you have to write—and they love it.

3. I answer lots of mail by photocopying their letter and handwriting an answer on its white space.

4. I carry letters and stamps with me at all times, so I can take advantage of waiting time. I also have several pre-stamped two-day shipping envelopes with me at all times, so I can send out important letters and documents in a minute (second!).

5. Sometimes a quick eighty-cent long distance call beats a thirty-minute writing marathon and 60¢ postage. Anytime a phone can give you "early," use it!

"When I write letters, I write one letter and make several copies of it, to which I add a personal note. If they are friends they will understand.

I do, say, one sheet of the major news in my life and then on the back I personalize it with things for that person in handwriting.

My Christmas mailing list is on a data base and I print out labels, saving all that addressing."

*"I keep a shoebox filled with all-occasion cards, a supply of stamps, and an address book and every Sunday night I prepare at least one card to send out on Monday. There's a calendar pasted inside the box cover so I have every family member and friend's birthday and anniversary at my fingertips. Sometimes an uplifting line or two can make all the difference in someone's life. I do this for selfish reasons, too—it makes **me** feel better."*

Meetings

Those meetings that are the bane of the business world… there are plenty of them on the homefront, too. They're a little more invisible or subtle sometimes, but they have just as much timewasting potential.

We have family meetings, homework meetings, school meetings, civic meetings, church meetings, Little League meetings, finance meetings, bank meetings, Neighborhood Watch meetings, our many club meetings, and so on.

As a Scoutmaster for many years now (and a Scout myself, as a boy), I know that the best way to ruin a good scout troop is to use too much time in meetings. The "going," not the gabbing, is what Scouting is really all about. Family counciling, too, is best done "on the hoof" in activities the whole family is involved in, not around a table in long, drawn-out formal meetings. I ran a church congregation at Sun Valley, Idaho, for several years under an organizational structure that included—you guessed it—numerous meetings. The longer they were, the worse the results.

Everyone dreads and puts off meetings. Some big helps here:

• *Make them shorter.*

They'll be more effective and everyone will dodge them less.

• *Even home meetings need an agenda.*

Home meetings can easily become chats that run on forever without accomplishing anything. It's hard to get to the point, interrupt, or cut someone off when they're deep into the details of their latest love affair. And often when the meeting's over you realize the two or three urgent questions the meeting was called for were never answered!

So make an agenda—just simple notes, or a little outline of key words to remind you. Then be sure to cover the "business" first. That way if talk turns to soap opera installments later, at least you'll have what you needed.

• *Never go to a meeting without knowing why!*

Going to a meeting anywhere, anytime without knowing why and having something ready is really the reverse of management. You use up time and contribute nothing and just set up the need to have additional meetings.

• *Bring solutions, not problems.*

It took me a few years, but I finally learned that meetings are for base touching, handing out assignments, and for brief reports on them, but not a place to solve problems. That is done by individuals, not meetings. I also learned to never bring a problem to a meeting, just solutions.

Watch what happens when someone (like you) in a home or family meeting brings a well-thought-through solution, idea, or resolve **written down**. It immediately organizes and directs the thoughts of all into something constructive instead of debating what-ifs and maybes and should-we's indefinitely.

Errands

You Don't Have to Do It in Person!

One great timesaving skill is realizing that "in person" is by no means always necessary to accomplish things. There are a few times and occasions when we must be physically present for something, by law, or when something serious might go wrong if we weren't. But you don't always have to appear to make an appearance, I've discovered.

We still seem to have that pioneer instinct to jump on our horse and go, but good managers avoid it, whenever possible. There is no such thing as a "quick trip to town."

One of the most magical words here is "**delivered**." Once I used to go get or run down everything myself. Now I've learned that the little extra charge for room service, for example, saves getting yourself presentable enough to go down to the hotel dining room and eat (and probably having to wait another half hour or more after you get there, to get waited on). If what you need can't be delivered, see if anyone else is headed that way, who could make a quick stop and pick it up or take care of it for you. Even many "must have your signature" things can be done for you by someone else via power of attorney.

I use the **mail** to run many of my errands, and prefer writing to making calls most of the time. Calling is better than going yourself, but there are some cautions here too. One call usually expands into at least two more to check things out further, make sure you have the right person or department, and so forth. And phoned instructions usually require some written confirmation in the end anyway. So most messages, requests, and assignments I do on paper, and make a copy. Then it's done, clearly recorded and understandable by all.

Checks are another magic tool here, too. There are plenty of people who run around for half a day after they get paid, paying bills and settling accounts and then boxing receipts. Checks are a far more efficient way to handle payment and documentation. I run half a dozen businesses and several organizations and I haven't been inside a bank in person for years, not once. They send things to be signed and I do the transactions sitting right at my desk for a few minutes.

Check, before you assume you must haul your body there!

"Errands can run and ruin you, wasting time, gas, and energy. The answer–LISTS, LISTS, LISTS."

"Get organized before you go! No good to head out without whatever papers or other things you need OR to go north, then south, then north again. I even 'order up' my stops on paper."

"I make a list of errands that need to be done and places I have to go. Then I attempt to plan my errands, do them all (or at least most of them) on a certain day or at a certain time. One can even plan the route in order not to be driving back and forth all over town. I do the grocery shopping last, so the popsicles won't melt.

Saving up errands, or methodical errand running like this will mean only half a day lost, instead of a couple of hours here, a couple of hours there, every day or so.

If an 'emergency' errand comes up, getting a part for some indispensible appliance, for instance, well, you just get in the car and get it as quickly as you can, calling ahead to see who has the part or whatever, and asking them to get it out of stock and have it ready for you.

Most errands can be evaluated, as to whether they can be postponed until a regular errand day, or less disruptive time. We've gotten so used to immediate satisfaction that delaying seems inconceivable. but it's really not that difficult to delay gratification, for not-very-important things."

"Errand running should be reduced to once or twice a week. I have a list of my most frequently required errands so that I don't forget them and shift them to someone else whenever I can."

Shopping

Most big corporations have a department called purchasing, and a purchasing agent–a trained professional–to get the right stuff at the right time at the right price. You are the purchasing agent for an equally demanding operation with a much more restricted budget. And the range and choice of things you have access to for your "provisioning" is almost beyond comprehension.

Just a few years back there was one–yes just one–"general store" (the mall of the day, newly upgraded from the lowly trading post). That store had everything you needed. Now, each shelf in the general store–shoes, for example–has sprouted into a whole store

of its own, dozens of them in fact. And the choices and deals never let you alone—more and better is everywhere: the item, the features and accessories, the ways to pay. Shopping is almost in the same league of importance and attention now as food and sex.

When your life and home management is subverted by daily shopping (the average person today is in a grocery store three times a week), little "lifetime" is left over. Shopping has become a job, and a full-time one. Not a way to secure necessities, as was its original purpose, but a way to waste most of your time, energy, and money.

I can't think of a better thing to say about shopping than:

DON'T

(unless you really need to)

You'll end up surrendering a day, just for sustenance, not progress. If you do go, buy once, fast, and get out. People who race all over town—or the county—to find the lowest price or a "bargain" obviously don't count their time, gas, or wear and tear on their vehicle into the total. It might be worth it for that one-time big purchase, but for three packages of paper towels and four pounds of ground round, it sure isn't. I see people spend a day to save a dollar. The day, not the dollar, is the real value in life. If you love or live to shop you'll probably never be a master manager. People who do 1,000 great things, you'll seldom see wandering in the shops like lost sheep. And as for cruising those "odd lots" type places—if you needed it, you'd already know it!

Asking others (experts in the category you need to make a purchase in) "where and what" is the smartest way to shortcut shopping.

How should you handle coupons? How many prosperous people do you see forever snipping and sorting coupons?

Read and know the fine print of the promise

It happens to all of us. We see a real deal or something "Free" and it sounds pretty compelling. But always, there are qualifiers and catches that come along with these once-in-a-lifetime opportunities. We all love freebies and bargains so much we never read the last 1/4 of the page, the fine print that gives the requirements and the costs, the obligations we take on with that "free" trip or dinner for two. Yes, you can have a free stainless steel fork and spoon… IF you sit through a two-hour sales pitch for stainless steel pots. Yes, you can have a free weekend in the mountains/on that tropical isle, IF you want to be badgered by real-estate salespeople before, during, and after. "You are pre-approved and this credit plan is really easy on you, only $56 a month…" Wow! But now read the fine print. The setup fee is $150 and the payments last for sixteen years and if you are more than three hours late with one there will be a hefty "delinquency charge."

Even the promises in the Bible have qualifiers, so always expect and be on the lookout for them!

"As for shopping, don't assume you are the only person capable of this chore. As soon as possible, induct anyone and everyone in the household into this important common responsibility. Just be sure to give people detailed (preferably written) instructions when they go, so you don't end up with the wrong size, wrong brand, wrong flavor."

"I keep a list by the phone for recording things as we run out of them. I don't do coupons and sales and special offers. Keeping track of coupons and what's on sale where and expiration dates is too time consuming. My time is worth more than that."

"A regular shopping time is a good idea, once a week or whatever is the best timing for your family. Go to the grocery when the shelves seem to be best stocked and when there aren't six people ahead of you at every register.

As for major expeditions to shop for school clothes, work clothes, and the like, I plan a day solely for this, seasonally, or as necessary."

"To keep track of what's needed by way of groceries, I put a magnetic dry erase board on the refrigerator. As any member of the household realizes some item is needed, they write it on the board (especially if they just used up the last of that item!).

Then on days when you're going shopping put these things on your buy list and after you get them, erase the board–it works really well.

This system is very good for multi-people families and people who can't remember even two or three things they need by the time they get to the store."

Home maintenance

I said this in *How to Have a 48-Hour Day*, but it's very much to the point here, too:

Have Nothing Around You That Doesn't Work

What's worse than finding the shovel handle split when you feel like digging, trying to start a dead lawn mower when it's time to mow, or limping along with scissors that won't cut? Think of all the things you own right now that don't work. **What good are they, not working?** They have to be fixed sometime, and that time always ends up being when you're ready and in the mood and need to use them NOW.

Broken or poorly working things, dull, half-functioning tools always ruin other things (including our temperament) when we try to use them. They slow us up, and never allow us to be a real go-getter. Fighting a sticky window or drawer over and over isn't smart management, and breaking it while fighting it is even less so.

Here's one of the easier management principles to put in practice: **Don't own anything that doesn't work.** It'll let you down at the worst possible time (it's cold, dark out, you're already late, etc.). The job won't get done, and you'll lose not only the time and dignity you spent fiddling with it, but your train of thought and concentration for hours afterward. This very day or week, repair or **get rid** of anything you have that doesn't work (divorces may take a little longer). If it doesn't work, fix it, change it, replace it, restore it, dump it, sell it, or give it away. It's better to have no jack at all than one that won't work.

If it won't work, it not only has no value, but wastes a lot of time waiting around and whimpering about it, tinkering with it and trying to fix it. Its potential to malfunction will guarantee you trouble, and add ten things to your mind that you don't need.

This "fix it or flush it" rule isn't just for tools and machines—it's for habits, procedures, systems, promises, and people—anything that doesn't work.

Preventive Maintenance

"Breakdowns" instantly convert a productive activity into a nonproductive one. The time and money lost can't usually be recovered, and breakdown can mean not only delay but death or injury, too.

One of the best business managers in the country (the person with the best production results in the whole huge Bell Telephone company) looked like just another ordinary Idaho human to me and all his colleagues. Yet, he led the national productivity index year af-

TORNADO AND HIGH-WIND WARNINGS HAVE BEEN ISSUED UNTIL....

ter year for the world's largest company. Nothing seemed to go wrong for him, his output was the highest and his expenses the lowest. An impossibility? The motors in his 120-vehicle fleet lasted longer, and they got 20,000 more miles out of their tires than anyone else did. His building maintenance costs were lower, phone installation times and repairs and other costs lower.

How did he do it? What was his secret? "I've learned an art called preventive maintenance. When I or any of my employees have free time, instead of standing around waiting for the next thing to happen, I analyze the age of the products in service, thus determining that in the next year certain items will be worn out. Then while everyone else is waiting for a problem to occur, I promptly change the old piece or product (which I'll have to do anyway). This not only eliminates the later replacement, but also the incoming complaint call, dispatching repairpeople, checking in and checking out."

He serviced, rebuilt, and restored machines, places, and people before they broke at the wrong time.

This man, a smart operator, also consistently won go-cart races (a family hobby). He and his sons had the same cart as all the competitors, but would beat them time after time. The secret again: Preventive maintenance. "How come your cart doesn't sputter and quit once in a while?" others would ask. The answer was easy: During the days and weeks when there wasn't a race, Les and his boys spent a few minutes maintaining things.

A popular piece of advice we hear is, "**Don't fix it if it ain't broke.**" That's as silly as saying, "Don't change or replace tires until they blow" (and make you late for an appointment, or kill someone).

We can't predict or foresee the exact moment that a worn belt, frayed piece of wiring, failing motor, cracked tooth, or withering friendship will finally give out. But if things are kept in good repair and maintained ahead, we do have some measure of control and protection against chaos and interruption. Some people may be impressed by how efficiently someone is able to round up all the cows that get out. I'm more impressed by the person who never fails to close the gate, or fix the weak spots in the fence.

Preventive maintenance is a word first for the home, then for human relationships, and then for business if you wish.

Housework
One big five-year hunk of management time

Is, you guessed it, housework! Many time experts have attempted to come up with a lifetime total of the time we spend on housework, and it ranges from four to nine years. Let's settle for five years of our life spent in cleaning and housework. Do we just live with that or… is there life after housework? (Some of us would settle for life **during** housework, and have been worried there might be housework after life.)

More than fifteen years ago now, I made people a promise that they could cut their cleaning time down about 75%… IF they made some sound management moves like forget the old wives' tales of cleaning, use the tools and techniques of the pros, get some help from those other household inhabitants, put

some mess prevention measures into effect, and get rid of junk. If you've missed out on this, you can find out all the secrets and details in *Is There Life After Housework?*, my first book, available in most libraries and of course, bookstores. Check it out, and you'll see why it's been a bestseller.

That never-lets-up laundry

I believe it was Margaret Mead who pointed out many years ago that as we humans find ways to eliminate and simplify the chores of life by inventing machines that do things faster, better, and more inexpensively, we end up somehow actually spending longer on the very same chores.

Like the lawn, for instance. It used to take an hour to cut the lawn with the old hand push mower. Then the gas or electric mower could cut the grass in twenty minutes. So now it takes many of us three hours to cut the lawn, because we have bigger lawns, and more elaborate landscaping that takes forever to trim around.

The same is true of the laundry. In my cleaning museum, I have a big collection of clothes washing equipment, including the oldest and earliest kinds. I've also seen the evolution here first-hand. When I was growing up we were far beyond the days of pounding your clothes clean on a rock in the river, but we got up at 5:00 a.m. on washday. We built a fire in the woodstove and carried all the water in from an outside well (sometimes in two feet of snow, too). Then in our trusty Turbo 4 gas-powered washer, we would wash... all day–that was Monday! We added blueing to the water to make the Sunday shirts good and white, and when we were done, we dumped the water (whole tubs full, mind you), and hung the clothes out on long clotheslines in the backyard (where the neighborhood dogs amused themselves by yanking things off). There was always a risk of getting scalded, or of catching your hair or something worse in the wringer. All of this required not only management, but endurance.

We all, rich and poor, did it this way once. Our washers today are fully automatic units with at least 41 dashboard selections of load size, temperature, agitation strength, and fabric setting. Many people wash every day, it is a continuous process. They wear things once and throw them in the washer, wash them to death. We have marvelous machines to wash, rinse, and dry for us, so we increase the number of clothes we have, the frequency with which we wash them, and the number of products we use to do it. Before you know it, it begins to look like we were getting off easy in the old days!

Laundry management is a whole subject in itself, maybe another book someday, but for right now:

1. Cut the carelessness (clothes thrown on the floor, feeding baby without a bib, wearing good clothes to go kneel in the garden).
2. Simplify your soaps and detergents, and the laundry aids shelf (don't believe all the ads).
3. Consolidate where you can—remember what hot water and electricity (for running the dryer) really cost.
4. Don't overdo—wash things when they're dirty, not just because they've been used once or twice, or someone them put in the hamper. I don't mean to shock you, but I believe in wearing work clothes a week, not a day. Bath towels don't have to be dumped in the washer daily, either. Remember, you're just drying—not cleaning—yourself with them. If everyone has "their towel," it can be used for up to a week and still be sanitary.

Food and cooking

If we spend five years in the bathroom, two years sitting in traffic, and at least five years cleaning, can you imagine how much time we spend on food in our life? Consider all the aspects of food management:

1. *Menu planning*

2. *Selecting and buying food, bringing it home and putting it away.*

3. *Preparing it to be eaten (cooking it, readying the table, etc.).*

4. *Consuming it.*

5. *Cleaning up after it and storing the leftovers.*

6. *Taking off the extra pounds it puts on us (exercise and dieting).*

Though home is probably the place we need it above all, most of the courses in "food management" seem to be for people who run restaurants, cafeterias, stores, or shipping companies. When it comes to food, so much of the advice (books, articles, and TV programs) around is on ways to complicate it further—how to have a greater selection of it, more (and more elaborate) ways to fix it, ways to make it more delicious, to decorate it. There is a world of experts on food out there, but when it comes to feeding ourselves and our family, we are the ultimate authority. So here is where the management comes in—in the life decision of whether we are going to class food as nourishment or entertainment. Whether we are eating to live, or living to eat.

I know people who do their food handling very efficiently, but it still takes them 25 hours a week because they are managing the unnecessary. There is a reasonable standard somewhere between gourmetdom/gluttony and sound nutrition, where food can and should be brought to a sane middle ground of health, satisfaction, and convenience. It's all the extra trimmings that take the time, the exotic ingredients, the sauces and appetizers, the frostings. These are the things that require the special pans and dishes, appliances and attachments, a larger refrigerator and pantry... all hard to manage.

Think about that and you may be willing to cut the fat off the food—all food—and get down to the real taste and value of it all. Watermelon tastes as good or better sliced, than it does diced, balled, brandied, and toothpicked. You can clean a plain old plate ten times faster than an embossed silver serving tray. If you've lost some management time or need some, food fondling is a good place to pick it up.

"I wait 'till people are hungry or else I cook and throw it away. I know that sounds like poor planning, but food is not the #1 concern of our house. We eat well but not tons and not by the clock."

"When I do cook, I cook enough for some leftovers, and the kids all know how to microwave."

"I cook three meals at once on Sunday, and then freeze them and serve them later. I make good use of a crock pot, too."

"Menu planning should be done once a week, before grocery shopping. Consult family members on ideas and preferences.

Make menu planning pages—have each member fill out an appropriate number of blocks with their desired menu. This way they're involved and can't always (kids, especially) turn up their noses at what you cook."

Children

Managing the "little monsters"

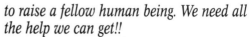

Right there is the first mistake we make dealing with kids in our efforts to "fit family into the action." They aren't monsters, and they **are** the action. Kids are the biggest and best part of the thousands of things we are handling in life, not one more obstacle or appendage to what we are doing. You don't manage kids, they are too smart and move too fast for any of us. You don't train kids, either–you train animals. Our only choice (right and rewarding choice, that is) is to **lead** and **allow** children. All the details of this would take a volume in itself so let me condense it quickly here.

You don't make room for kids, they take it. You add them into, not onto your life. Kids don't respond to what is said, only to what they see **you** do. So lead them in the course you expect of them, **be** what you want them to be and be it **with** them. Don't day care them, day share them.

Being bored, mischievous, or underfoot isn't a child's weakness, it's the parents'. Kids tend themselves once they are fueled with direction and example. A functioning family unit self-manages because its cause, direction, and support is built-in.

"We each have our own ideas about how to raise our children. Encourage, and listen to any and all advice, and then decide if you agree with it. Use what you can, and forget the rest."

*"**Don't be afraid to get help!!** Today's society is a very challenging arena in which to raise a fellow human being. We need all the help we can get!!*

Take parenting classes–at churches, Parents of Teenagers Anonymous, etc. Check at libraries, community centers, schools, colleges, churches, and in newspapers for courses.

It's especially important to be with other people who have similar situations– infants, toddlers, teens, or a child with special gifts or needs. So you can talk and see that maybe you're not alone."

Tammy's taxi service

A young mother of two stood in front of me at a seminar and said with drooping shoulders, "My daughter is in dance three days a week, my son has four days of baseball, and they both have meetings and clubs and parties and…" (by now she was almost in tears) "my husband and I just pass each other in the driveway anymore."

What is one of the biggest frustrators, time killers, and interrupters of modern home management? **Chauffeuring**, and it's not confined to the 250 activities of the average kid today, either. Little League and "lessons" alone consume a goodly slice of the average home manager's life, but then there is also running errands, picking up parts, dropping off repairs, making deliveries, visits, and emergencies.

No doubt much of this is necessary to keep the gears of life today turning, but most home taxi drivers are ready to say "enough" as they run the tires off two or more vehicles. We had eight teenagers home at once, so I know.

Chauffeuring, like shopping, makes sense as long as it's a necessity. When it becomes habit, convenience, spoiled, and too much, you are just spinning your wheels (and handling 1,000 things at once isn't a matter of how many thousands of miles you put on the odometer). I'd suggest:

1. Pooling the effort and taking turns. Don't let yourself always end up the designated driver.
2. Make at least some of the passengers share the cost—help pay for gas, repairs, and insurance (watch this cut mileage!).
3. Stack your trips and errands together instead of making all those single-purpose jaunts.
4. Be gone when people want to go—they can find another way, or walk. When I was a teenager myself, I walked or ran six miles home every night after ball practice (in the snow and when it was twenty below, too). And believe it or not, I lived!
5. As soon as the older kids get that long-awaited license, let them help out.
6. My favorite: pay for someone else to do it— **buy their gas**. They will be thrilled (fooled) and you get off cheaply and none of your time used either!

"If I have to take someone somewhere, I ask one of the other kids if they want to come with me too and I use that time to talk with them and catch up. I try to work some of the errands and other things we need to do in with the chauffeuring–stop at the bank, go to the chiropractor, etc."

"If simply waiting through an activity (rather than making two trips, one to deliver and one to pick up a child) seems the simplest, you can take some work with you, such as reading or craft work. Or you can use the time to go the library, or to lunch with a friend.

Band together with neighbors, if possible, to 'carpool' to such things."

"I hire a teenager to drive the kids somewhere sometimes."

"This is a tough nut to crack for working mothers. Train your kids early to use mass transit if it's safe and available. Our town has a van-type bus service that you can call say, if your daughter gets out of school at 3:00 and has a ballet lesson at 4:00 though you don't get out of work until 5:00. For $1.50 they will pick up your child at school, home, or wherever and bring them to lessons, doctors, etc. It's well worth it."

Launching people

They make a big thing of the space shuttle, getting it ready and getting it off, tracking it… and then getting it back safely. Big deal, we do this around home every day, and with much more complicated missiles than those metal and plastic ones. We do this with living, breathing, touchy and delicate people.

Launching the loved ones begins back in preschool days and most of us are still doing it when our launchees outweigh us. The woman of the house, especially, is often getting some helpless husband ready for hunting or fishing or just getting him off to work for the day or on that big business trip. The big ones are school and work—someone always needs to go, usually first thing in the morning, too.

In some lives, this has become an accepted scramble of scurrying, scraping up lunch, lunch money, caps, cases and just like at a missile launching, looking nervously at the clock all the while. Once our launchees are out the door, we wonder if they stayed on course and actually got there safely. Then, after a little breather (and a chance to clean up the launching site), the process of bringing them home begins… picking up dropped clothes and jackets, cleaning out lunchboxes, gathering up and putting away papers, etc.

How much of your life is just this, getting people up (out of bed, off the couch) and getting them off? Many people just accept and follow the course of push and panic… forever. Some do make standards and rules, but once a launchee gets late or behind (they're too tired, or they lose something) the whole thing is thrown back into desperation, and so much for the best laid plans of mice, men, and mothers.

Is there a management cure? Yes, there is—a one-word cure called accountability, which few people are willing to put in effect. Once you look after someone and do for them (and they know you will), you have made yourself, forever, the launcher. And the launchees will exploit and enslave you forever. The best progressive launch program I've seen is called "back off management." Tell them they're on their own and let them miss, be late, and have the consequences of it a few times. 95% of them will finally get the message of self-launching and do it thereafter. Just don't cave in at the first mishap or disaster of their launch failures. It will take a while. I know tiny kids and whole families that get up themselves, make their own breakfast, wash and dress themselves, and catch the bus, entirely by themselves, every day. That's what happens when a determined person calls upon and uses management magic!

Guests

Guests! We love 'em. Even the duds and unpleasant ones make good dinnertime conversation later. We prepare for them, in fact we break our butts for them. We do care for the folks who live here the rest of the time, but when company heads our way, we go into overtime. Instantly a new realm of quality comes over the house. We'd eat hamburger, but for them we get "guest food." No easy way out of meal-fixing or menu planning while guests are here. We might eke by on $75 worth of grocery money every two weeks (30¢ coupons are critical), but when a guest is on the way or here to stay, we can blow our whole wad on one Sunday dinner. For us, it would be milk or water, but guests have a selection of beverages. "Oh, I think Grandma Utterbeck drinks *Diet Pepsi!*" and we rush to the store. When guests come there are fourteen snack and refreshment selections at least, plus those special purchases to fit the guests' special dietary needs.

Then there's guest cleaning! Always a cut above the regular level (we wouldn't want them to see how we actually live). And **guest scheduling!** Anything and everything remotely regular (including the most sacred rules we live by) can be altered or broken for guests. For guests, we'll stay up 'till 1:30 a.m. on weekdays, wait forever to get into the bathroom, listen to their favorite music, eat dinner at 11 p.m., ignore the washer and dryer running at all hours of the day and night, and manage to smile when a guest's pet commits some unpardonable act. Let's not forget guest dressing, either–now we have to make ourselves presentable even to make our way from our bedroom to the shower in the morning.

Last but not least, there is guest emotion. From the moment they cross the threshold until the hour they leave, we sweat what we say and do so we won't hurt their feelings–are oh-so-careful not to mention the divorce, the cancer scare, those molesting charges, their impending bankruptcy or failed re-

election, their smoking and drinking habits, their bad language (that we generally don't allow in our house), and on, and on!

And there we are, the host or hostess, in need of a miracle of management. When we have guests we have more time constraints and other pressures on us than in the worst week at any workplace. Visitors can be wonderful, but they always massively affect our "to do" lists and interrupt any efficiency flow we have going. Plus special arrangements always cost time and money–ours!

Guests are indeed a two-edged sword, capable of carving us out a better slice of life, or cutting our heart and home up like the sharp hooves of a stampeding herd of cattle. Guests can set back our homefront agenda about five years in one visit, or boost it ahead the same by their inspiration and contributions.

If you just let guests bleed and trash you (which lots of us do), now is the time to put a stop to it. Don't turn to mush when they strike–manage them!

Start with the very timing of those visits in the first place. Don't automatically say "Great!" when Cousin Christopher announces he may drop by on his way back to Chicago. If that is in serious conflict with what you already have planned for that weekend, say so. Don't kid yourself that a visitor won't make any difference. Then, together work out a better time for some togetherness, when it has a better chance of really being fun. This is why people ask, so we need to answer honestly.

One of the best guest suggestions I've ever heard came from a sharp hostess who said, "You don't have to make a whole new routine for guests and visitors. They're visiting **you**. So let them find out what you're like and how you live; let them adapt and live by your rules. It's good for you and good for them."

In forty years of living in a house with seven bedrooms and a giant yard, complete with volleyball court, merry-go-round, playhouse, and go-carts, my wife and I have had our share and then some of guests, announced and unannounced. We finally learned to do just that—remember that it's **our** place and they're coming to it. So we hold to the everyday rules and systems and levels and time laws and let them adapt.

And the guests? They love it. They never feel like they're imposing—if they drop in, we just drop them into what we're doing. If we have special food or cold juice we give them some, if we don't, we sure don't run to the store and get it. If we can eat chili or Cocoa Puffs for supper, so can they. If we have something scheduled and they show up or invite themselves over without warning, we've many times driven out of the yard to our event, with the surprise guests looking out the window of our house watching us go.

If you aren't doing it already, start today to manage guests instead of upturning all your scheduling and commitments to accommodate them. Don't just hand all your time over to them as we too often do. Let them share it with you—on your terms.

Most guests, for example, arrive released of all their timetables while you are still on yours. Some are looking for a talkfest, others anxious for you to take them golfing or fishing or hiking. Others just want to sleep on your couch, watch your TV, or read a book while the visiting goes on around them. If they're going to want to be chauffeured around to see the sights or for you to take off work to spend time with them, you'd better be prepared ahead to handle it. A statement **before or when they first arrive** as to your schedule and obligations goes a long way toward making things manageable. Being busy is actually an advantage in dealing with guests (almost a magic potion)—you remain in control because they can't and won't question busy.

Finally, always have a little "maid basket" of cleaning supplies at hand so they can clean up after themselves—they'll be happy (and secretly relieved) to do it!

"When you have an outside job, housecleaning often takes a back seat to other more pressing needs. So make the most of those rare occasions when you do get the whole place to 'company's coming' condition. If you've deep cleaned and decluttered the whole place because Mr. and Mrs. X are coming over, don't waste it. Invite someone else over you've wanted to visit with, too, while the door and window glass still sparkles and the kitchen floor is still freshly cleaned and waxed."

"When neighbor kids are over and you're getting ready to go somewhere, or have just had enough of them breaking your kids' toys and picking fights, it's EASY to send them home if you say, '15 minutes left to play... 10 minutes till the pool closes... 5 minutes till you need to go, so find your shoes and clean up now.'"

The Holidays

Peppered throughout a full year of time are those special days—originally created, designed, and placed to pro-

vide a little festivity to enhance our quality of life. Certainly, many of them do just that. But these occasions don't just come and go by themselves. We have to do the celebrating, arranging, and spending for them.

These days are seldom single, either. There are at least three phases to each of them.

1. Before—getting ready, preparations.
2. During—living it up and doing the day.
3. After—recovery: cleanup, catchup, and heal up. All special days have their hangovers, not necessarily from food or drink, but in those credit card and long distance charge statements, thank-yous, follow-ups, etc.

Holidays were intended to give a lot, but many of them are now taking from us, actually becoming a monkey wrench in the gears of our management for a better quality of life. There are so many holidays now, so much that has to be found and spent, so often–time, place, and money–that many of the special days are becoming a dreaded "have-to" instead of the "get to" they were meant to be.

It falls under management's major enemy... TOO MUCH!

I heard one woman sum up the three main holidays of the year in just those terms:

Thanksgiving: eat too much.
Christmas: buy too much.
New Year's: drink too much.

I thought that maybe as one who employs several thousand people, has a big family, and a big circle of friends–all with their own special days to celebrate, that I might be alone in this opinion. But no, I hear it from everywhere. We are now looking for plain ordinary days, relief days you might call them, so we can rest, save a little money, and get something useful done. Fun, merriment, recognition, and rejoicing have their place, occasionally, but when the frosting gets thicker than the cake, the cake is ruined. Look at the days that have crept up on us, the days we should and ought (and merchandisers will never fail to remind us) to recognize and do something for:

National Holidays

New Year's
Martin Luther King Jr. Day
Washington's Birthday
Lincoln's Birthday
Easter
4th of July
Labor Day
Memorial Day
Thanksgiving
Christmas

The Minors

Valentine's Day
St. Patrick's Day
Good Friday
Mother's Day
Father's Day
Secretary's Day
Grandparent's Day
Sweetest Day
Halloween
Election Day

Personal Days

Birthdays
Anniversaries
Vacation
Graduation Day

Then there are still other special days that have to be recognized and funded, and that interrupt the regular flow in some way: opening day, spring break, etc., etc.

Add up these special days that we all as individuals and citizens have, and they come to at least thirty. Now add in the before and after days we put in for each of these and we end up with **three months**—one quarter of the whole year— in some way "handling" the special days. You can see why many are crying, "enough!" and most are crying, "too much!"

Now let's add to this the "weekend." *USA Today Weekend* sent me, as one of their contributors, a study done on "The American Weekend." It is clear from this that the average person now almost lives for the weekend, plans for it like an event or holiday or celebration. 104 more days annually spent looking for some life enhancement, and mostly resulting in more headaches from "too much."

What and how you celebrate in your life is entirely your business, but it does have to be decided upon and disciplined some. If you just slide along accepting and responding to everything that comes along, you'll spend most of your life managing "accessories" and have little time and energy for the real things.

Going all out for every occasion is not necessary (or wise). You'll only end up disappointed, discouraged, unful- filled, and short of accomplishments and cash. Lots of us are now finding quiet days at home as the superior "play days" of the year. (Using some of those holidays to organize all of your other days is a good idea, too.)

The bottom line here is… construct your own holiday calendar. Remember that none of them are mandated or re- quired. Celebrate them only to the ex- tent, and in the ways, that you really want to. Make holidays a matter of "I want, we want" instead of "we must observe." Let them fit you, don't worry about fitting them, and watch your qual- ity of life and management improve.

Calendared holidays, and scheduled "days off" from our work routine are by no means the only holidays and days off around. We can be thankful on many more days than Thanksgiving, or fish on many more days than opening day. In fact, many are listing the official holi- days as "horror days," because when they try to do something they are caught up in a mass with everyone else trying to "holiday."

You need the change and revival that holidays can offer, but why not take them when they fit you, not when they fall on a calendar or someone else's schedule? Don't let free time just hap- pen to you—make it happen when and where you want it.

When it comes to holidays, too, be sure to plan and look ahead instead of waiting for the day to dawn on you and then in desperation trying to decide "what are we going to do now?"

"When I write a birthday on my calendar, I make a reminder that it is coming at least three days earlier.

I have the birthdays of loved ones who are not longer with us on there, too, so we can go get an ice cream cone on Grandma Burridge's birthday. This is the closest I get to genealogy!"

"Include as many family members as possible in things like this. Never assume that you are the only person who could pull it off. It just AIN'T SO! Birthdays can be planned a year in advance. Pick up party favors or gifts when they're on sale."

"Traditions carried through make everyone happy, so it is worth the effort to observe the holidays that are meaningful to you. If special meals, desserts, or whatever are part of the celebration, as much as possible should be done ahead of time. Many foods can be prepared well ahead. Children and other family members can help with cookie baking and the like. Vacation time or days off from your outside job may be necessary to cope with the details of more ambitious entertaining.

Some families have 'carry in' meals so that holiday togetherness can be enjoyed without elaborate cooking that no one may have time to do. Or do potlucks, where everyone brings something, perhaps prearranged specialties, and this helps divide the labor."

"Cut back and enjoy! Lower your expectations, spread Christmas out over the entire month of December. Do cards the first week, decorate the second week, bake the third week. Go to a church or community potluck on Thanksgiving. It's great—you only make one dish and you get lots of great food and company (and no cleanup or turkey carcasses to deal with later). Spend less time entertaining in your home for holidays (so there'll be less cleanup and cooking), and invite the friends you would have had over to join you at a holiday function–Easter egg hunt, Christmas musical, volunteer to help feed others at a mission, etc. Doing a life-enhancing task with a friend can be more fulfilling than overeating and sipping coffee.

As for birthdays, you can get a real lift by surprising your birthday person–a balloon and flowers and a small gift goes a long way if it's delivered to school for a child, to work for an adult, or to the door for the homemaker.

If it's a kid's birthday, give up–do the pizza parlor/McDonald's thing. That's all kids want anyway, and it spares your home."

Trips
It's not all there when you get there?

How often have you left on a trip or visit and when you got there, slapped your forehead and said "Holy cow! I forgot the _____!" (Always something important, too–often the main reason you came.) This is easy to do because when we're on the way to other things and places we always have a lot on our minds like: where, when, what, who, and how. By the time we go through all that, even the best mind misses something. And those misses cause all kinds of messes. We have to call, go back, re-buy, or go without.... We feel stupid (and bring it up at least forty times to tell everyone how absentminded we're getting these days).

As my trips became ever more ambitious and detailed, often involving six different destinations and twenty business contacts as well as a dozen or so personal projects to handle en route, I had to transfer my preparation (packing) list from my mind to a physical record. Here's what I do and it will work for you too.

1. At least a week ahead, go through the whole trip in your mind and jot down on paper the events and what you need for each—write it down.
2. Now—EARLY, EARLY (days, not hours or minutes ahead)—round those things up, all of them, including any notes and papers you need, and put them in a "GO" pile or box.
3. After you've assembled all this, don't leave your list in the pile. Carry it with you, and go over it again sometime when your mind is fully awake and alert—you'll pick up some new things.
4. On the day of departure itself, first clean yourself up and dress. Yes, dress **before** you pack. If you dress last, you'll forget something and leave it behind, or need something that's already crammed deep inside a closed and locked suitcase out at the curb. Dress three hours early and then go back over your final collection of things to be packed. You'll be ten times sharper, and able to worry about things instead of yourself!
5. You're about to leave (good and early!). Now stop for a minute or two in the car or the doorway before you go and for a fourth time now, do a quick rundown. You may not believe this, but you'll probably find one more important thing you've forgotten... get it and go!

*"Family trips: Although where and when you'll be going should be a joint decision, the **how** should be masterminded by one person.*

Everyone should have a say in deciding where to spend the vacation. But traveling plans, reservations, organizing the trip, and coordinating everything should be overseen by one chief, who instructs everyone else on their assignment and responsibility."

Avoiding a pileup when you get back

One of the bad parts of even the best trip is facing that buildup when you get back home. Going and being somewhere different brings a real rush of restoration and relaxation, but into every brain gradually creeps the dread of facing the music when it's all over. You left to get away from it—and you did—but most of it, as you know, didn't go away. In fact, most things left unattended only gain problems.

This situation dampens many a trip, and often people attempt to correct it by making it clear where and how they can be contacted at all times during their absence (vacation, honeymoon, convention, or camping trip). I hate this myself. When I leave to do something important—play or work—I don't want a pigtail of problems trailing behind me every step of the way. I watch almost everyone around me during meetings, cruises, and flights, fighting phone calls and faxes from the things they left behind.

The big secret here is to organize and prepare well enough before departure to reduce buildup while you're gone. **An ounce of preparation before going** (facing up to and fixing things) **is**

worth a pound of patching when you get back. The most important part of packing for a trip, in fact, is putting all your responsibilities in order. I pay up, come out and ask those touchy questions, get that commitment, and set up the rules–all the what-to-do's if and when–before I go out the door. One big help here is giving someone the authority to act in your place. It sure beats not being able to get into your place when you get back.

Then, even with the two homes and four businesses I run, I can return from a month's absence and in half a day or less everything is caught up to the moment again. Does that ever make my trips fun and focused! Managing long distance is so inefficient.

"When I worked in an office, one of my worst moments was returning from vacation and finding papers dumped all over my desk, as if someone had upended a wastebasket on it. When my boss went on vacation, I made three files for the incoming materials: 1) Flames, really hot stuff; 2) Coals, need attention soon; and 3) Ashes, outdated materials, junk mail, etc.

I never did that for myself. But now (when I come home to a big pile of accumulated mail and other papers) I do!"

Interruptions

Businesses talk about interruption as a problem. We all know the interruptions at home are at least thirty times worse and usually of a more critical nature than the interruptions we get in business. Remember, business operates in a framework and home operates in a free-for-all.

You'll never manage to eliminate interruptions, they are a part of life. Several interruptions a day, however, is much more manageable than several dozen a day (which many busy homes have). The secret is in keeping some control here, instead of just letting it all happen to us.

First, don't assume that you have to be 100% available all the time. You don't have to drop everything and run at every beck and call. I credit one of my college teachers for a good concept (the only one I got out of the whole course, but it made the course worthwhile). Mentioning the phone as a disorganizer and interrupter, he made the statement: "My home and life is not open to any fool with a dime." People can call back later, leave a message, write, send a foot messenger, etc. There are lots of options.

Recently, during the busiest time of my life, I worked at home for a month while supervising the construction of a new house. I was full to the brim with jobs–home jobs, business jobs, church jobs, community jobs, Scouting jobs (a three-page list full of them). Yet I managed to perform miracles of accomplish-

ment and focus. Was it my brilliance? Nope. I'm the same old janitor I've always been, I just had a stroke of management blessing. Someone damaged the underground phone cable to my house (a ranch twenty miles out in the country), and the phone was basically unusable... for a month. It was wonderful, and I think others got more done too, because I wasn't calling them. I just stacked my calls and time to call because I had to, and I got by. I cut the interruptions of phone calls—I controlled them.

We reach a time in our lives at home when we have to control the traffic, or there will be no life—only interruptions—to manage... and where does that get you? Choose your own system of immunity, and respecting those of others, just start using it. Doing 1,000 things is sure more fulfilling for everyone than 1,000 interruptions.

Interruptions can't undo an undeviating course!

We all know the value of an undeviating course, however, we have convinced ourselves that the reality of interruptions, especially when we have small children, totally shatters the straight line between any two points. But a course is a path, a way, a road to a predetermined destination. Yes, we may have to stop, sit in traffic, or follow some detour signs, but not deviating from the road is the key here. Delays, distractions, breakdowns, disappointments, and all the rest are part and parcel of the highway of living. Just stay on the road. It's when we try those questionable side roads and shortcuts, or make a sudden impetuous change in destination that we end up in trouble.

Don't let a family squabble derail a family schedule; don't let a postponement put off a good goal; don't let an emergency or disaster snuff out an idea or make you abandon a destination. Set and pursue a course to the good thing you want, stay on the path, and don't let unforeseen happenings de-path you. Interruptions can't undo an undeviating course!

"Interruptions? Expect them, be glad someone's needs met, glad to be busy, adjust list."

"I long ago resigned myself to the idea that I was very seldom going to get through a day accomplishing exactly what I had planned."

"Isn't that the name of the game? I think attitude helps here—doing your best, but realizing right at the beginning of each day that something is probably going to come up. You aren't going to get everything done that you wanted to, and you are probably going to make a few mistakes. So don't get married to a rigid list or schedule, no matter how well thought out it is."

"Deal with interruptions as they roll in, following your instincts. Don't let yourself lose additional time doubting (and rethinking and rehashing) your decisions after you do. Then get on with what you were doing as quickly as possible."

"Interruptions are simply life. So cease the activity in hand, deal with the interruption as efficiently as you can, and get back to what you were doing. It helps to compartmentalize, and close and reopen those mental compartments as necessary."

"As for 'drop ins' (as in 'drop dead') be courteous, but try to dispose of them quickly. I often palm them off on my husband, who's retired, to chat with. With relatives or others you don't wish to alienate, you control your frustration and visit with them as best you can. It does help to have daily chores which CANNOT be postponed. You have to do these things, and your drop-in can be made to realize it. Or you can plead an appointment, that works sometimes.

If someone calls and wants to visit or drop by, whatever, and it's not convenient, tell them so nicely, offering an alternative time and date, if possible."

"It's great to have a tight, strict schedule, and to get tons (thousands!) of things done, but allow for interruptions–be prepared so you don't freak out. I know it's hard for us conscientious, non-leisurely, driven types. We want to list, list, list, achieve, achieve, achieve. But interruptions are unavoidable, they will happen. So chill out! Psyche yourself so that when an interruption happens you can relax instead of flipping out.

Practice an attitude something like: 'At least it's not life threatening.' Even try to enjoy the interruption as a pleasant change of pace from your routine and schedule.

Emergencies

We know they'll come, in the form of injuries, accidents, forgotten things, fights, spills, and losses, and it'll always be when we're in the middle of something else. We don't have the luxury of stopping life to fix an emergency, yet we have to deal with them. If we let every "emergency" foul up the entire course of things we'll end up basket cases.

Those magic words EARLY and READY help even with emergencies. When you're early and ahead of everything, nothing (almost nothing) by way of a surprise will totally derail you. When you run early and prepared, a glitch, even an emergency–will be only a small or not too serious interruption in the flow of things.

We can't be ready for all the consequences and demands of something like a surprise death or serious illness or injury, a flood, fire, or a lost job, but we still have to manage them. As emergencies accelerate the demands on our situation, we have to accelerate our demands on ourselves. None of us travels at our load limit anyway. Like a truck, we can carry more than we usually carry. Not for very long maybe, but for short trips and when an emergency occurs. Our only choice is to overload and overtax ourselves a little. We can and it won't hurt us. That's a lot wiser than pushing all our other "to-do's," including the daily family demands, out of the way for a week or whatever. Watch top managers handle emergency situations… you'll learn a lot.

When something "happens":

1. Get the true details. News reports/announcements (even from dear friends or apparently responsible media) are often exaggerated, distorted, or incomplete. Find out what really happened and why—most "first reporters" are news mongers or gossips, who get things second or thirdhand and add or eliminate things to heighten color and excitement. A few minutes of inquiry into what, where, how, and why will bring many "emergencies" into better (and much more handleable) focus.
2. Place it before you face it. Don't try to handle it until you place it:
   - A. I must deal with this immediately.
   - B. It can wait.
   - C. I can't fix it, I need someone else to help.

"In an emergency, cover bases, be sure kids are safe (or take them with), smile and go with it. Cussing doesn't help anything—from getting stitches to cleaning up spills to hysterical kids. So breathe deep and FIX THE PROBLEM."

"Every emergency is different of course, so I guess attitude is the main thing—learning to relax. A good phone list helps here, for those emergency numbers or just someone to hand-hold or help transport someone or something."

"In a medical emergency, don't go to pieces. Remain calm. Get the patient quieted and stabilized. Call the ambulance, or take the injured/sick person to the emergency room immediately. Everything else has to wait. If other children are home, all must be loaded into the car, or drop them off at a neighbor's, or have a neighbor come over. Dithering about, crying, and panicking are not allowed. Only counterproductive."

"You can be prepared for nearly any emergency, and this should be a real priority in any family. Make sure you have a complete set of emergency numbers, a box of emergency equipment, and well-stocked first aid kit (not one of those little ditsy ones you buy, but one you make up yourself).

Don't just know the number of the police, fire department, and ambulance—check around your neighborhood and learn the phone number of doctors, nurses, people trained in CPR, etc., who might live nearby. Charts inside my kitchen cupboards have step-by-step instructions for artificial respiration, the Heimlich maneuver, CPR, what to do in a poisoning emergency, and what not to do."

"You just have to stay calm and do what you have to do. If the kids get hurt, don't fall apart 'till they're all taken care of and bandaged up."

"Make a directory of all the doctors (including specialists), dentists, chiropractors, opticians, veterinarians, and so on, that you use. Include their name, address, and phone number, so if a person other than yourself needed to contact one of them in an emergency, they would know who to call for what, for each member of the family. Include the same info for the local hospital, clinic, or other health care facilities you use.

Have the name, address, and policy numbers of medical insurance and the location of the policy or handbook noted. Have instructions concerning precertification spelled out.

Include the name, address, and phone number of pharmacies you use and prescription plan name and policy number.

List the name and number of your plumber, electrician, water and power company, gas company, cable company, etc.

Also include names of persons to notify in case of emergency–relatives, friends, babysitters to care for children if necessary. Where family members can usually be reached–work, home, church, wherever.

Your children's friends' names and numbers are especially important if you have teenagers who usually only tell you that they'll be at 'John's house.' John who? Where?

Update the directory every six months.

Of course, have emergency numbers on the phone, too–tape them onto it if you must. In the excitement of an emergency brains go numb, and you need this info NOW."

Juggling home management and an outside job

A comment I often hear is: "I sometimes have trouble juggling my home responsibilities and my outside job. How do I find the right balance here?"

We can divide our management arena into three main areas:

> *Self (personal) management*
> *Home management*
> *Outside job management*

Looking at this list, if we each made a "pie graph" of where our management time and energy goes, those diagrams would be vastly different.

This of course, is up to us. It's our own choice. We are free to allot our ef-

forts as we see fit. But we do have to manage all three of these at the same time, and if we can't or don't find a livable balance, life can be a real pain for us and others. Big family, big job, and big personal doings can all coexist. In fact you **can't** operate them separately, they all go on at the same time, and vary daily in demands and urgency. Life management overall is coordinating these big three. People who try to separate them soon find out that management isn't a process, it's a set of principles, rules, boundaries, judgments, and motivations that apply almost equally to all three areas. Things like:

- *on time • communication*
- *steady application • prudence*
- *loyalty • wise cash use*
- *compassion • dependability*

are the principles and tools of life efficiency, and we use them in everything we do. We may vary the application at home and in our personal lives with a little more compassion and patience, or adjust the consequences a little, but the basic principles are the same. And whether we are managing home, work, or community activities, it is all the same person doing it–us.

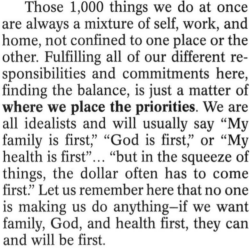

Those 1,000 things we do at once are always a mixture of self, work, and home, not confined to one place or the other. Fulfilling all of our different responsibilities and commitments here, finding the balance, is just a matter of **where we place the priorities**. We are all idealists and will usually say "My family is first," "God is first," or "My health is first"… "but in the squeeze of things, the dollar often has to come first." Let us remember here that no one is making us do anything—if we want family, God, and health first, they can and will be first.

It all comes down to what is really important to us, what we really value. The emphasis we end up with is a simple choice of direction—not a matter of skills or mechanics. It's a question of where we want to put our time, thought, and money, and how much we really care about our home, work, or self. For some people, their job is their life, they treasure it more than home or health. Many care less about their job, it just exists to fund and underwrite their home life.

Remember none of these areas—self, home, job—stops while you work on one, they all go on at once, at home,

work, and play. Managing well is learning to coordinate all three and find a good mix. (And all of these areas feed into and back on each other.) For example, when you enjoy your job and do it well, self management is happening and home life is blessed. When home is managed well it's easier to be a success in business.

There are no rules for coordinating home and work—we have to make the rules, according to what each of these areas means to us and our values and ethics.

"I use a spiral bound notebook about 8" x 10" for my lists. I open it to the second page so I have a separate page on each spread for work and for home.

This way I can flip it open and see my work and my home needs at the same time."

"My outside jobs are: teaching gymnastics and cleaning and painting, and much of the time when I am doing them my kids are working alongside me, taking class, or watching each other at home. I have only short time periods away from the kids because I KNOW (and am glad of it) they are my #1 priority… my real job."

"When you have an outside job too, lesser details of the home duties will usually have to be let go. If other family members can fill in, so much the better. One can sometimes hire a cleaning person, but other times it may be necessary to give some things a 'lick and a promise.' Using convenience foods or eating out isn't so terrible."

"Your priorities must change immediately. If you're used to having meat and potatoes on the table every night by 6:00, forget it; some nights pizza will have to do, and life will go on. If you've always done laundry every Monday, forget it; do a little laundry Monday, a little on Tuesday, a little on Wednesday, etc. Life will go on if all the laundry isn't done on Mondays.

As quickly as possible, designate authority to other family members, such as starting supper, doing a load of laundry, or vacuuming. Kids should be learning to do these things anyway."

WHAT SLOWS HOME MANAGERS DOWN THE MOST

undisciplined kids
broken or unfixed things
waiting for someone else to do it
fighting finances
surprises of any kind
illness
visitors you're unprepared for
tending junk and clutter
running out of anything
running late and behind
hunting for something
"shouldn't have been necessary" trips to town
worrying too much about unimportant details

being under- or over-tooled
fights and arguments
traffic
spills
dull tools
having to wait for something
slow or late repairpeople
unsolicited salespeople
telemarketers
being hit with a new, unfamiliar schedule
a good book half read

The Big Three:
Junk, Help,
& Money

We might all have slightly different candidates for the three biggest subjects to beware of, but I'd like you to look at the three I selected, my "Three Musketeers of Mismanagement"... Junk... Help... and Money!

DEJUNK!

If all management problems, needs, frustrations, struggles, opinions, and facts or truths were fed into an all-knowing computer in an attempt to identify THE biggest single negative influence on home management, without question the answer would pop out on the laser printer: JUNK AND CLUTTER!

Dodging around, hopping over, and wading or pawing through all the junk and clutter around our home and yard and vehicles and in our closets and drawers (and wallets, purses, and toolboxes, too), is unquestionably the biggest enemy of good management. It's the champion waster of time, space, emotion, the great alienator of friends and loved ones and associates. Junk and clutter love to coax us into the loser column. They never sleep or release their grip on us either. Even if they're out of sight, deep in the basement or way up in the attic, they're never out of mind, and we're never free from the need to deal with them.

The bottom line is (and I know none of you reading this would argue with it): **DEJUNKING IS THE GREATEST ORGANIZATIONAL STRATEGY EVER!** Scores of articles and books have been written on this subject, and the best two ever are *Clutter's Last Stand* and *Not for Packrats Only*. Read and follow them, and your management efficiency will double.

Let me give you a short course now to warm you up, so you can make some instant progress right away, today, and taste some of the coming rewards.

Dejunking eliminates management problems because:

It reduces housework about 40%
It makes you more efficient at everything you do
It gives you back a lot of space, time, and money, too
It frees you up to handle more important things
It puts an end to all that "hunting"
It removes distractions
It eliminates fights and arguments
It assures more energy and better sleep at night
It generates self-respect and self-esteem

I've been a professional cleaner for more than forty years now, and I discovered early in my attacks on disheveled homes that about half of cleaning had nothing to do with dirt or germs, brooms or vacuums. At least 40% of housework/cleaning is just handling junk, litter, and clutter around the house. Most of this stuff is **worthless**– deceased, defunct, broken, obsolete, outdated, or worn out. But we keep it so it still requires a keeper, and guess who that keeper is? YOU. Your time, your resources, and your space are taken up by anything you **own** or **keep.** You have to sort it, arrange it, store it, protect it, insure it, dust and clean it, manage it, move it from place to place. Good, truly useful things are worth it. But all those other things are just a maintenance and management nightmare. Bury the dead! Much progress and accomplishment has been slowed down or stopped by carrying around things (even ideas and intentions) that have long outlived their usefulness.

I remember when I was six or seven, trying to make an old flashlight work. I cleaned it, oiled it, took it apart, and replaced different pieces of it for about three hours straight. Still it showed no sign of life. Mother finally came in with her hands on her hips and said, "Donald, quit beating a dead horse!"

How many of us have tossed a spent pen back in our pocket or the drawer, or finally identified and removed a burned-out Christmas bulb and gads, it still looks good–maybe it's just tired and wounded–and tossed it back with the good ones? Do that with enough things and you'll spend hours rummaging, testing, and rechecking–that uses time! That's poor management. All it does is cause confusion, take up room, and call for more tending, accounting, and keeping track.

A friend of mine, Dave Sanders, was a splendid marksman with the bow and arrow, he won every match he ever entered. Yet out in the woods, matched against Wile E. Whitetail, he never bagged a buck. One evening, driving back through the beautiful Sun Valley mountains from a construction job, we came around a corner and a herd of deer appeared, headed by a splendid buck. It was hunting season and Sanders had his bow handy. He eased out of the vehicle and up to the deer, and now that buck was standing broadside, motionless, just fifteen yards away–point blank range. Sanders could hit a mosquito at that distance. He smoothly drew an arrow out of his quiver, aimed, and let that bowstring go. "Thang!" The arrow veered wildly and stuck in a tree and the deer bounced silently into the forest. Dave's big chance had finally come and he muffed it. His aim was perfect as usual, it was the arrow. Three days earlier, he'd split the arrow practicing. It was ruined but he just couldn't bring himself to toss it, so put it back in the quiver (like we all do with junk) to deal with later. That was the one he'd pulled to shoot! We often miss our marks for the same reason.

We must have "keeper" cells in our brain somewhere. We're all sentimentalists and love to keep remainders to remind us of the tough times and the good times. Even dead things we keep for evidence, and to keep memories alive. What if you walked into a surgeon's office and found it strewn with old kidneys, tonsils, and appendixes, bone fragments, used heart valves, gallstones, and all the old casts that once did a good job for someone? Or walked into a car dealership and found piles of old gaskets and piston rods, rusted out tailpipes, worn brake shoes, broken wrenches, and anything that ever failed and was replaced? Ridiculous even to think about? **We** keep the equivalent of this around all the time!

One of the most important management moves you can make is to rid yourself and your surroundings of outgrown, no good, or no longer needed things–dreams and grudges as well as broken tools, too-tight clothes, and old papers. If you're done with it, do away with it! It's so inefficient to keep carrying around or caring for garbage. It sabotages any management system. Haul it off or it will haunt and hurt you.

Anything dead will undo your management—so bury it, cremate it, or toss it. In the course of your life you'll wear out and use up lots of good things. I know they've given to you, but give them up now. Dragging their decaying remains with you (in storage, filed, etc.) burns your best fuel—for nothing. Anything you have to feed, fix, or fiddle with for no real benefit should be on your "chuck it" list.

That high-class junk called luxury

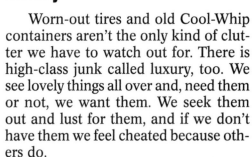

Worn-out tires and old Cool-Whip containers aren't the only kind of clutter we have to watch out for. There is high-class junk called luxury, too. We see lovely things all over and, need them or not, we want them. We seek them out and lust for them, and if we don't have them we feel cheated because others do.

Before you exhaust yourself in the effort to find and own all those frills, be advised that luxury is the very worst kind of thing to tend. It makes you pay more interest and insurance, calls for more coddling, more space, and more precautions, you constantly have to post signs and say things to friends and family like, "Oh, oh! Don't touch!" "Stay back!" "Get out, you can't eat in there!" Even if you're rich you can't afford luxury because of the **time it takes**.

We've all heard of what a drain overhead can be in business. Well, at home luxury items are **all overhead**, those things that have to be locked up and guarded, tediously cleaned and maintained, polished and appraised, things that may impress the public and the neighbors but we hardly ever enjoy or use them. Luxury takes more than its share of the slice of management. It just gives us a bunch of extra-high-anxiety things to count, catalog, and store, and keeps us working extra jobs and hours to pay for them.

Often it isn't that we are poor or inept organizers, it is that we are spending too much time lining up new stuff that really won't fit or isn't needed in our life. Anyone would be a struggling organizer with too much, and many of us are, because our energy for accomplishment is sidetracked into a spin of stuff.

Don't manage the unnecessary

Remember always that good management's first law is dejunk! Unburden yourself of things (yes, even valuable things) you don't need or want—dejunk! This can mean people, places, or habits, too—not just old clothes, cars, or cartons of paper! Tending too many twinkee friends, for example, can take a lot of life and time.

I heard someone on the radio once appraise this life as 5% struggle, 5% fun, and 90% maintenance. I was impressed with the accuracy of the observation, but depressed by the thought of how unnecessary most of this is. True, life does include some struggle, but think:

if the maintenance part was reduced by good management, the fun and joy of it would have a bigger slice of the pie. So let's not have or keep unnecessary things around us that require maintenance—here lies one of the big secrets of doing 1,000 things at once.

You have three basic choices as to when to dejunk: Now, later, and when you're dead

- *LATER it only gets worse and prolongs your suffering.*
- *WAITING TILL YOU'RE DEAD causes others to suffer and remember you (not necessarily kindly) for your stuff rather than yourself.*
- *So NOW—right now—is the only time to do it.*

And where to start???? (Not with others' junk, as we always seem to want to do.)

The starting place is with yourself— your personal things

Your carry-along clutter: in wallets, purses, briefcases.

Your parked stuff: drawers, closets, desks, lockers, jewelry cases, your toy and hobby collections, photos, notebooks, tool boxes, tackle boxes, anything you alone own, use, or occupy.

Then and only then, on to the public, common area, or co-owned stuff.

How:

Get up at 5:00 a.m. (you'll be cold-hearted and objective then).

Wear no clothes… that have pockets.

Put on some dejunking music (not *Carry Me Back to Old*

Virginny or *Send Me the Pillow You Dream On*—something like a Sousa march or *Got Along Without You Before I Met You, Gonna Get Along Without You Now*).

Now get out four big sturdy boxes for the:

4-BOX SORTING SYSTEM

A way to get junk judging, and the rerouting of objects that follows, down to a science. Get four boxes, label them, and then everything you come across has to go into one of these:

JUNK

Obvious trash, and stuff so awful you don't want to sic it on anyone else, even if it's in perfect condition.

CHARITY

It's still good and useful, but not for you—you don't want, need, or like it anymore. So put it in here and pass it along to a relative, friend, or the charity of your choice.

118

SORT

It's something you still want or need, but it isn't doing you any good where it is now. Drop it in here so it can be put in position to actually be used.

EMOTIONAL WITHDRAWAL

Things you know you should get rid of, but you can't quite bring yourself to do it yet. Like that collection (original boxes, lapel pins, and all) of every corsage you ever received in your young life. Half the petals have crumbled off of them, they're full of dust and impossible to clean, and you can't even remember who most of them were from. But you also can't pitch them right now. So seal them up in an Emotional Withdrawal box and put it on the shelf for six months or so. By then you'll have adjusted to the idea of disposing of them, and the sight of those faded, shriveled rosebuds and mummified gardenias will have faded from your mind. Pick up the box—without opening it—and dispose of it.

PROBATION

If you insist, we'll create a fifth category here: Probation. When you come across something about which you are truly not sure, slap a "Probation" sticker on it. Note on there how long you're willing to leave the item in limbo, until whether or not it is a "keeper" is resolved. Now put these probation items somewhere you're forced to look at them, or better yet to actually use them. Then there won't be any doubt when that "three months" or "six months" rolls around.

As you work your way through your hoards, pour the contents of any containers of anything out onto a big blanket, so all of your sins are in plain sight, and you'll have to pick each thing up and weigh its worth. If you junk out of a box or trunk, you'll never get to the bottom.

Your judgment criteria are:

Don't love anything that can't love you back.

Does this enhance my life or the lives of others? If not, pass it on to someone else, pitch it, recycle it, or sell it, but get it out of your management area!

How to stay dejunked

First announce to others that you are clutter free, out of the business of managing junk, and they'll quit dumping their unwanted things on you and quit inviting you to garage sales. Don't hang around or visit junk dives such as malls and "whatnot shoppes," or spend all your spare time shopping or flipping through catalogs. When the fever strikes, study your credit card balance, balance your checkbook, and go buy groceries if you have to buy something (that will shock you and your wallet into good sense).

Remember and repeat every morning to yourself:

Anything Kept Requires a Keeper

You're that keeper. So make it count, or count it out right now. Sift through your physical and mental stuff right now and hold a funeral for the unfit and watch your management effectiveness double!

GETTING HELP

People who handle 1,000 things at once and manage to keep on handling them don't do it alone. It might look that way, or they might hog all the credit for their accomplishments, but don't be fooled. Behind every good man and woman you'll find some often silent and unnoticed helpers. You aren't alone!

Your "better half"

Our main resource for pursuing and performing the 1,000 worthy works of our choice is of course ourselves, our own head and heart. But many of us have a right arm closely connected to that head and heart, often called "our better half." All of the helps in moving the mountain aren't a matter of heaving and hauling rock. They may also come in subtler forms like encouragement, teamwork, pinch hitting when necessary, or trading "we" for "me" at times when two heads are better than one, four hands better than two. Our closest know us best and can champion our causes quicker and more efficiently than anyone. But pride, stubbornness, or pettiness too often cut us off from this, simply because we refuse to include our mate. The closeness and often the briefing is already there, so don't make

communication one of those big impossible "relationship" words. Just keep each other posted on what you're doing, and if there truly is a love and mutual respect there, help will come forth and be exchanged voluntarily, both ways. It's usually that simple, just letting each other know what is going on, when and why. Husbands and wives who "team up" and plug into each other's goals, direction, and patterns will consistently triple the accomplishment of those who don't.

I know you are thinking right now that Aslett is writing from the idealism of the perfect, stable, two-parent home, where teamwork is easy. I am, and it is my hope for my children and grandchildren that they can get to such a situation. But your thinking is right on. Over one-third of the homes, even here in rural Idaho where I live, are single-parent situations. Years ago we had maybe 10% widows or widowers, and a few "single" homes in the aftermath of some tragedy. Today, with divorce, abandonment, and new independent ways of thinking so omnipresent, many of you reading this book may not have a two-person team going for you. And you might love to not have all the burden, worry, and responsibility for everything solely on your back. Tough as it might be, we're seeing single families that not only have earned their way, but are squared away with their children, homes, yards, church, and community—all in all much better managed than the "complete compatible home" folks. I often shake my head in amazement at what single-parent households can do and how well they run things. I don't know if I could do it.

Just because you don't have a team member built right into your household, doesn't mean you can't still take advantage of the teamwork process.

Remember the Lone Ranger, determined to "clean up" the crime and the town and the whole west? All of the other members of his Ranger team were killed in an outlaw ambush and only he survived. But he quickly teamed up with Tonto—not a relative, not a race match; they didn't even speak the same language. And not only did they work well together—help, support, and advise each other—but they always used the local sheriff and townspeople and ranchers, too, to help solve any problem they were up against, and share the credit. The "Lone" Ranger's success was actually a "we," not a "me" process (even if all the movies and TV today seem to feature a lone, rock-muscled, fearless cop/soldier, taking on whole cities and countries with one 44-magnum, and a bountiful supply of four-letter words and beautiful women). One person, single or whatever, has the capacity to creatively recreate the team process along new lines. Do it.

"Spouse, partners, family, even small children can help. Even single parents need 'support staff.'"

"My neighbor gets home from work around 4:30, however her second grader gets off the bus at 3:30. He gets off at my house, and in exchange she runs errands for me twice a week, since she works in town. My sister brings my son home from school since she works next to the school. In return, I gas up her car once a week."

The family

Here is a BIG, BIG boost toward those 1,000 things at once—the family.

Take notice here. Most high achievers and mighty managers have a healthy functional family. One of the big reasons for the stress and disorganization that is blamed today on "society," "the workplace," or "the world" is the shortage of old-time family support. Society, the workplace, and the world have been around for centuries, often inflicting more pressure, injuries, injustices, inequalities, and unkindnesses than today. But before, there was a firm family organization behind almost everyone. It's people that help people survive, not government or do-gooder organizations or TV talk shows. I'd say 75% of my own accomplishments are strongly interwoven with family help. If a family remains a team generation after generation, they have a network of help and checks and balances that no Fortune 500 company could even comprehend.

If your family is weak, estranged, or lost, start today to renew and rebuild it. It is the foundation of accomplishing much. As I watch families grow apart to do their own thing I see efficiency decrease and problems increase. Fighting problems takes time and resources that could be doing 1,000 much more worthwhile things.

When we leave home to get married and form new relationships that is supposed to enhance, not unhook, our family bonds. The availability of a family to call on all the time (not just in times of pleasure and pain) is a social secret that has almost been lost. I know that family help can be abused as well as used, such as in the case of kids who never leave home but leech on their parents forever, or others who bring all their failures and burdens back to their aged parents and grandparents. But in general, a close and intact family helps prevent failures and ease burdens and heals the unprevented and unfortunate.

Society hasn't destroyed the family, it's us, as individuals, and society can't heal the family either, it's us who has to do it. I've seen one person (a peacemaker) enter a fighting, aloof, selfish, apart family and slowly—by letters, visits, and helping hands—bring that entire family spread across the U.S. together as a team, willing to give time, love, and money to each other. In my own family, no baby is born, illness or surgery endured, moving day or vacation planned that someone isn't there to take the kids, stay and help, make a loan, or share the days, weeks, or months of weakness, and 1,000 things still get done.

When a family is functioning **no one has to ask for help,** it is offered. So fix your family if it needs fixing—become that peacemaker, get grudges and pettiness out, start offering and watch how your management improves. You'll find out what the "grand" means in grandparents, how the psychological contribution of parents even surpasses their biological one, that brother/sister, in-law, or cousin isn't a label, it's a position of support.

If you are missing your family machine remember it won't heal itself—**you do it**. You need that family, and it needs you.

If you don't have a family, join one and contribute and you won't have to worry about bloodlines. Being "adopted" by a fine family is every bit as good as being born into it.

"How do I get it all done? I'm not well organized. I have help (my children and husband, and relatives)."

"What is my #1 secret for getting 1,000 things at once done? My mother-in-law—if it wasn't for her, we'd go under/be on Welfare."

"Grandparents can be the greatest asset around for a thriving, fully functional family unit. They are the foundation."

"There is a lot to be said for the old-time idea of families living close by each other. I have a sister living on either side of me and one that lives a quarter of a mile away. Anytime a problem arises, someone loving and caring is there to lend a hand or offer moral support. If something happens and I can't be home for my children, they have the security of knowing some other family member is there for them. It's the ultimate security."

We're always being told to take care of our assets, and certainly family and friends are among our most valuable assets!

Teaching the coming generation to manage

Now here in this business of knowing how to do 1,000 things at once and do them successfully and well, is an entirely new aspect to consider. An important one.

In our world today where almost everything is done for our kids and paid for them, and almost all decisions, when you think about it, are made for them, the opportunities available to them to manage things, even common everyday things in their lives, is almost zero.

You don't just reach a point (such as when you come of age) when you suddenly know how to run things. I've seen straight "A" students, high school seniors, and even college kids, unable to manage even the most elementary form of organization, because at home and even school, everything was always outlined and organized for them. Our self-rising, fast cooking, instant results, push-a-button-to-get-it society leaves the sorting and lining up muscles in a young human totally undeveloped.

So when your schedule is more than full and those children around you have to help with a lot of it, they learn. Kids that grow up with everything done for them–cooking, cleaning, choosing, earning–when they do come of age, you've got troubles. Because with growth, adulthood, and family responsibilities come 1,000 things to do. You don't learn this in school, either. You learn it from wise parents, who line you up with one, two, and then a half-dozen or more chores and explain what and when and how. And then leave it to you and have high expectations.

"All the kids in our house do their own laundry and if they make a boo-boo and ruin a favorite thing, or run out of undies, well, that's how you learn. They all have an assigned day for laundry. When you have a lot of kids, it's the only way."

"By the age of five, children should be 'kicking in' with real help–picking up after themselves, running the vacuum, dusting, fetching, carrying, etc."

*"Maybe it's an old-fashioned idea, but I think an allowance is a good idea for children, teaching them to earn/save/spend money early on. It also rewards their efforts to help, which bolsters their sense of self-worth. I see nothing wrong with a little bonus for extra help–**incentive**."*

Handling our home helpers

Whatever size of "potential help pool" we may have, there comes the question of how to best get the help out of them. Should we beg, bargain, boost, or buy our way here?

Delegation

It appears everywhere–in miracle management articles and books, seminars, and lectures–that magic word for getting things done, DELEGATION.

Delegation is supposed to "free us up," by assigning some of our jobs and responsibilities to someone else. Well, in business there are a few (even though you're paying, darn few) eager beavers standing by to do things for you, but at home we're lucky to find

even one. Those other people on the homefront are just like us; they all have forty things of their own to do and deal with, so they're not anxious to be sent on any fetching missions. Making good assignments and spreading the chores and responsibilities of a home wisely and fairly through the family or people you live with is fine, in fact, smart. But handing **your** duties over to be done by them is questionable.

When you tell a harried homemaker with a big family and a barely-get-by budget to "just delegate" her problems, be sure to also tell her:
*Who to? **and** Who pays?*

The best way to delegate on the home front is to get others to help and share of their own accord. Just pouncing on someone and asking them to drop, delay, or postpone their own activities to save you in yours is a dastardly deed indeed. Far better to make what you need and want clear and visible or audible *before the crisis*. You can draw up a plan or list of what is needed so others can see where they might be able to help. Then be sure to say please and thank you, and then live the please and thank you by doing the same, errands and help, for others when they are in need.

Showing is better than telling

Somewhere along the line it was established that the best way to get something done is to "order" it done. Shoot or shout out an order and send someone scurrying to deliver the goods for you. We hear orders all the time around home, like:

- *Clean your room right now!*
- *This is the last time I'm going to ask you to put that away!*
- *Haven't you washed the car yet?*
- *Do I have to plead with you to iron those shirts?*

Amazing, isn't it, the day we discover that giving orders doesn't automatically get jobs done? The Lord can only get about 5% of us to obey his commandments, so why are we so surprised that our attempts to give directives and duty assignments around the house so often get nowhere? If you're looking for a magic solution to this, you're wasting a lot of good management time because there isn't any. As you know by now, there are times when our hypothetical "home helpers" prefer verbal bludgeoning to cleaning the bathtub. Boy, does that confuse the management process!

What do the real ace home managers do to get something done? They become shepherds instead of sheepherders. A shepherd who goes out ahead of the sheep and gets in with them (instead of behind them yelling orders) can handle a whole mountain full of sheep. This works for fathers,

mothers, kids trying to direct other kids, and even in the neighborhood. Show and lead and exemplify what you want done–few people can resist that management style! Think about the people who are trying to get *you* to do something. Don't you respond to leadership and example five times faster and better than a commandment or order? When you want a repair, a clean room, a less chaotic checkbook, anything neater, or better around the home, then you personally act out and demonstrate the directive to the kids, your husband or wife, dad or mom, or the in-laws, instead of just orally requesting it. You don't have to shout "and soon, please!" When and if *you* begin to run, they all will.

Good management is **doing things with people** and **being involved with** what you have going instead of just commanding or "delegating" it done. Working with someone on a project, even for a while, is magic. It's far better than just setting yourself up as the boss, supervisor, or advisor.

I've run Little League spring training for thirty green, loud boys at the same time and parents were amazed that I could get that many kids all doing and going. They found it a struggle to even handle ten kids at once. The reason was so simple. They gave orders and pointed and herded and spent all their time outlining and handing out rules and orders and threatening and reading the kids the consequences. I dressed like the kids, ran the bases and slid home, wrestled and biffed and fought and cooked. I even ate the awful food they cooked because I found indigestion far preferable to the heartburn of always telling and ordering them how.

Working right on the job with them has always been the secret of my success in running large cleaning and painting crews. Never ride around in a pickup with a clipboard or send kids to do things, take them. It's the same whether you're writing books, heading up community projects, or at home getting kids to clean their rooms. Move the same amount of rock and heave the same garbage cans they do, because in the long run it's the easier, not the harder way. It's hard to delegate and direct and worry and fret and fume from afar. It's so much easier to be right in the herd, leading by outworking instead of out-talking them. You're teaching without having to talk much, plus building loyalty.

"If you try to do it all yourself, everyone will always expect you to. You'll be resentful, and they won't have the satisfaction of being involved.

So have a family meeting and discuss and document what needs to be done daily, weekly, monthly, yearly, and occasionally. Have members pick what they want to do."

"I've found that attempting a repair myself will almost always trigger assistance."

"Getting help around the house can be real tricky, since no one wants to do something for nothing and we can't always afford to pay for help. I've found trading services the best answer. If my son wants me to take him fishing, for example, he has to unload and reload the dishwasher. If my daughter wants me to watch her son on Friday night, she has to wash my windows on Saturday. If another daughter wants to borrow my car, she has to clean it up first. It works!"

"Always ask your helpers nicely, don't give orders, and do give praise. Thank them and tell them how pleased you are, how helpful and responsible they are. (Or let them overhear you telling someone how helpful they are.)"

"Don't criticize!! This makes anyone grouchy and uncooperative."

Make your path public

One of my most solid secrets of handling 1,000 things at once (and accomplishing them, too) is that about half of them are done by other people, and no, I didn't ask for or delegate this either. All the things I want to do and am doing, I always make public knowledge. I tell everyone around, even strangers, what I'll be doing, when and why, even print it up and post it. I show my commitment and enthusiasm for the projects, and thanks to human nature, I get help. Most of us, of our own free will and choice, will jump in and help whenever we can. So the minute you let people know where you are going and why, if it is a worthy journey or

objective, they will plug it into their subconscious. And when they come across an item or idea that could help you, they'll pass it on. I help thousands of people a year and more than that are daily helping me. It's like having a platoon of part-time helpers, free. Call it brotherhood, sisterhood, volunteerism, altruism, or whatever, it **works.** And we save each other lots of work.

Most people are reluctant, even terrified, to make their direction and intentions, their wants and wishes, public. ("What if I fail?") But just do it and watch how many people become your loyal assistants, and truly enjoy doing so, too.

Hiring it out

Hiring it out is sometimes a good management tool. If you really can't or don't like to do something, and you can afford to, **hire it done**. One friend of mine, for example, hated the bookkeeping part of his home business, but was determined to do it. He bought all the ledger books and computer programs he needed to do it, and it was actually a fairly small and easy job. But he disliked it so much, he put it off and made it into a big undertaking that easily cost him $300 a month worth of time and struggle and then it wasn't done right anyway. I finally persuaded him to hire a local accountant part time, who charged him $35 a month and that included his taxes at the end of the year, (which he generally paid $500 for alone every April 14th and 1/2).

The home services available are ever more expanded and economical these days. This is the day of "available professionals"–the Yellow Pages can help turn your 1,000 things goal into gold. Almost anyone with an ability is willing (for a price) to perform in areas you lack the time and skill to deal with. So if you have phobias, special needs, or run into any snags, there are options. Just check out those A to Z listings for help with things like:

cleaning
lawn and yard care
plumbing
carpentry
cabinetmaking
electrical problems
painting
refinishing
repairs
sharpening
remodeling
interior decoration
furniture upholstering/repair

mending/alterations
moving
delivery
transporting
shipping and packaging
shopping
gifts
catering and party planning
entertainment
photography
child care
home nursing/medical care
counseling
accounting/bookkeeping
computer services
secretarial services
pet care
pest control/removal
snow removal
storage
tool rental
travel planning
tree service

Watch these people and learn! Next time you may be able to cut the amount of time you need them, or do it yourself.

Herding the hired help

This, unfortunately, doesn't always work as smoothly as dialing does. Some of these so-called pros are problems, and their work, price, and schedule ends up a pain instead of progress. You are right to expect what you pay for and they promise. Getting it on the front end

instead of after the fact (a bad job/no show, etc.) is the way to go.

Here is a little checklist to help assure that:

❏ 1. Find out **how long they've been in business**—endurance is an endorsement of its own. If they've been around for less than two years, be careful.

❏ 2. Always **check references**. Call and ask other customers how satisfied they were, especially any friends or acquaintances of yours who have dealt with the company or contractor in question. Don't just believe everything it says in the ad or brochure. And you might ask for their last three customers, not just **any** three, so you don't end up talking to their best friend, cousin, and brother-in-law.

❏ 3. Get **proof of insurance**. If an accident happens on your premises or to your facility and the workers involved aren't properly insured, **you** could be in big trouble. Make sure they have professional liability insurance. Legitimate contractors have it and if it is a private individual who will be doing the job your homeowner's policy probably covers them—check it out.

❏ 4. Get a **bid or price quote** before they start. Anyone who really knows their business can tell you what something will cost before they start. Get it in writing and hold them to it. If they can't or won't give you a firm bid (or at least an estimate), don't hire them.

❏ 5. **Never pay in advance**. Only a small part of most jobs is material, so paying in advance isn't necessary (or wise). Besides, if they have an investment in the materials they will finish faster.

❏ 6. Find out **who** is coming to do the job. A clean, sharp, convincing manager might sell and set it up and then shifty-looking, surly people (who act as if they were hired last night) show up to work. Ask who is coming—it's a good preventive.

❏ 7. Get a written **WHEN** out of them—when they will start, when they will finish.

❏ 8. Pay **by check**. Cash often eludes memories, yours and theirs.

❏ 9. Always thank the people who did it when they're done. There isn't a person alive who doesn't take pride in their work. A few cookies, a compliment, or even a tip for a job well done is a good investment. There will be another day and another need and this will give you an edge for your 1,000 things.

"There's plenty of incompetent help around and it can be a big problem. They pick up a hammer and call themselves a carpenter, pick up a pair of wire cutters and call themselves an electrician."

"You just have to stick with the ones you know are good/will deliver. You find them by asking people you know who did the work that they were happy with."

"Calling in outside help should be a mutual effort in the family, so that in case of a mess, no one person is to blame. If the kitchen sink starts leaking, talk to your mate about it first, he may be able to take care of it. If you go right to calling in outside assistance, it could cost a lot of money, plus if it isn't done right, your mate will be mad because he or she wasn't consulted."

"Don't take anything for granted!! Don't sign anything unless you really understand what it says. Get references and check them out."

It isn't getting done when and how you need it?

A little visual can sum the basic problem up nicely here:

Today	Tomorrow	Two weeks later
1,000 things I gotta and want to do	The most things I can and will get done on my own The "I need help things"— assigned, scheduled, or hired out to others	(THE PROBLEM) Others didn't act! They said they would fix it They promised to pick it up I paid them to do it, too They've put it off again They've made 1,000 excuses (and are still making them) I'm totally ignored They have time to fix the neighbors', but not mine They can, they should have, but they haven't shown When will it (or will it ever?) get done?

This is pretty typical of things you don't do yourself. "Assistance" we get free and that we pay for are often about the same when it comes to this. It doesn't get done when and how we need it.

Yet, on many of those items in the 1,000 we really need the help, we can't lift or transport something, hang the door, set the computerized sprinkler timer, reassemble the stereo, or lay the pipe without it. We're dependent on someone's word or service, and when they don't come through, it blocks our progress. I'll bet there isn't one of you reading this who can't stop and make a list of ten things you need done that you have a promise on, but aren't done. And you are still waiting and wondering if they ever will be, and it is holding things up in your life.

So what can you do?

NAG!

Even those of us who hate nagging finally resort to it. We rename it, of course–nudging, reminding, prompting, bugging, ordering, and insisting. Finding ourselves whining and complaining constantly to others here is enough to irritate us as well as them.

You don't have to beat and beg–there are better ways to manage help. Such as:

- *Develop a reputation for not accepting being put on the back burner. It only takes a few times and the word will get around that if they welch on their word to you, they won't have you as a friend or customer.*
- *Get **someone else** on it. If you have a "deadbeat" for a contractor, spouse, or helper, get someone who **does** do things to do it instead. Losing face resurrects more*

welchers than you can believe. Having someone else come to do your job is a sharp (and effective) prod.
- *Get a **time or date commitment**, always! Never let anyone off without an answer to that big question "WHEN"? I hate it when people do it to me, but it works 100% of the time. If you can't get a date or time, that tells you something right there.*

There are other ways to get people moving, but these three will basically correct your problem. And by the way, don't bargain, beg, and bribe. I've seen people use food, favors, bonuses, sex, gifts, and anything to get people to do the things they gave their word on or have already been compensated for. If you start doing this you will always have to do it, increasing the booty each time. Bargaining for the already committed is low-class!

"Nudging and prodding others to keep things moving is a pain in the butt, but it must be done. Hints: positive reinforcement, family discussions, coercion–i.e., if ten-year-old Bobby can't do his chores then you don't have time to take him to soccer practice!"

"Remind them of something they can do when the work is done. It takes more reminding than I'd like."

"A tough one. If you say something twice in a week, it's 'nagging.' Mostly I dangle carrots, I guess."

"As household manager, it may be necessary at times to direct others to do certain things. (That's why we're getting the big bucks, right?) It's demeaning to nag and you should try to avoid that sand trap.

'You get more flies with honey than you do with vinegar,' my mother always said. Tactfully, if possible, but firmly, give instructions, make needs known. Mean it; don't make empty threats. Carry through on discipline if requests aren't met. A household will be in constant turmoil if one member flouts the rules set down for the comfort of everyone. Each member needs to carry a share of the responsibility. It really cripples the family if one member isn't doing this. Young or old, all must do according to their abilities to keep things running smoothly and get chores completed."

"We have a family chore assignment chart, but I still have to do a lot of 'reminding.' Work must be done or no play, no computer, no friends over, etc."

"All major chore assignments in our family rotate every week and you can't _____ unless your chore is done by Friday (even if it slips into Saturday). This works pretty well if enforced."

"I've found that the '1, 2, 3 strikes… you're out' system works well. When my teenage son refuses to do something he's been asked to do, he gets three strikes, and then he loses a privilege or something important to him."

MONEY

The most common home management nightmare, and killer of the kindest home situation, good old money!

Money has achieved a massive take-over of our lives; it rules, it dictates. Almost all of us of think of money as the solution to our problems, to better management of our lives. We've all said things like this to ourselves: "Gee, if I just had more money…"

I'd get more done
I'd have more time
I wouldn't have all these worries
I'd lose weight
My marriage would improve
My kids would mind better
I'd be more religious
My house/yard would be cleaner
I'd be better liked in the community
I'd eat healthier food
I could work less and relax more
I'd be more thoughtful
I'd visit folks more
I'd help the poor

The list goes on forever. We really believe this, too, that more money would iron out our problems and we'd be happier and more in control. Sorry, but more money in the home coffers won't improve a marriage, your sex life, make you more spiritual, make your

kids mind better or stop your dog from peeing on the neighbor's lawn. More money won't make you skinny or more popular or take away stress and worry as we're all so sure it will.

All of the above could be done with or without money, we've just let it become our overall excuse for any lack anywhere.

You don't have to be well-off to manage well. In fact, it can make management more of a nightmare. More money only means ever more tending and inventorying and eliminates the motivation to care about accomplishing more. Haven't we all noticed that people (ourselves and others) with excess cash make bad decisions–given enough time, they inevitably do something with it that plagues and complicates (if not self-destructs) their lives? They always seem to load, not lighten, their lives with it.

With money, it isn't really a matter of how much we have, but how we manage it!

Ahead is happy!

There have been innumerable books and articles on managing money and finances, but there are really only a few things you need to know about it.

One **BIG secret** is simply learning to **live ahead,** instead of behind with your money. Most people live owing, and most of that "behind money" is not only costly, but used carelessly. That money gauge in our life really works strangely. When the money we have coming in goes up, so does what we spend, so we seldom get ahead. And when what we're getting goes down, the "what we spend" needle often doesn't. We still spend the same as when we had

it to spend. We may read the gauge, but we don't pay any attention to it.

When we're racing to cover overdrafts and plotting how to pay all our charge accounts at the end of the month, we're trying to stretch money that isn't there. Those thirty days in a month add up to a lot of turmoil and struggle, a pressure that never lets up. We're slaves to it, forever juggling our money around and working off what we have in the bank rather than what we need to pay. Get yourself out of this position for a few weeks or months and you'll automatically shift into a better management gear (without any fancy financial advice seminars, either). "Catch up, keep up" takes ten times more management energy than keeping ahead. Eliminating unnecessary management is management's finest hour.

Nothing beats paying cash up front, and forgetting all the accounting and figuring and bills coming in and rushing to cover payments. As my brother who paid cash for his new $23,000 car answered a friend who asked him how the payments were, "Well, the first one was pretty grim, but for the ten years after that they were hard to beat." Money ahead we treat with respect; money behind instills a spirit of waste and avoidance.

Reviewing the year-end report in my cleaning company one year, I noticed we showed a loss of over $18,000 on unpaid-back advances, meaning money I advanced my employees before they earned it or had it coming. A big percentage of them didn't pay it back even after the courtesy and kindness of getting it before it was due. We advanced money because some of our employees seemed to be struggling to their last penny and "couldn't make it" without a regular cash transfusion. (Due to their style of living in debt or being behind, perhaps.) Unable to tolerate such huge losses any longer, plus the dishonesty of not getting paid back at all, and all the extra accounting occasioned by sixty or more people constantly asking for advances, we put out a ruling that advances were for emergencies and special hardship cases only. Guess how many of those we had next time? All sixty! That did it, we eliminated all advances, period. And guess what? Everyone survived and got along fine, in fact better. A true testimony to how much of a plain old habit using debt money to sustain yourself can be. A bad way to live or manage.

So just reverse where your money use is right now, pull it up front, go without, sell a few toys, and surrender a few trips for a year or so and you can do it. Then operate that way and life will never be the same! You'll be rich no matter how much or little you have.

Even all you "poor" people reading this have more and enjoy a higher standard of living than kings and queens did a few years ago. So SPEND LESS (you can!) Most people, when faced with job loss or divorce, manage to cut their expenses 50% (unbelievable!) and admit they live as well if not better than before. How?

- *Quit buying "stuff" you don't really need—in food, clothes, tools, furnishings, decorations, cosmetics, toys.*
- *Cut down those entertainment expenses, too (expensive dinners, etc.). Try progress instead of play, it's cheaper and 1,000 times more rewarding.*
- *Cut up most of your credit cards.*

- *Keep your old car—the average car is good for 200,000+ miles!*

When you get money, keep it until you are ahead and **then** buy, use it off the front instead of the rear, and you'll keep yourself unburdened. Sure you may need to finance a few things, but the less the better. You pay dearly for other people's money—with **your life, your time**, and that's all we have in the end. Borrowed and credit money is easy to spend and waste, and always takes longer and is harder than we imagined to repay. When you borrow or finance $2,000 for something, long term, it seems to not hurt, but it does. The knife is going in slow, but it is cutting. When you have the $2,000 in your checking account and go down to buy the same thing, there is a difference, a big difference. Now it is YOUR real money and you'll be wiser with it. "Ahead money" feels so secure and pure and good that we spend it better and more carefully.

There are no secrets in money, just simple arithmetic. Just spread the margin to the positive between what you make and spend and watch your management and accomplishment improve as your money worries disappear.

Remember: paying back is ten times harder than borrowing.

Know where you are

An old shopkeeper I know gave me one of the simplest and best summaries of business success I've ever heard, "You seldom fail or go broke if you are making a real profit." This agrees with the #1 reason for financial failure at home as well as in business: People don't know where they are.

Let's take a look at this down on the farm, for example.

Many farmers my rancher father and I knew lost their farms or were gradually squeezed out when farming got more sophisticated and competitive, no matter how hard and long they'd worked. Many of them milked cows, receiving a big milk check every month which came just in time to make payments and buy groceries. The check was such a boon that the expenses that went into getting that check were seldom charted. One farmer, for example, was getting a $2300 milk check. He milked night and morning and fed and catered to those cows constantly. Every month he and his family went deeper in debt, but that milk check kept coming. Finally, they lost the farm and they moved to the city and got jobs in stores and at a plant.

Still disturbed by what had happened (because he was actually smart and had worked his butt off), the farmer finally did something too many of us managers never get around to and that was to calculate the true cost of producing that milk check.

He raised the hay he fed, so he'd never figured it into the expenses, it was just there. But the cost of raising the hay, cutting and baling it, the twine, etc., was cash out of pocket. Because he didn't sell the hay, he fed it, until now he never knew that his hay cost per month was over $2,000! His vet bills per month were $80; the grain for the herd was over $300 a month; the utilities for the barn and manure disposal system another $150; taxes on the barn

came in at $20 a month; the payment on the automatic milker $101; the hired boy made $200 a month; udder salves and other miscellaneous cow care items ran about $50 petty cash a month; the pasture he irrigated with a pump surprisingly cost him over $300 a month. Since he had it and owned it, he just used it. It never occurred to him that these expenses were quietly mounting up every month. They were invisible to him because he never actually received a statement or invoice detailing their cost in black and white. When he added the expenses for the dairy all together they came to $3201 a month. And then, because at least one cow died every year, there was a replacement cost to be considered (easily overlooked because they reproduce for free, right?). Wrong, the cost of replacements–he'd always gotten loans for that–averaged out to $160 a month.

So the total expenses of his milking operation were $3,361. Bottom line: **he was losing $1,061 a month**, not counting any of his labor involved in all this!

Many of us are using and spending

much more than we take in. However, because when those big checks come in we get some short-range relief, we don't properly evaluate the long-term deficit. That deficit slowly but surely adds up and catches up to us, even though other people and other accounts may defer and absorb it temporarily.

Another common money loser thought to be a money maker are some part-time home businesses. We may sell things on the side, for instance, and the size of the occasional checks that come in may blind us to the daily dollar drain on our resources. One woman I know sold cosmetics in a rural area. She drove seven to twenty miles to sell a bottle of lotion for $7.95, and then when it came in she delivered it. She paid $4 for the lotion and calculated herself a nice $3.95 profit. But the calls and car expenses for the sale came to over $6, plus her time, postage, and home space devoted to this undertaking.

At the end of the year, her total profit from this franchised home business was $500, and her costs, absorbed by her husband's income and the household in general, were over $1,000. So she lost $500—all that time, scheduling, and sacrifice to **lose** money (which means more unnecessary scheduling and sacrifice in other areas).

Money is the root of many management problems! In most cases, money is managing people—very few are managing it. Banks, finance, and credit companies of all kinds feed and prosper on our inability to manage money.

Taking control of the money in and around your life is the biggest of the big three steps to gaining good management skills and a happier life.

"It doesn't matter how often you hear that a marriage or partnership is a 50/50 proposition—only one person should handle the finances. He should keep the other informed at all times.

Likewise, for recordkeeping, only one person should be responsible."

"'First things first,' such as paying rent/ mortgage, utilities, insurance, and so on. We economize as we come to less pressing needs. This is a very individual matter, our own finances, but unlike the government, we can't spend money we don't have. So there comes a stopping place."

"I keep all bills due in one place. I used to have an elaborate chart that listed everything that came due every month and when, but it was so time-consuming we abandoned it and just went back to 'as needed.'"

"Money is a difficult subject because 'budget' is a dirty word today and over-spending is a symptom of our 'out of whack' society. Hints: have only one credit card. Having more is a temptation and hurts your credit availability even if you don't use them.

Have everything possible paid automatically out of your checkbook. If you don't see the $ you can't spend it. If you can't do this through your place of work have the money sent to a bank account you keep separate for bills only.

Do your saving by automatic deposit also.

Savings bonds are good because you can't cash them for at least six months. They give good interest right now and their very appearance makes them look 'sacred' and inhibits casual use."

MORE SECRETS OF MASTER MANAGERS

1. **Carry a longer measuring stick**. Most "life" accomplishments can't be measured in short spans, yet our modern mentality is "fast food," "nonstop flight," "quick fix." Good management has a pyramid-building mentality—think and work ahead, then wait patiently for the outcome.

2. **Bite, don't nibble**. True, nibbling may save us from a surprise mouthful of hot peppers or awful casserole, but nibbling is slow and leaves a lot of crumbs (and meanwhile the meal at hand goes stale). A bite commits and stains and we might be forced to chew fast, swallow quick, or even spit it out. Bites outperform nibbles three to one!
   For example, if we want to:
   garden
   dejunk
   remodel
   paint
   learn how to do something
   overhaul something

   Instead of diving in and just doing it, we often peck at it, timidly doing a tiny bit of it here and there, in brief, part-time, halfhearted efforts. We nibble, when we need to bite it.

3. Run your own switches and set your own schedules. Example: Calling a cab or limo to the airport. I tell them the time I want to leave, and they immediately ask "What time does your plane leave?" That is really none of their business, is it? They shouldn't make the decision as to what time I want or need to be at the airport. Set and pursue your own course and schedule, and you won't fall into the traffic and trials everyone else does.

4. Don't accept the "RE" words. Things done right the first time don't need a "re" word. Managers that accept the "re" words as what's to be expected (par for the course), often double their management traffic. I'm talking about repair, redo, repeat, recover, reconsider, refinance—don't RE!

Redo: *Plugging, patching, or covering poor management with more poor management.*

The Only
Time Expert-YOU

The truth about time control

There must be ten million "time control" techniques and shortcuts out there and you've heard or read them all as many times as I have, and still time has not been magically multiplied. "Time management" is a wonderful buzzword, but the hard, hard truth is that **we don't control or manage time.**

There are no time experts out there, not even old Father Time.

Time goes on untouched and uncaring, no matter what, why, or who. The only claim, influence, or effect we can have on time is to USE it! We can only get better at dodging the timewasters and snatching any empty spots or spaces.

Trim down those not really necessary activities

An obvious way to use time better is ELIMINATION–cutting down on the "not really necessary" things, especially the ones you don't enjoy anyway. Now that works. Take big formal social events, for example. They are nice (especially if you cherish and keep score of engraved invitations, enjoy ironing tablecloths, and don't mind driving things back and forth from the dry cleaner). But they sure can take up a lot of time. When I decided to cut not only formality, but fanciness of any kind (clothing, food, furnishings, decorations, etc.), boy did it make a difference. I actually have a more satisfying life now, and I can dress and groom in ten minutes and get on with it while many of my glamorous friends are still painting and preening and polishing and matching and parading in front of a mirror an hour later.

Here are some things you can let go a little and steal some "spare time" from right now:

Primping (including elaborate and time-consuming hairstyles, makeup, and outfits).

Deep cleaning–you've probably already figured out how to cut some corners here.

Laundry–there's a lot of unnecessary washing done in this country. A towel, for example, doesn't have to hit the hamper after a single use.

Cooking–you don't have to make a formal four-course meal every night for just the two of you, unless you really want to.

Eating out

Telephone time–a biggie.

Overplanning (at the expense of doing).

Fidget habits–such as smoking and coffee drinking. Count up the time (and money) you spend on things like this in a day or week. It'll amaze you.

Shopping–especially going to the store for just one or two things, and idle shopping or mall cruising.

Playing–especially those activities you don't really enjoy all that much anyway.

Spectatoring (TV watching, etc.).

Gossiping and chatting.

Organization memberships and other group activities that aren't doing what you hoped they'd do for you.

Traveling

Lawn and yard work (you could always cement your yard over, or put it into ground cover).

Pets (you don't have to keep the whole litter!)

One woman, running almost beyond imagining to do it all, keep up with it all, stay aware of it all, prepare for it all, sat down, shrugged her shoulders, and said, "You know, folks, we are over-evented."

We've all felt or thought that at least occasionally. A few or some events are really events, but preparing for and participating in 75 events in every season, however (even if they're all worthwhile) is back to that good old "too much."

Cure yourself of Mediaitis

Where have I picked up the most extra time at home? Curing myself of mediaitis. If you just hang around the house with them, the media—TV, newspapers, magazines—will consume almost all of your time. And worsen your mental condition in the process; all it is is pages and pages of pain and more pain and negative and more minute analyses of the musk ox's sex life or the history of masking tape, channel upon channel of sickcoms and commercials. You can just dump most of it. Anything truly important, you can get in a capsulized form a day or so later anyway, and save watching and reading and listening to six hours of analysis and rehash and opinions of experts that aren't experts. Those of us who have done it are now smarter and have more free hours and less paper trash and lower electricity bills and anxiety levels. We also feel about ten times better than we did before. My life doesn't need to stop while the riots or trials are going on in L.A. I can have compassion and interest without having it totally preoccupy me.

The best management channel on TV—ABC? CBS? NBC? CNN? TNT? Nope, it's OFF!

Snatch those time fragments

We might have some free time at work, but at home, it's rare indeed, especially if we have children, an aged parent, or a home and property of any size. We're not very likely, in the average fully scheduled home, to find any stretches of unoccupied or spare time to do a personal thing or handle an unforeseen new chore.

Getting to everything we want and need to do is literally survival of the fittest, because "fitting" to-do's into any available time is the key.

Using those precious little units of time called "fragments" is definitely good management. I write most of my books in airports, on planes, in motels, and in dull meetings!

Where can we find those fragments around the house?

Just a few examples here:

1. Very early and very late in the day there is always 15 minutes or more that can be used (that time we usually spend gearing up and ungearing ourselves).
2. While waiting—in lines, on people and appointments, on clothes dryers or recipe stages (see page 140).
3. During TV time. We can give the tube 1/3 of our attention and use the other 2/3 to accomplish something.
4. While on the treadmill or exercise bike.
5. When traveling anywhere, there is tons of time (as long as we don't have to drive).

"One of the most helpful hints I found in your book How Do I Clean the Moosehead? *was the idea of doing housework in snatches of time. This was a real eye opener for me. There was a time when I was so preoccupied with housework (BC– before children!) that I wouldn't even find time to visit sick friends. Now I have time to spend with four children, among other activities, and get no less housework done."*

Little blasts are often better than one big boom

Getting things done is like saving money. If you keep dropping in dimes and nickels, you'll be surprised how much you've accumulated by the end of the year. Often we envision a marathon solid month to do something, and for sure we won't find that month coming along and offering itself to us. If we just chip away at that project, on the other hand, instead–little minutes here and there–by the end of the month it might be done!

At the entryway to our ranch, for example, I decided to build a large (I mean large) rock pool monument to my wife's late parents. Something with beautiful stonework, plants, and a series of cascading waterfalls. Just looking at the preliminary drawings made people moan at the work involved. Probably two full months worth, and if I contracted it out it would cost over $10,000. But I had the rock available right on my ranch, the tools, and a few hours a week I could devote to it, in the late evenings and early mornings and on holidays. Besides, what's better exercise–mental, physical, and emotional–than lifting 50 or 100-pound rocks, mixing mortar, and creating a lasting monument to two people you loved?

Once it was planned, every time I had a backhoe or cement truck on the premises (for one of my other projects) I'd have them take fifteen minutes to help out with my rock pool project. Some nights when grandkids or friends were over, we'd run up and pick up a few more rocks and add them to the pile. That pool grew seemingly at snail speed, but I kept pecking away at it– even five rocks mortared a night is 150 rocks in a month! Suddenly, there it was, finished. A miniature mountain, and it was worth it. And I never had to schedule it in.

Likewise, cleaning the fridge a little at a time as you use it is sure smarter than a big monthly purge and purification. Cleaning, weeding, cross-stitching, in fact in almost everything (even romance), keeping at it consistently, every free minute you get, sure beats a big all-out campaign.

We always have the chores and emergencies of regular living, and those new opportunities that pop up and need to be tended. These things never take a week off. But that big, big project, I mean the biggest of all books or building projects will get done, too, if you gather it under the scope of your other goals and find and use the spare minutes, even seconds. How quickly they add up to days and the days to weeks, and the project is finished, and finished well.

Reclaim that waiting time

Learning to manage waiting time isn't an option, it's part of the basic equipment for modern life. Often, we don't know exactly when something will happen, or come. We have to remain in control of our time and not surrender it to oblivion, aggravation, or even the urge to kill. What can we do?

Whenever possible, avoid or refuse to honor waiting like:
1. Lines (don't just pick the shortest line, get there before or after the line, or go somewhere there isn't a line).
2. Traffic (go before or after rush hour). When you go at an off time, lots of yellow lights are flashing, but no stoplights are working and you can zip through town twice as fast.
3. Being put on hold on the phone (call back, or call at a better time to begin with).
4. Waiting an overlong time in the doctor's office when your appointment was scheduled months ahead. Make sure you get the first appointment in the morning after they open, or the first one after their lunch break. Call ahead to see if the doctor is running late because of emergency

surgery, delivering a baby, or the like. You can also develop some sudden shooting pains in the waiting room, or switch doctors.
5. Waiting to be waited on.

"When I'm in need of a clerk and none is in sight, I sometimes sing out cheerily, 'I'm shoplifting.' One usually comes right away. (I've never been frisked yet.)"

6. Waiting for that repairperson, carpenter, installer, appraiser, etc. Make them tell you not only the day but the hour. Or at very least, whether it will be a.m. or p.m. And call the evening before to **confirm** that they're coming.
7. Late employees. Let them know that you notice lateness and make them realize that it inconveniences and costs you. If that doesn't do it, make it cost them (in minutes and hours deducted from their paycheck, or the sudden need to find a new job).

Many of our waits (bank lines, supermarket lines, phone lines, traffic) can be cured by coming at a less popular time, moving to another location, or taking our business elsewhere. Mixed with too many other "waiters," we can quickly lose patience or our belief in the nobility of man.

Another big key here is not letting yourself fall into the "can't really do anything until..." mentality. Just because something is pending or coming, doesn't mean you can't keep right on with all the other things you have to do. Don't just hang around or fidget in limbo.

Some lines and waits can be avoided entirely by doing the thing (such as getting your new driver's license, or the plane tickets) ahead by mail, as you could have, if you'd just bothered to read the fine print or been willing to get to it a little sooner.

Think portable

Einstein made a statement we all ought to remember: **"The kind of work I do can be done anywhere."** Make the waits you can't escape into productive breaks. Think portable. Carry what you need to keep your "to-do's" going when your go-to's are delayed. Then you keep control of your time, and it's a lot better than staring into space, drumming your fingers, or working toward your degree in "insults and horn honking."

To carry my own work along, I have a super sized briefcase for travel and a cardboard box for around home. I strip all the mail and other "incoming" to the meat and then sort it into marked file folders. Many times I've had five or six trade magazines to read, and done it in twenty minutes, in those time fragments in waiting rooms and lobbies!

Waiting time: A good home manager never wastes it.

We can either fill up and use waiting time or it will be filled by someone else with something else.

Some things you can do during waits:

1. Read (for information or pleasure)
2. Write
3. Study
4. Plan
5. Make lists
6. Update your address book
7. Draw or sketch
8. Exercise
9. Have a friend wait with you and catch up on your friendship
10. Have a child wait with you and share some time together
11. Dejunk
12. Little cleaning chores
13. Needlework or mending
14. Empty the lint filter, check the pressure in the fire extinguisher, etc.
15. Sing
16. Pray
17. And any of thousands more!

"I never go somewhere without something to do! I have TONS of reading to do. I try to keep up on the subjects in which I have college degrees as well as other areas I am concerned with (from heavy social and medical issues to the political arena). I carry journals and papers everywhere and read at stoplights, waiting for kids, etc."

"If I have to take someone to the doctor or dentist, I write in my journal, make out bills, write letters while they're in there. I can't waste all that time when there is so much to do."

Take advantage of travel

Students of time use tell us that the average American spends **four years** of his or her life traveling in automobiles alone. (Six months of that waiting for red lights to turn green, nine months sitting in traffic.) Add in other travel, and that's a big, big slice of our life and time.

Think about that a while, and I think you'll suddenly discover that travel offers some prime time to deal with and get things done–for ourselves or with the kids. Those time scientists, again, say that the time we actually spend on a one-to-one basis with our children is 37 seconds a day. As one mother told me, just driving to the babysitter and back in her case takes a half hour a day. She uses this time with her son to talk, listen, teach, and look at school treasures. It's actually more uninterrupted time than many of us get together at home in the "living room" (which is more like the "rush through" room for many of us today).

In the old days of horse-drawn transport you were doing well to hang on, keep warm, and stay aboard the bouncing buggy. The only shock absorber was the personal padding on your backside. Travel time could easily be torture. Today traveling is so inviting and easy, a turn of a key instead of a twenty-minute crank or harnessing up a balky horse. When we travel, we're usually free of most of our usual routines, and our mind is free so we can do mental chores. If someone else is driving, then both our mind and hands are free, often in complete peace and privacy. It's far better than the average home or office situation. So don't waste that travel time!

Use those before and after hours

When Interstate 15 came through Idaho, the state needed straw to spread on the freshly cut gaps, to keep them from washing and eroding. They arranged with local organizations to gather the straw from local farmers. Our church group committed to provide fifty loads, as a fundraiser for our youth camp. When it came time to actually do it, however, enthusiasm eroded worse than those road slopes. Our bishop begged for help and politely tried to fit the project into the perfect time for everyone, but he got little or no support from an "overcommitted" congregation. Finally, a less patient and much larger man (whom everyone respected, if not feared) got up, lumbered to the podium, and cheerfully said, "I know, brethren, we're all busy all of the time..." Religious nods of agreement came from all sides. "Well, then–how many of you are booked and busy at 2:30 in the morning?" A slight gasp, fidgeting feet, but no hands went up. "Good, then we can all be there?" Some weak nods followed. "Every man be there with a truck at 2:30 a.m. tomorrow, Johnson's field. Anyone not there, I'll personally come to your home and tip your bed over and get you there–in the name of the Lord, of course." We had a hundred percent turnout at this

"perfect time" and finished the whole project by 8:00 that morning. Thanks to timing... and possibly some slight persuasion.

Likewise, we have a man in our community that if you looked up the word "manager" in the dictionary, his picture would be there. He's unquestionably an impressive, outstanding individual. I've known him thirty years and watched him move mountains and change and influence lives all that time.

Noticing one day his third cutting of hay down and rowed nicely, almost as if by magic, I asked him, "Reed, how do you get all of this done?" "I do most of it while others are sleeping," he said.

This may be one of the secrets of management you haven't tried. Often we sleep a lot, not really because we're tired, but because we're bored or depressed. Once you break out of that mold and start getting a lot done, you'll find yourself on a high that just doesn't seem to call for as much sleep.

Good managers really take advantage of those before and after hours. They're usually our least cluttered time—just about everyone who has a demand of some kind on us has wound down (or isn't wound up yet). That leaves us... freedom!

"What is my #1 secret for getting 1,000 things at once done? Staying up late at night, doing stuff after the kids are in bed. I get organized, make school lunches, etc."

The Secret Saturday

Once we had separate days for work, rest, washing, shopping, ironing, playing, paying, partying, etc. Today we've blended ourselves a week where activities on each or any day can barely

be separated. I'm sold on Sunday to rest, change, edify yourself, worship, and reunite the family–all in all refuel for the big 5 (Mon.-Fri.). But Saturday, earmarked for centuries as bath day, ruckus raising and play day, is a key day for the homefront... a management day.

It offers, if you take advantage of it, space and place to plan. Four hours of Saturday spent fixing (friendships or broken ships), writing, filing, outlining, organizing, cleaning up, or whatever can cut twenty hours worth of trouble out of next week.

Make the most of mood

We all know how poorly we function when we "just don't feel like it right now." No matter how much something needs doing, how worthwhile it is, or how important it might be to us or others, when we don't feel like it, we want to let it lie. As we've heard so many people say, "I couldn't even force myself to do it!"

Other times we don't just feel like doing it but pant and paw and snort to do it, because we're "on a roll." It's not only ecstasy for us, but the job gets done five times faster and better. And everyone around loves us and our attitude.

We've all seen the home team kids be losing badly and suddenly little Deven Dork (who hasn't hit a ball all season) nails a homer and the team's mood switches to "Now anything is possible." They go from lose to win instantly and the opposing championship team can't contain them.

Mood is a real powerhouse when it comes to hitting the duties of life. That's the big reason we hate interruptions, they break the mood and the flow we're in!

Mood breakers

At home, because of all those interruptions mentioned earlier, it's extra important to take advantage of whatever "clear channel" time you do get. This is why good managers and movers at home or anyplace don't tie their life and limb to "schedules." They use them to regulate, but never dictate. They seldom let a phone call, mealtime, bedtime, quitting time, golf game, bad or good news–anything–stop them when they really get going. You can and will accomplish more in three hours then, than in three days slugging it out with a mere sense of duty.

We can't make ourselves click into a mood at a moment's notice. Nor can we wait to make dinner, change a diaper, or pay the bills, until we're in the mood. Lots of things we have to do with determination and not mood. But we **can stay on a roll when we do happen into one and use it as a catalyst for major accomplishment.**

I asked a group of ordinary, everyday people what the worst mood breakers were, so we can keep an eye out for them and avoid them whenever we can.

(I've left space for you to add your own at the end)

The telephone
Food and eating
Alcoholic drinks that make you silly, sleepy, etc.
Sudden have-to's such as an appliance failure, or the need to run to the bank to cover an overdraft
Can't find something you need (such as a key)
Missing ingredient or material while cooking or on a fix-it project
Getting sidetracked on some new problem or project that comes up

A big surprise expense
Sickness or injury to yourself or someone close
Coming across something that makes you mad
Salespeople
Visitors
Wrong comment from spouse or other
Music we dislike
The TV news

_____

_____

_____

_____

_____

_____

_____

Don't go to town if you don't have to! **Things like this do more damage than just the time they occupy, 9-11 a.m. or whatever. The dressing and hair curling, etc., and the mental torquing of the whole day to the fact that you have to make an appearance this morning or afternoon, can end up derailing half the day, or more. (Often part of the day before, too.)**

Do it right the first time

As we age (and gain responsibility and ambition with the years), time becomes our most prized and sought-after possession. We'll do anything to get more of this elusive commodity. We pay for services, conveniences, and shortcuts meant to give it to us, and are forever searching and maneuvering for "more time." How would you like to save about four years of it over the rest of your life?

How much time do you spend explaining mistakes and dealing with the foulups, reversals, and setbacks that follow? Many of us spend least an hour a day. And where do most of those reversals and setbacks come from?

Not doing it right the first time. Example:

- *We don't sign that important paper on the right line, so it's sent back to us for redo. Meanwhile, the loan/merchandise we were so anxious for is delayed.*
- *We make a mistake balancing our checkbook. Now we have not only embarrassment, but a lot of money wasted in bad check charges. Plus all that time wasted calling or going to see people to straighten things out.*
- *We don't check or change the oil in our*

NO, OVER THERE... **NO.** OVER HERE...
... I MEAN **THERE** ... OH, NO, I MEANT...

vehicle (20 minutes and $20). As a result we eventually have to replace the motor (2 days and $900).
- *We didn't see why we should pay extra for an "underlayment" when the installers were putting down the vinyl flooring in our new room addition. Now, less than a year later, every nail head in the plywood subfloor beneath is faithfully reproduced in little vinyl bumps, as is the big uneven ledge near the door. Replacing this now will not only cost plenty, but surely gouge and scar all the now-finished woodwork and trim, and at least ten thousand things will have to be moved out of the way to do it.*
- *We didn't wear protective gloves or goggles when we should have, so instead we spent two hours and five hundred dollars in the emergency room, plus a week or a month recuperating. Not to mention all the pain, lost work, and inconvenience involved.*

Everything not done right the first time stays with us to be 1) done again; 2) repaired; 3) multiplied; and 4) carried in conscience and notebook. We spend millions of dollars a year on psychologists and seminars to get relief, and breathing room from the "load" of living. I'd bet 65% of this is "didn't do it right the first time" stuff. You can cut those millions; you can cut your load! Do it right the first time!

If you don't have time to do it right, when will you have time to do it over?

We hear poorly done things referred to sometimes as "survivable mistakes." Most mistakes **are** survivable. Repeats and repairs to revive and survive, however, carry a heavy price tag. As we deal with the breakage or bombout involved, our entire focus and direction is shifted out of the progress mode into a recovery mode. Fixing is no fun and uses much more time and money than building it right in the first place does. First times are usually single-person operations, which is the simplest, quickest, and most cost effective. Any redo generally multiplies the people and mechanics involved, thus complicating the situation and raising the ante.

A fifteen-minute job, for example, not done right the first time usually takes three times as long (forty-five minutes) to redo. It costs a few more dollars in parts and supplies, more postage or phone time. But that is often meager compared to the effort and emotion involved in explaining it, reporting it, and arranging and following up on the redo.

Before we're through, the original $5 cost ends up $50.

There is another price we pay, too, the inner feeling of disappointment, disgust, and irritation with ourselves for having "blown something." It punishes us before, during, and after the cash and care administered to fix something. Not doing it right the first time always puts us behind. There is always "too much" when you are behind, always that uneasiness of being "behind the eight ball."

Another cost often overlooked is our credibility. We all know the difference between the person you can trust to get something done and the one where you know you better make a note to yourself to follow up because it probably won't get done right otherwise. None of us want to deal with people who are always forcing us into the "redo" mode because it is frustrating as well as risky.

Redo's cost us momentum, too. Notice that when you "get off on the wrong foot," your jump is only half as far. A business or team with momentum is virtually unstoppable, and what can break momentum? Not weather or opposition; not challenges or new ground. In fact, these often fuel momentum—we are all eager for and enthusiastic about something new. What will dampen the discipline of even the best is having to break rhythm and go back and "pick up" or redo something that was done wrong. We don't mind being pressed on a new task, but have little or no desire to squeeze in an old defunct one.

Why don't we do things right the first time? It isn't because we don't know how. We somehow manage to do things right if our very lives, our vanity, or something very dear to us is involved. We generally don't make mistakes packing our parachutes because the potential impact is so great.

During military training, National Guardsmen like myself were required to dismantle a 50-caliber machine gun. Once the rear breech cable was snapped off, there was a set screw to turn exactly one-quarter turn, that locked the reconcile spring, so when you took the unit apart, the spring wouldn't fire back. (It had enough power to go through a wall or more to the point, through you.) It was scary and important. If you didn't do it right the first time, death or destruction was your payoff. I've watched thousands—morons to master's degrees—take those guns apart, and still haven't heard of one getting pierced. They don't want a second chance. They all do it right the first time, and every time.

Notice we always have the hot water adjusted just right in the shower, before we get in.

And how many times has anyone dropped a tiny baby? I know thousands of people who handle babies thousands of times a year and have never dropped one once, in spite of all that squirming.

Think about driving, too. We can drive along and do much or most of it right but when an officer appears, it's amazing how 100% performance is possible–right speed, right signal, all belts fastened, etc.

Why is it that we focus on doing certain things right while on others, we spend years of our life fixing and redoing?

It's partly because of plain old carelessness, and partly because we don't see fixing and correcting as the waste of time it is. We have absorbed the thought somehow that "troubleshooters" are effective managers. Troubleshooters ought to be shot themselves. Trouble-preventers are what the world needs and doing it right the first time is what makes for smooth management and trouble prevention.

Don't wait till you're filling your tank for a scuba dive or checking over the rocket ship for your journey to Saturn. Save yourself a lot of time and trouble **every day**, by running your eye down this list of lesser things it **is** worth doing right the first time. (Many of these are things we do at least weekly.)

- *Giving directions (such as to the Fire Department or ambulance as to where your house is)*
- *Taking down/getting directions (so you don't spend an extra hour circling and backtracking and asking more people and getting mad and flustered and ending up still **late** to something important)*
- *Making notes (so they can be READ later)*

- *Deciding where something (such as a fence) is to be located*
- *Putting the lid on something (so it doesn't suddenly come off and splash all over clothes or furnishings or whatever)*
- *Identifying what something is (so you don't end up using the wrong stuff on the wrong thing, destroying something, or poisoning yourself)*
- *Picking up the right suitcase from the airport carousel*
- *Explaining what you want done (...don't take ANYTHING for granted)*
- *Explaining yourself/picking the right excuse to put forward*
- *Picking the doctor for your facelift/nose job/brain surgery, etc.*

NOW, HAND ME THE NEW NOSE SHE WANTED, DR. WATKINS.

- *Picking the right grade of sandpaper to use*
- *Doing something it is very hard to get in position to do (such as washing windows four stories up, installing the weathervane on top of the building, or planting your flag on Everest)*
- *Giving instructions (...don't take ANY-THING for granted)*
- *Fixing something (...a couple sheets of metal are loose on the shed roof; you don't fix it right, and the whole roof is torn off by the next big wind)*
- *Closing the gate or locking the door before you leave*
- *Turning off the power, or the water*
- *Checking for termites*
- *Using birth control*
- *Mixing up mortar*
- *Applying epoxy*
- *Attaching jumper cables*
- *Putting a tire/wheel back on*
- *Meeting your fiancee's/boyfriend's or girlfriend's parents for the first time*
- *Deciding whether or not to cut down that 100-year old tree*
- *Addressing that important letter*
- *Packing for that ten-day backpack trip into the wilderness*
- *Washing/cleaning that $275 sweater/ $1600 throw rug*
- *Giving the dimensions for that expensive custom-made_____*
- *Being sure that person you've got your pistol pointed at is an intruder*
- *Washing something extra-fuzzy*
- *Loading your camera before the big event*
- *Picking a mate (redo costs particularly high here)*
- *Putting in the decimal point*
- *Engraving your name on something*
- *Deciding whether something is dead or not*

- *Deciding where to plant a tree*
- *Driving to town on an icy road*

- *Applying herbicide*
- *Deciding when the steak will still be rare*
- *Deciding how much salt to put in something*
- *Deciding which papers to throw in the woodstove*
- *Looking before you back up/pull onto the highway/cross the RR track*
- *Deciding that the ice is strong enough to stand/skate on*
- *Setting the oven temperature*
- *Choosing the setting on a pressure washer*
- *Attaching something (such as a trailer)*
- *Tying something on, such as a tarp (an extra minute or even few seconds here can prevent lost things, water-damaged things, things scattered all over, things escaping and damaging other things)*
- *Measuring the dose (especially of poten-tially dangerous or life-sustaining medica-tions)*
- *Picking the right bottle (before you swig it down or put drops of it in your eye)*
- *Picking the things to trash on a computer*
- *Preparing the surface for painting (if you don't do it right the first time, you'll be removing peeled paint and smoothing rough surfaces and other time-consuming,*

aggravating jobs before you can even repaint)
- Pointing the nozzle in the right direction (whether it's spray paint, or Mace)
- Indicating which building you want demolished
  ...Which trees are to be cut
  ...Which branches to prune off
- Remembering which chemical was the "1" and which was the "5" in that "1:5"
- Cutting those $40 apiece oak boards to size for what you're making
- Spelling that important person's name right
- Signalling the auctioneer
- Knowing which are the weeds and which are the flowers
- Putting the price in the ad

- Making sure that something is level
- Deciding where you want to put down concrete
- Deciding where to put the house on the lot
- Making/Building a foundation
- Installing anything lasting
- Deciding what color carpeting you want
- Making the basic structure of something strong enough
- Deciding where you need to cut the hole in the wall
- Putting out your campfire
- Installing electrical wiring
- Using indelible ink
- Burying that deceased pet (so it won't be dug up by predators, etc.)

A job/task
Done wrong or too quickly

Needs adjustment

Needs to be redone

Causes a problem/have to solve the problem

Causes a misunderstanding/have to make an explanation or apology

Ruins the tool or the materials/have to get new/ then do it all over again

Facts/tools/supplies may be unavailable or hard to come by now

Makes someone mad/have to calm them down

May be too late to do it now

May cost more to do it now

Penalties assessed

Upsets the authorities/puts us under scrutiny

We lose the "iron is hot" moment

Tools: Bigger? Better? or Bummers?

I t's ten-thirty, the TV news just finished up, and you're ready to call it a day. But before you can turn off the TV, a convincing personality is asking you a pretty direct question. Holding up a luscious salad (that is a piece of art indeed), he asks, "At your next dinner party, what would your guests think if you presented them with a salad that looked

like this?" You sit back down in the chair thinking, "Now that would be something!" Then the announcer really gets your attention. "You can do this, without any experience at all, in only a fraction of the time you now spend making a regular **dull** salad!" You have certainly been a dull salad maker, and this sounds like real results! He now offers to show you how a simple, inexpensive tool efficiently glamorized those cucumbers, radishes, peppers, and cauliflower–in fact, the whole vegetable family. In awe, you watch a big chunk of carrot being reduced to small systematically diced squares, then ZIP! he changes blades and now they're chips! Then curls! Then strings! Then flowers! Then balls! Then triangles! Incredible what that little tool can do, and in no time at all! It worked on TV, you saw it, and there was just an ordinary human like you operating it. What a salad manager you'd be!

Someone gave my wife and I one of these wonderful things as a gift, and the timing was perfect. Some neighbors had just brought by a basket of vegetables and lunch was a couple of hours away. From the other room, I heard the package being unwrapped by my wife, then the rustle of the instructions, then a silence for three minutes as they were read. Then for over an hour, I heard whirring and grinding, the sound of parts hitting the counter, and the sink running, so I imagined the celery was soon to be salivatorized. Then things got slower and slower and I heard murmurings. When I went in to investigate, the entire counter was covered with parts and blades and shreds of all different vegetables. There were pieces of greenery flung all over, too–it looked as if a James Bond chase car had hit a fruit and vegetable stand.

"How did it work?" I asked.

"I could have made this salad by hand with a paring knife in ten minutes," she said.

How often in our lives have we bought a magic tool which either doesn't work, works for a short time and then self-destructs, or requires more effort to operate than the "time it saves"? If you were making salads full time or three times a day, a SuperDuper Salad Slicer would make sense. For an occasional one, it costs you. It's the same with things like a screwdriver attachment for an electric drill, sure they're fast and easy, if you're putting in lots of screws. But generally you're not, and one or five screws can be done in few minutes by hand (better and neater, too)–while it takes ten minutes just to set up the drill to do it.

Snow blowers are another good example. For a few serious and consistent snow situations (such as Antarctica or Buffalo), they may have merit, but for most of us, they're a waste of time and money. Even here in Idaho, 5,000 feet above sea level, where we get snow in abominable amounts, there are very few times one is needed. There may be three or four significant snowfalls a year (over the two months of deepest winter) that merit unearthing and rolling out the blower. But the rest of the time–most of the time–the walks would be cleaner, and less fuel and human energy expended, if we just used the old ($7.98) snow shovel. We'd be finished in minutes, plus there'd be no snow sprayed all over the neighbors' yard and cars. Yet, in every block of homes in mild-climate cities, you see at least five families storing these monsters (and paying for them) year-round, cranking them up and gassing and oiling them, then heaving them out of the garage—all for a few inches of snow. It's enough to bring on that heart attack we bought the blower to prevent!

Or consider all those four-wheel drive vehicles. I always ask owners why they've got one, when off-road needs for most modern Americans are nearly zero. Not one in twenty can answer "because I really need it." Maybe they just needed something to stimulate the economy, burn gas, and wear off rubber... or reinforce their ego.

Walk through a nice neighborhood any Saturday afternoon. All the garage doors will be up as the proud owners putter in the yards of their fine homes, squeezed into a sixty-foot lot. Just about every garage contains a magnificent riding mower, contractor's wheelbarrow, and enough lawn and garden tools to farm 100 acres.

There's a psychological hangup here that says, "If I own a better tool for it, I can/will do it better." That's like saying "if I own more clocks I'll always be on time." It simply isn't true. We want to lose weight so we have all kinds of slimfeast formulas, doctor's-office-quality scales, belly firmers, rowing machines, and stationary bikes to help— all tools that do zero good without our contribution.

I've known literally hundreds of people who, frustrated with their housecleaning, watch a great vacuum cleaner sales demo, then pay up to $1,000 for a souped-up, state of the art vacuum cleaner, with 44 ingenious attachments. Of course the quality of their vacuuming—how they vacuum or how often—doesn't change a bit. But it's the promise of what that tool **could** do for them.

Some people can't cook, so they buy cookbooks, blenders, food processors, freezers, juicers, shredders, slow and fast cookers, timers—great tools, but those folks carrying them home proudly from the store still can't (or don't want to) cook.

Likewise, right after the home show or county fair, almost every home is blessed with some kind of implement or electric gadget that gets tried out once or twice (probably just fiddled with on the way home in the car) and then relegated to the back of the bottom shelf in the cupboard. A friend of mine told me he'd never used his impressive Father's Day present, a shoeshine kit complete with foot rest and brass-latched wood case and every piece of shoe-shining equipment imaginable. Then three more of us chimed in that we'd never used ours, either! Most of what little spit shining we do is far away from our handy-dandy, magnificent kits. At least 95% of the exercise equipment bought for the promise of a beautiful, healthy body only develops the bugs' and spiders' muscles from dodging it, down there where it's stuck under the bed or in storage. The same is true of elaborate repair kits, automated tooth cleaning equipment, and yard gizmos that promise better and faster performance. If you just have them around, they won't do a thing to make you better or faster.

Buying and wearing a new $500 digital watch with alarm, two-way radio, pager, cellular phone, recorder, and computer, is not the answer for someone who can't or won't tell time, follow up, or get up. It's just another trinket to make payments on.

If you let them, tools will convince you that they're the key to keeping up with the demands of managing things. They aren't, they're just tools.

A few examples of overtooling

- *A seven-thousand function calculator (when all you really need is add, subtract, and multiply).*
- *A ninety-cycle washer/dryer (no one reads far enough into the booklet to find out what the other 87 cycles are for).*
- *An expensive pro quality camera (when we'd be happier with an Instamatic).*
- *A "survival knife" capable of cutting a tin can in half or stopping a grizzly in its tracks (when we never venture beyond the back yard).*
- *Programmable, stereo sound VCR.*
- *Souped up guns.*
- *Souped up cars.*
- *A boat–a tool that takes unending amounts of time to tend and tow, and that we're forever throwing money at, all for a few hours of "fun" every summer!*

I had a simple goal one day, to be sure to be off by 4:30 the next morning to catch a plane. So I sent someone to get me an alarm clock. All I wanted was an alarm, not to be entertained, informed, intrigued, or anything else. Just awakened at my chosen time. My errandee returned with a clock radio, and the thing was a mass of buttons, setters, and adjusters. It literally had twenty different services for you–you could be awakened by buzzers, alarms, or the musical station or selection of your choice. There were snooze, presnooze, extended snooze, and heavens knows what other settings. A complicated little instruction book came with it that could easily take all the time between now and 4:30 a.m. to comprehend. It was literally, for an ordinary human who just wanted to do an ordinary job, unworkable. I had to call in the genius grandson to set it. It took up

a lot of space, and if the electricity happened to go off for a few seconds it flashed and blinked like a radio tower, keeping me and all the mosquitoes awake. Finally I sneaked shamefacedly into a supermarket and bought a plain old windup alarm clock for $6.95. It told time and had only two levers on the back, one to set the time and the other to set and stop the alarm. It did the job, just what I wanted done and no more!

I noticed that others at home here are using the twenty-option clock radio, and then setting my alarm clock too, using it for a backup, because they don't quite trust the complicated one.

Anytime you spend more time, effort, and money managing a tool than the problem it's supposed to solve, you don't need it!

Then there's the combination tools, the "Swiss Army knife syndrome." We all have to have one–the thing is three inches thick, weighs four pounds, and in twenty years, we never use a third of the clever trinkets on it. Yet it's a promise (like a reversible raincoat–which never works) that we can't resist.

I have seen a few clever combination tools, like an antique baby rocker that had a butter churn built into the

headboard and by the time the baby was asleep you had butter. Great! (If you have a baby and if you churn your own butter.) Remember, how useful something is is determined by how much **you** need it.

Don't be taken in by every "better tool"

It's better to have ten tools doing 1,000 things, than 1,000 tools doing ten things.

Don't be taken in by every "better tool" promise. Keep up with and get the good ones, the proven ones. The rest of the time, remember that it's our hands and brains that give us 95% of our management results.

My wife and I have a sixty-acre ranch here in Southern Idaho, and about five acres of that is yard. Most of it needs mowing, and for years we only dreamed of (or coveted) our doctor neighbor's riding mower. We mowed our lawn entirely by hand, every year. When we could finally afford a nice riding mower, we continued with the hand mowers, gradually removing all the rocks in the yard and straightening the edges and in general making things level and safe for the great riding lawn mower now on the agenda. We began to relish the thought so much—the time-saving and ease and salvation of the new riding mower to come—that the hand mowing didn't seem such hard work anymore. You know how it is when you're looking forward to relief, it always eases the pain of the present.

The spring of '92 was the year—everything was green, and the grass was growing like a new baby skunk. The rolling hills of our yard were filling out so nicely and the willows and weeping birches and pines and cedars we'd planted were setting off the distant view so handsomely. So for the last time, I set the hand mower to low and in a couple of days of spare evening minutes mowed the entire lawn, hillsides, fence edges and all. It was manicured so nicely that some little kid said to his mother when they drove over the hill near our place, "Mom, does the President live there?"

Feeling rich and noble now, and preparing to leave on a two-week trip as a seminar teacher, I gave my wife an open checkbook and told her to go next week and get our mechanic son to help if necessary, but buy the best riding lawn mower she could, one she felt good on and one that would last. I left and three days later she called me in Washington bubbling with enthusiasm. They'd delivered a deluxe top-of-the-line Toro. It was self-starting and rode like a sports car, did everything to the lawn but re-seed it. My wife could hardly wait to attack the lawn the next day. When we were talking again a few days later, I asked how it worked. A short silence, then, "Oh, it's fun to ride, but takes some getting used to." Then she proceeded to brag about the features—how the motor shut off automatically when you got out of the seat, the fourteen different speeds it would go, the neighbor's awe, etc. Now I couldn't wait to get home and see my beautiful place—and for a change, without having to labor over all those acres by hand. When I did arrive, I was quivering with anticipation as I drove into the yard.

I was only halfway down the driveway and I slammed on the brakes—it looked like a war zone, or like a barber had gotten drunk with a pair of scissors in his hand. There were big cut and half-cut swathes in all directions. Huge hunks of grass had been dug out and turf was missing all over. Everywhere you looked, there were raw scrapes and red paint rub marks, nicks and gouges out of posts and tree trunks, and extension cords and hoses chewed to bits. Shrubs and flower beds had been massacred down and sideways. There were ruts and holes in the lawn where something had been stuck, and not one cor-

ner was cut right. You couldn't have planned an uglier landscape.

I wondered if my wife had been the first woman in history to get a DUI operating a lawn mower, but she didn't drink, so it had to be something else. I was too devastated to even be disappointed or angry—I was just plain stunned. I was standing in the middle of a small patch of injured lawn shaking my head in amazement when Barbara came sheepishly out the door.

"Gadfrey, Dear, what happened?" I asked.

"Well," she said, "for sure these things don't run themselves, I'm learning!"

"Learning! It's lucky you're alive, woman!"

Now she defended herself, "Well, you should have seen it before I fixed it yesterday with the hand mower."

Since then, we've both gotten better on it, but a riding mower wasn't the cure-all we'd imagined it to be, not much faster either. It's just another tool that needs to be used the right way at the right time by the right people (with the right acreage).

Tools are assistants, not assistant managers

A cry I heard from a frustrated home manager: "I have a PC loaded with information, but just because you're computerized, doesn't mean you're organized!" "Information" is the tool of all tools, but it's not a manager. Only you, a human, can manage, and you're the only organizer.

We see advertised, an "Executive Planner Kit," with forms and notebooks to "organize" us. You probably have one, in fact, most of us have tried them. The first fallacy here is the assumption that all executives plan well and we should copy them. It also assumes that the planning pattern that worked for one type of person is going to work for another—it seldom does. I've seen people buy and use a big day planning notebook or binder and actually get worse—now they spend forty minutes extra a day entering things and hunting for entries.

A tool is to aid the process, or simplify it, not do it for you, replace you, or repair bad planning.

Using tools to Band-Aid a bigger problem is one more caution in management. Adding another accessory like air bags to cars is brilliant gesture to save lives and will save some each year. But selling alcohol at every gas station and convenience store affects the death and injury rate a thousand times more than those ingenious air bags do. It's like using pills and plastic surgery to accomplish what saner sleeping, eating, and drinking habits would.

Even when tools do what they're supposed to, in the kitchen, backyard, or garage, there are times they can "mismanage" or slow you down. One afternoon on my ranch we had three post holes to dig. I handed my son Grant a shovel and said, "Let's go for it!" Grant, a modern computerized man, said, "This is stupid. We have a post hole digger that can dig these holes in one minute each." True, we did have a magnificent post hole digger, that takes about an hour to mount and dismount on the PTO of the tractor. It's a super tool if we're doing a whole fenceline of holes, but for this short job, it would multiply our time by four. With the mechanical digger, it would take us an hour and three minutes; by hand, the two of us could do it in **fifteen minutes**!

Often on our kitchen counters, too, we have tools—mixers, blenders, processors, and so on—that can do a chore in seconds but we're smart enough to leave them alone because setting them up and cleaning them up takes fifteen minutes, while doing the chore by hand only takes three minutes. And even if something can shred three pounds of cheese in ninety seconds, who needs three pounds of shredded cheese?

I'm not a believer in cleaning floors on hands and knees, but sometimes in the bathroom or other small areas, thirty seconds on the hands and knees eliminates ten or more minutes of doing it the modern way. Modern equipment doesn't offer us magic, just choice. So don't be blind to looking the situation over. When handwriting is still faster and gets the message across or the job done, then the heck with the computer. There are times when simply accomplishing the purpose outranks perfection. With tools, always back up and evaluate before you buy "the ideal," or even the "I need it now" tool.

Gadgets only get you ahead if they save you time or money or make things physically easier. The words "automatic," "electric," or electronic" are by no means always superior to "manual."

"The reason food processors are so popular is that most people have never had a really sharp knife."

UNDERTOOLED is as bad as overtooled

Think back through your entire life to how many times "if you had a pock-

etknife" it would have cut out tons of tussle. It would have saved your time, hands, nails, and teeth, and begging, hunting, damaging things. Just a simple tool you didn't have when you needed it.

As a professional painter, I'd lay on the floor and groan when I saw people walking home with some of the throw-away brushes, flyweight dropcloths, and wimpy pressure-feed paint sprayers pitched to us today. They turn a three-hour job into a nine-hour job, plus you pay for it.

Somewhere between toolless and overtooled there is "toolsmartville"– having what you need when you need it. Once you decide your course, destiny, talent, family size, interest, and location, tool up for it. Figure out what your essential equipment is and be sure you have it.

I carry scissors, scotch tape, a thesaurus, twenty pens, several legal pads, a rope, and my famous toilet souvenirs, in an enormous briefcase all the time– 24 hours–these are some of **my** tools for managing better and faster. Others might never leave home without a calculator and scissors in their purse, or a trowel, thermos bottle, and big flashlight in their car trunk.

Your tooling has to fit you, not the general public. Fit the file cabinet (should it be a paper or metal one?) or the frying pan (electric, or old reliable cast iron?) to your temperament, your requirements, and your work flow.

"If it's good enough for the office, it's good enough for the house. I have a desk tape dispenser, a good stapler, and an easy to read calculator at my desk. I am not going to struggle with one of those disposable plastic tape dispensers that break if

you sneeze on them. Give me a heavy desk model that doesn't move just when you need to rip off a piece of tape to prevent your whole gift wrap from unraveling in front of your eyes."

"I have a jump rope, cat's cradle string, bag of jacks, small book of games, and toothbrush I carry everywhere. This fits my lifestyle, and I've never been sorry. My van has a box of books and a rack of travel games. I do kids, and these tools work."

When I say "tools" I don't just mean those electronic gadgets, I mean real tools that save time, bless you and others, and give you some flexibility. For example, trust me and buy a good set of expensive, heavy-duty jumper cables. (The discount store ones can't transfer enough juice to jump a head set battery. And every time you need to use them on your car or that of a friend or neighbor in distress, it takes thirty minutes of clamping and adjusting and motor-revving.) With a good set, it's magic—in ten seconds that dead car is resurrected, and you glory in it and go!

TOOL TESTER

All those tools we've bought, thought of buying, or had given to us– wouldn't it be great if we had a little meter to run them past, with a needle to register: Useful or Questionable, Keeper or Caster, Asset or Liability?

Well, we can do our own evaluation of the "bility" of a tool. Just for fun, pull out some of those doubtful tools and run them through this quick...

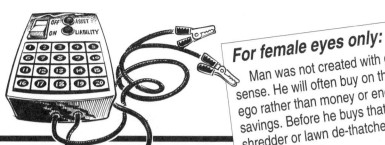

Tool Tester

	POOR	FAIR	GOOD	EXCEL

Affordability .... ☐ ☐ ☐ ☐
How much of a strain will it be to buy it right now?

Versatility .... ☐ ☐ ☐ ☐
How versatile is it, how many things can it be used for?

Seasonability .... ☐ ☐ ☐ ☐
Can you use it/do you need it year round?

Fuelability .... ☐ ☐ ☐ ☐
Will fuel, energy, batteries, etc., always be available and accessible? How expensive are they?

Maintainability .... ☐ ☐ ☐ ☐
What will it take to keep it working, and how often will it have to be done? (Cleaning, adjusting, tuning, oiling, etc.)

Durability .... ☐ ☐ ☐ ☐
How long is it likely to hold up?

Breakability .... ☐ ☐ ☐ ☐
How easy is it for you or others to hurt or ruin it?

Repairability .... ☐ ☐ ☐ ☐
If it dies or gets wounded, how easily can it be fixed, how hard will it be to get parts, how much will the fixing cost?

Storability .... ☐ ☐ ☐ ☐
How much room does it take up, and how easy is it to hang, store, or park?

Availability .... ☐ ☐ ☐ ☐
When and where you need it, will it be there?

	POOR	FAIR	GOOD	EXCEL

Crippleability .... ☐ ☐ ☐ ☐
Is it safe for you and others to use and be around? Will using it do anything bad to you, physically or mentally?

Portability .... ☐ ☐ ☐ ☐
Can you use it here, there, and anywhere, or just here?

Loseability .... ☐ ☐ ☐ ☐
What are the chances of it being lost or mislaid?

Borrowability .... ☐ ☐ ☐ ☐
Will you be able to keep it on the premises?

Stealability .... ☐ ☐ ☐ ☐
Is it attractive enough to "walk away"?

Extinctability .... ☐ ☐ ☐ ☐
How soon will it be obsolete?

Depreciability .... ☐ ☐ ☐ ☐
How long and well will it hold its value?

Responsibility .... ☐ ☐ ☐ ☐
How does it affect the environment/ society?

Disposability .... ☐ ☐ ☐ ☐
When you're through with it, will you be able to sell it or otherwise dispose of it?

Inevitability .... ☐ ☐ ☐ ☐
How badly do you need it? How often will you use it? Will its lifetime usefulness to you be worth what it costs?

Common
Mistakes of
Home Managers

Funny how some lessons stick with you forever. I remember how in our little country grade school (four grades in one room) our teacher taught us the value of habits, good and bad, in health class once. She had a student hold up his middle and index fingers and she wrapped a thread around them, tied it, and asked him to break the thread. The student did so easily. Then she wrapped two threads around those fingers and said, "OK, now break that." And with a touch of strain he did. Then three threads were wrapped around the same way, and the student struggled a bit but did break them. When she moved up to four—just one tiny strand more than three—he was redfaced and grunting, but couldn't break the bind.

This is exactly how managing things at home works. Two or three little mistakes or bad household habits can cause a little problem or adjustment, but five or six, ten or twenty common little mistakes added up can mean your progress (like the student's hand) becomes immobilized.

Failing to attack/ charge/strike!

To help us see our problems in perspective, let's take a look at an imaginary American Indian Chief in an earlier day.

Chief No Scalps is just like you and me; he has lots of things to do today, tomorrow, next week and next month: food gathering and cooking, circuit training, trimming his horses' hooves, repairing the teepee, playing with his children, cleaning the outhouse, trading for some new hides, sending some smoke signals to his friends, catching up on his quillwork, shopping for a birthday present for Mrs. No Scalps, and more. And that's only his regular "To Do" list. Big special jobs come along all the time: a party for some visiting Apaches, the warrior graduation, a wedding, a trip to Pocatello (to visit great chief uncle), a funeral, dealing with the two tribe vandals who tossed a rotten buffalo robe in the drinking water spring. And as if all this wasn't enough, a big surprise "to-do" has to go to the top of the list now. This came up this morning when it became clear that some pesky settlers were treading on tribal territory again. So a management problem, a priority *goal* has emerged, "PUSH BACK THE SETTLERS."

Right now, today!

First, as all good managers do, he checks his **resources** and he does have a tribe, family, helpers, and teammates, trained and loyal to his direction.

Second, in all good management, you have to have good **intelligence sources** and he does know where the settlers are and when they're coming. His scouts did their work well!

Third, a good manager can **appraise** a situation wisely and accurately to determine what's needed—how many, how much, when and how—and Chief No Scalps does this.

Fourth, good management requires **leadership**, the ability to rally together, inspire, and motivate your colleagues to action toward your goals—no problem here.

Fifth, in all management, **money** pops up. Selecting and purchasing wisely, for example, is essential. Paying too much or too little for things you need can really affect management results–here too No Scalps truly shines.

Sixth, managing to **communicate** well so that others understand, help, and support you in your quest, is key. And who better than our chief?

Seventh, **public relations**, keeping the family or tribe aware of your intentions, facing the task with full bravado and fanfare. No one knows media like No Scalps.

Now you would think that with all of these virtues and skills of good home and tribe management, the chief would have easily subdued the settlers. He had the game on his home turf, the element of surprise, and his forces outnumbered the settlers ten to one. But he didn't stop them. Why? He did all the planning, preparation, motivation, everything (even inventory!) so well....

But he didn't execute the critical action in managing anything. He never did attack. He just rode around the panicked train, whooping and hollering and threatening, kicking up lots of dust. He never gave himself or his followers the signal to go for it. (Now you know where he got his name.)

He had plenty of time, plenty of Indians, and plenty of ammo, but he couldn't reach his goal if he didn't attack.

After forty years on the firing line of home and business management, it's clear to me that most of us can get things organized well, but fall down on the most important factor: **doing**!

Strategic plans don't manage, nor do goals or programs. They're all just gold-embossed and (hopefully) wise intentions. It's like climbing the ladder and posing gracefully on the diving board. That's all positioning. You have to jump or charge to make it happen.

"My mother spends half the day making out her list, and by the time she gets done, there isn't much time left to do anything."

Remember, putting things in order is only planning. Don't forget the DOING!

Imitating someone else's style

To be a good manager, we do have to use the skills of good management, but how, when, where, and on what we use them isn't cast in concrete, it's up to us, and it's called **style**. War was No Scalps' style, had he attacked, it would have done the job. But now,

down the trail a ways, the settlers ran into more chiefs. They all had the same goal (push the settlers back), but different styles, and they all planned and prepared and rallied their followers accordingly.

One chief, Fire Big, and his tribe went on ahead and burned all the grass so the settlers couldn't feed their animals and had to turn back. Another chief, Swipe Wheels, crept in at night and snatched all the horses and oxen off the picket line. Chief Entrepreneur contracted settler removal out to the Shoshone and Blackfeet, and Chief Red Tape sent a medicine man and lawyer to negotiate the settlers' return. Chief Buffalo Chip stampeded antelope and buffalo through the settlers' camp every night, 'till they finally got so pooped on and discouraged they headed back.

No management style was wrong or right. Even Chief No Scalps had a good one, he just needed to carry it out.

There is no **one way** to manage, there are lots of good ways, and you can usually find one that fits you and your temperament and situation. You can get as much done as anyone else, or as expected, and yet do it in a totally different way.

I like to encompass the whole objective, spreading myself thin if necessary, while my wife, an equally good manager, approaches the objective a piece at a time. Some of us have no limit to our ambition or drive, and we thrive on risks. Others are more attuned to detail and move slowly and softly, maneuvering all the while, and still accomplish as much as the loud, aggressive dudes.

You have your own style, so don't try to copy and wear someone else's. You can watch and learn from, gain information and insight from someone else, but you **can't *be* them**. That's a fashion-magazine mentality, a dumb and ineffective way to live. I see companies hold classes, for example, where some shy, timid soul is enrolled in "Advanced Aggression Management." There's no way it can or ever will fit that person.

There are some good management principles that apply to almost anyone, but don't bother copying a style that might not fit your personality, schedule, size, weight, energy, ethics, sex, or background.

In high school, I was serious about baseball, as were many of my teammates. And we were all very much aware of a young Rookie-of-the-Year named Gil McDougald. He was a great New York Yankee second baseman who came from our small team in Twin Falls, Idaho. He was our hero and definitely had his own way of hitting. He held a bat like a spear, and he would stand there waiting for the pitch with his left foot stretched out and his big toe extended, a truly awkward and contorted pose. His stance in the batter's box distinguished him from all other players before and after, in both the minor and major leagues. So all of us "would-be big leaguers" adapted his statuesque pose at bat. The only difference was, Gil batted 350 for the year, and none of us could even hold the position, let alone hit anything once we achieved it. We concentrated so hard on trying to look like old Gil that we had no strength left to swing. Some of us finally figured out that we weren't going to be on the team very long if we kept this up. So we went back to a practical position that felt good to us and started producing hits and runs again. Those who were still locked into that spastic stance struck out and were finally sent off the team.

When you watch and study management styles, watch good home operators at work. Be sure to focus on the principles and processes, not the prancing, of the person you admire.

Bear in mind, too, that just because someone is rich and famous, or old and wise, it doesn't mean their order or system is the best way to handle things. Ask three good home managers to do the same job and watch. Each one will come up with a different way to do it. One may be better than the others, but they'll all work. Too many "one wayers" are entrenched in the teaching systems of the world and home, and we're all still following them like sheep.

It's not that we can't learn and gain from the management methods of others, because we can. But every home, family, situation, and set of relationships and constraints is different. Too many of us, trying to find the ideal way of doing something, will see it working in the Smith home with their kids, cars, checkbooks, grandpas, and allowances, so we get all the details and follow their recipe to the letter, yet it never seems to come out as well as theirs did. If we could just adapt the heart of what they do and how they do it to our own personal situation and home environment, **then** we'd have something.

My purpose in these pages is to provide you with some principles–not methods–of good management that you might want to include in *your* style.

Running out

Have you ever noticed that master managers seldom run out of anything? They always seem to have enough of things when and if they need them.

I KNEW I SHOULD'VE TOPPED THOSE TANKS OFF WHEN I HAD THE CHANCE.

On the other hand, the disorganized, struggling, and behind folks are forever on the brink or the edge. They're always out or about to be out of something, and have to stop and run to town, or start calling all over frantically. Their cars hold about the same amount of gas, but the good managers run off the top of the tank. The others are always draining the dregs at the bottom, praying that the fumes will at least carry them to the side of the road before their car glides to a halt.

It makes a big difference in management and results, the practice of NEVER RUNNING OUT.

Look at the time you waste when you're suddenly out of milk, bread, butter, or laundry detergent. A minute of top-of-tank management earlier on would have saved thirty minutes of complaining and then another thirty rushing off somewhere to get some. Right at the worst possible moment, with not a minute to spare, you're out of pantyhose, cat food, salt for the water softener, batteries for the flashlight, or that prescription you can't do without. Or you're about to step out the door for the airport and don't even have enough cash on you to put in a meter! You're dead! Situations like this are just an invitation to chaos and time wasting and raw nerves and recklessness and rushing and even accidents, because you're so rattled.

It's like the gas, you have to buy it every so often anyway, so why not keep ahead instead of behind? Ahead costs you the same, but behind costs you an hour or more of wasted time in addition (if not a cab fare or tow fee). At home, at work, or en route anywhere, if you run out, you suffer! The sad part is we often run out knowingly. We've noticed there's just enough milk left for one more bowl of cereal and we're walking right by the dairy case, but some loose neuron in our brain shouts, "Maybe I'll wait until we're out."

Or you're painting and estimate it'll take at least four gallons of paint to do the job—so you buy just exactly that many. You should be able to make it if you're careful. The paint is $20 a gallon, and you don't want to waste it.

You get home and get started and it looks good, but it's going to be close.

So you agonize and squeeze and sweat to make the paint stretch. It takes twice as long going at it this way (wasting two hours of your time) and then you run out anyway!

You live fifty miles out of town and took time off from a good-paying job to paint, so now you have two choices—neither of which is good: 1) Stop and clean up and wait until next time you go to town to get it (and then have to take the time to get all set up to paint again, plus the time for another cleanup); or 2) Waste two more hours and a hundred more miles (plus the cutting edge of your ambition) to go get it now. Either way, you're paying a lot in time and expenses. You'd be far ahead if you'd just bought an extra gallon in the first place, even if you just pitched the excess or painted the pigpen with it.

At the checkout of a lumber store once, I noticed several contractors purchasing materials. One company, as was obvious from the two people there to buy supplies, wasn't going to win any management awards. They spent fifteen minutes debating over it, then got only a pound and half of nails (eighty cents worth).

"Think this will be enough?"

"Well, should be. Should be... if we run out we can run back in."

They proceeded this way through several items, cutting the amounts close. With the amount of their combined wages they were wasting ($30 an hour), they could have doubled their orders and been out of there in minutes.

Nothing is worse, when it comes to management, than running out. You end up an exasperated errand runner for your errors of judgment. And when you run out of *things* you need, it's easy to run out of energy, patience, and courtesy, too. A stockpile is the best stock you can own, a good investment in life management.

Playing "catchup"–a game you can't win!

I heard one of my uncles describe his farm failure to other farmers at his bankruptcy sale. Trying to explain why he hadn't made it, he kicked the dirt and said, "It just seems like I'm always a day late and a dollar short."

He had indeed, better than he knew, described his managerial abilities. He could have gone by the name of "Old Catch-Up." He was always catching up, and working hard at it. We all play catchup once in a while and know it's not fun. He operated his farm and his whole life that way. He was always waiting until something broke, to fix it; waiting 'till the cows got out, to mend the fence (and round them up); waiting until crops drooped and turned brown before watering them; waiting until the baby had diaper rash, before deciding to change him more often; waiting until all the shirts were gone before washing and ironing. He was just as fast and efficient at fixing, watering, herding, diapering, and washing as the successful farmers, except he always worked from a behind, catchup position.

You may have played catchup on a hike sometime. Once you fall behind the main group, you seem to have to work harder all the way. The group stops to catch their breath, rest, visit, laugh, and pass the canteen around and just as you arrive on the scene, finally "catching up," they're strapping their packs back on and on their way again. So again you drag and lag behind and fall back again, only to repeat this little scene over and over all the way. Everyone walked the same distance, only you never got a rest or a breather all day and missed all the fun because you didn't keep up.

That's the curse of running your life in a catchup mode. It's not a position you're put in or assigned to, or the spot you deserve–it's where **you choose** to place and keep yourself.

Working or being behind seems so insignificant, so innocent, even something to joke about. But it's no joke, and it gets no sympathy. People are irritated and disgusted with, intolerant and critical of those who are constantly behind. They get so fed up, they begin to wish you'd get farther behind and entirely out of sight! "I work better under pressure," some will say. Behind isn't "pressure," it's procrastination... proof you can't manage or function on your own. It's a big sign that says you need others or external forces to coax or demand performance out of you. When you delay anything, you lose control over it and let it or "they" (the circumstances) run the time clock and you.

Bringing up the rear is not the road to a happy life.

Catchup or working behind is simply more time-consuming, involved, and risky. Here's twenty reasons why (there are more):

1. When you finally do get back to or around to it, you have to reread the instructions and reintroduce yourself to the situation.
2. You have to find your place again (hunt for it).
3. You have to explain again (and again and again) why it's late.
4. Finding help is harder.
5. You need to re-enthuse any help you did have.
6. Have to update everything you were doing.
7. Repair any damage that's occurred meanwhile.
8. Waiting 'till the last minute makes you irritable, edgy, and more likely to forget some critical detail. Rushing means errors, period.
9. You have no room to maneuver or make mistakes (so you end up serving raw potatoes).
10. You have to do things at odd times and in odd ways (often imposing on others in the process).
11. It makes you likely to ask unreasonable things of others to cover your butt.
12. Costs extra in Fed Ex, overnight mail, faxing; and extra charges for "rush" services.
13. You have to make extra, timewasting phone calls.
14. You run the risk that there's no room—no seat or reservation left for it or you.
15. You have to take what you can get, because you don't have time to shop around or find what you'd really like.
16. They may be out of something you need—or it's been discontinued.
17. You miss opportunities.
18. You disappoint others (especially your family).
19. You make people mad.
20. You're left out; never asked to be on a committee or invited to things.

Putting things on layaway

It's a big meanie that always gets you: the old "LAYAWAY PLAN."

Postponed obligations are so easy to incur:

"Sure, I'll take those old windows if you decide to get rid of them..."

"Just call me when you're ready to paint/ move and I'll come running..."

"I'll take ten of those when they are printed."

"Just stop by any time and we'll crank up the old boat..."

"I'll send you a check in a couple of months."

"I'll be glad to read your aunt's novel when she gets it written."

"If Queenie ever has puppies you could keep us in mind."

"I'll be glad to pick that up for you the next time I'm in the city."

"OK, we can have lunch the next time I'm in town."

At the time it was a way out, a way to get rid of some pest, a way to state your intention or to sound sympa-thetic, yet delay action. Or even a genuine, though poorly thought out, impulse of the moment. But that later always comes and usually at the worst of times. Your word is at stake, so you almost have to do it, no matter how stupid it is or you were.

Whenever you are posed with something to be done later, pretend that it has to be done today. If it still seems desirable and doable, then long-term commitment to do it is fine. If you feel yourself hesitating, don't start listening to the whispering of the evasion elf. Half-hearted intentions are hard to schedule in… and hard to pay for when the IOU comes due.

Hunting

We spend at least five years of our lives just hunting for things around the house. We can't start or finish anything until "it" is found, so hunting is one of good management's most notorious enemies. How much time have you and other household members spent hunting for things like keys, glasses, screwdrivers, scissors, pens (that work), baby pacifiers, hammers, phone books, address books, the remote control to the

168

TV, cleaning gear, play gear, etc. And now that phones are portable we often have to hunt for them when we hear a ring.

Too many of us have "hunting homes," where the common cry is "I'll find it" not "I'll get it." Every project launches a miniature safari to bag some rubber bands or packing tape. The project itself only takes about five minutes, the hunting and finding fifteen minutes! (And a lot of growling, yelling, blaming, and stress!)

Hunting just kills momentum, schedules, confidence levels and patience, of both the hunters and the waiters. Cure it and you'll eliminate a lot of management messes.

It's easy to get disgusted with this big rush to retrieve every time you want to get something done. "Don't hunt" is easy to say, how can you make it easy to do?

Dejunk!

Get rid of all that excess, unused, and worthless stuff, so you can find, and have room for, the things you really care about and need. (See Chapter 8.)

Store things where it makes the most sense

In other words, keep the dog food where you feed the dog.

Set up work stations

Knowing most of us won't change our bad habits very fast, you can do something called "setting up work stations." Establish and design a specific place for doing a specific thing, such as getting things ready to mail, or wrapping presents. Always do it there, and make sure everything you need to do the job is there, and handy. Likewise, you might want to have a home office, a sewing/mending station, an official work-bench for home repairs, or even a houseplant tending station.

Establish a clear-cut place for every essential tool

Just doing this with extension cords alone would extend most of our lives at least a year!

Or consider cleaning gear, for another example. Generally we have fifteen minutes to clean, and spend twelve of them finding, rounding up, assembling what we need to do it. Get a little plastic "maid basket" or cleaning caddy or several of them to hold all the equipment you need, and keep it/them in a certain place–ALWAYS THE SAME ONE.

Enforce the everyone-put-it-right-back rule

Everything is used by everyone at home, so you only need one "non-putter-backer" and the best organizational plan is plundered. If you're tired of saying "Well if you'd put it back where it belonged, you could find it," what can you do to make your fellow users pay attention?

Make "Put it right back as soon as you're done with it" an ironclad rule, and enforce it with penalties if necessary, for anyone who breaks the rule, including yourself. Putting tools away the minute you're finished with them doesn't take any time at all, yet we have a way of dodging it, so the only way to deal with this is to make replacing things a reflex.

Have duplicates where they're really needed

- *have and leave a shovel in the garden*
- *a toilet plunger by each toilet*
- *have a TV pillow specifically for the TV room*
- *have an extra vacuum in that inconvenient spot you vacuum a lot*
- *have an outside and an inside knife*

- *have three brooms (not one) and put them where they're most needed*
- *Etc.*

Anchor it!

Anchoring things so they're always right there when you need them will cut hunting, too. We've all used the tethered pens in banks, and it was surely a mother tired of hunting for mittens who first tied them to the kids' coat sleeves. You can do this with other things, too, such as a measuring cup in the laundry room, the scissors in the children's craft area, or the padlock that's supposed to lock the shed door.

"Everything in our home is stored near its point of use. Detergent by dishwasher/clotheswasher, tools by workbench, keys by door, dishes by counter, dishpans between stove and sink."

"Having all the stuff for something in one place is a big help. If the sleeping bags are here and the mess kits there and the tents somewhere else, it's hard to remember everything for camping and takes longer to assemble it all. I now have all the camping stuff, for example, under the stairs and it's great."

Borrowing

For sure some money has been saved, and some good friendships started because of borrowing. Borrowing is such a quick fix when we need something, that some of us get too good at it. Borrowing seems to be a winning situation, after all it's there, the person isn't using it, and all you have to do is ask. Borrowing saves us lots of bucks and gives us a chance to keep in touch with/get acquainted with our family, neighbors, friends, or even strangers.

But before you're too quick to borrow, remember that not all the relationships that result from borrowing are positive, and many times the "money saved" is only an illusion. Probably 25% of the time, borrowing is an okay management decision around home, but the other three quarters of the time it isn't. Have you noticed that **super managers almost never borrow**? If something is close and it's handy, borrowing may pay, but not if you have to travel and call to get it. I had a woman tell me how much she loved my book *Is There Life After Housework?*, for instance. "I've checked it out of the library four times now." Twice she made a special trip to get it, and she lives eighteen miles from the library. Remember that borrowing takes two round trips, one to go get it and one to take it back. I added up the costs for the use of her car, parking, and her time to make the trips and it came to four hours and $22 in expenses. She still didn't own the book, and it only costs $10.99 new!

MAY I BORROW A CUP
OF SKY PIECES?

I built a day camp for the Scouts on my property, and the Scout office (twenty-five miles away), had all the tug-of-war ropes, bows and arrows, and other equipment for the boys. Before going in to get it (borrow it) I sat down and figured out the cost of the trips. It was cheaper (in expenses alone, never mind my time and energy) to just buy these things and own them and keep them right here. So for a total investment of $200 I bought the works and used it for ten years. Others borrowing the same equipment from me or the Scout office spent at least $1,000 over those ten years coming and getting it and then returning it, calling before, thanking afterward, making arrangements, etc.

Remember, anything you borrow is generally used and is often closer to the breaking point than new, and if and when it breaks (and it will), the percentages are against you. You have to fix it or replace it, or the lender will never forgive you. Then how do you decide on a fair price for something usually more worn and abused than the lender realized it was? Or so old "they don't make them like that any more"? Most borrowing takes time, too–a call (or several) and conversation to ask and arrange, a call and trip to pick up, a call and trip to return, and so on.

I try to avoid borrowing myself, but lots of people borrow from me, and in most cases they lose money over just buying the objects themselves. Most of them never return the item until I ask and then they are always at a "desperate moment" and have to disrupt and drop everything to bring it back, and they hate me for it. Seldom is the item returned clean and in good condition. Lending is generally a losing proposi-

tion, too, when you consider all this plus the time you lose anguishing over whether you should lend something or not, when you know you don't want to and that you'll end up regretting it. I enjoy lending for the 25% of the time that it saves money and energy and the environment, but if you want to be a good manager, be careful about the other 75%, when borrowing (or lending) really costs you–in time, money, irritation, and anxiety.

Labeling reduces "losing"

It's easy for things to get lost, not only with people we lent them to, but right in the middle of our own household or family. To help keep my cleaning crews and jobs straight at work, I started putting identification on all my cleaning tools. This worked so well I started labeling all my possessions, from trucks to tools: rug shampooing equipment, suitcases, dutch ovens, lawn mowers, ladders, quilt frames, hammers and wheelbarrows.

Once I did that, they kind of managed themselves. I didn't have to stake a claim to them or describe them to anyone–everyone knew what, where, and whose.

Label lendables with at least your name; you can even paint some "your color." You'll be amazed how much hunting, arguing over, and recovering of things will be eliminated. If your labeling is done in a permanent form like etching, it will even help discourage thieves.

"My father puts 'This was stolen from Paul Harris' on his stuff."

"I think a lot of people borrow things and then honestly cannot recall where to return them. A label will fix that, too."

"I keep a list of things I have loaned out (and I know of others who keep records like this in an almost library-like way). Stickers with your name on them help here."

Concluding before you collect

Just about every one of us are sometimes kicking ourselves for something we did that was "real stupid." It was a dumb thing to do, a totally bad decision, and we can't believe we did it. If we take a hard look at it, what will we find usually caused it? Reaching a conclusion before we collected the data.

Flying off the handle right after we've received the first bit of information, the request, the news, the bill, the schedule, the report is so common at home (and for that matter in business, too). Before we even take a minute to find out if, when, how, what, why, or where, we are marching off to mend the situation. Like when we've told our kids curfew is 10:00 p.m. and they come home at 11:10. Nine out of ten parents are so irritated they've already passed sentence by the time that teen walks in the door, so they don't hear what or

why. I've seen people grab bills and tear down to the sender in a rage before they even looked carefully and saw that statement actually registered a credit, money back. Do we ever retreat sheepishly when we do these things!

Years of experience finally taught me that even when a genuine piece of bad news is dropped on you, look, think, set it aside for a while, and consider all the whys and wherefores of what happened before you do anything. It'll keep you from doing one of those real dumb things we kick ourselves and others for, and may well end up a positive, teaching experience.

"Grouping" isn't always a good idea

There is a management tactic that always sounds good on paper, saving time and money, like putting four kids in one bedroom or buying one bike to be used by all.

In the business world this is called consolidation, and it's the process of taking a number of problems or people and putting them under one umbrella. Sure it might be "more efficient" and cheaper, too, but it's not always a good idea. Consolidation may sometimes mean a savings in rent and service, but accountability may be lessened in the process, causing a need (yes, at home, too) for detective work and administrative headaches that add up to ten times the cost.

Take those loans and credit cards, for instance, they (like kids) get away from us sometimes, and suddenly we wake up and find we owe $25,000 when all of those balances are added up. Right now our income has a hard time stretching to keep up with all those payments, so a loan expert smoothly talks us into a "bill consolidation" loan. This means just one "easy" payment, less than all those other payments. People fall for this by the millions, but when you do this, you still owe all that money, and now you've paid loan fees and points and stretched the payoff out for months and years, and added LOTS of interest. You haven't fixed anything or really gotten any relief either. And maybe worst of all, you've forgotten just how you ended up owing all that (what you bought or did that maybe you could have done without), because it's all been merged into one bland, anonymous, seemingly necessary "debt."

There is a miracle in maintaining individual accountability, with children or adults. Joint accounts never work as well as individual ones—one of the account partners is always being brought to grief by the other. Blanketing problems under one simple heading is seldom the answer. Good management keeps problems and people separate so accountability can be maintained and measured. You tell me how a group dog, a group car, a group stereo, or a group instrument (a piano might be an exception) ever works in home to anyone's satisfaction. Public space is always no man's land when it comes to cleanup and care. "Ours" never works like "mine." It's just one more little management key that will save you agony and arbitration.

Looking for "The Ledge"

A big time waster most home managers fall into is the search for the elusive "ledge." Once on life's road we only pick up speed, pick up loads and rules and responsibilities and opportunities and dreams, and more and more and more to do. Sooner or later it begins to get to us, and this is about when the idea of that "ledge" is formulated in our mind.

Somewhere… ahead… there is or will be a place, a ledge, a sanctuary, a rest stop, where we can leap out of the stream, or jump off the merry-go-round. Time will stop there, and noises and demands, too, and we can just lie there for a while and pant and recover, catch up. After we've nursed our road wounds and calmly collected ourselves, we can do all that letter writing and meditation, complete all those undone chores and waiting projects. Then, all restored and rested, we can leap off the ledge and back into the fight of life, much the better now with no backaches or backlog.

Everyone has their dream of the ledge. Maybe it would be a minor in-

I THINK I SEE A LEDGE AT ABOUT 80,000 FEET.

jury that put us safely out of commission for a while so we can give ourselves all the time we need to catch up as we convalesce. Maybe it's a vacation, a spell in prison, being snowbound for a few months, any wild dream of a place to duck into and out of the sniping and lightning and milling of the everyday hassles and demands of living–making a living, caring for a home and family. We just need that little ledge–**that release from the rat race**–to stop and service our vehicles, to fix and heal and refuel.

Most of us are still looking and waiting for that ledge, as our salvation from society's demands and our crazy schedule and all those commitments, before they drive us insane or work us to death. There isn't a single one of us who hasn't been on the watch for it. In fact, we anticipate it, with a great list of the things we are going to get done when we finally find or reach it.

I've been looking for mine since about the age of twenty-one, and at sixty now, I finally realize that there ain't one! And anything I thought was one, wasn't–instead it was a road shoulder just loaded with more.

"**Stopping to catch up**" is unfortunately one of those idle wishes. How many of us ever get time to stop? Few of us do, or will, and with each passing year it only gets harder to find stopping time to catch up. How many retired people have you seen bragging about finally being caught up in life? They are usually clutching for more time as it slips by more frantically than any thirty- or forty-year-old. And even if you can manage to stop the clock, it probably won't aid your management. Most of the time, when people do stop to catch up, they're so relieved to be stopped, they fall further behind.

The bottom line is, you are going to have to stay on the road and fix yourself **on** the road–en route, out in the open of the fast lane. You don't get to stop to get more done, you have to do it on the run, and you can.

"Some time off will give me time to catch things up." **Ever notice how often students who take a year off from college to work end up in debt and further behind at the end of the year than if they'd stayed in school and worked full time? There's something mysteriously self-consuming about time that is taken off to catch up. Always ahead of the game, good managers fit catchup work right into the regular onslaught of life. They never wait for a relief to come in and pitch a few innings for them so they can catch up.**

Forgetting to manage yourself

We've all been really sick and miserable sometime, unable to move, just lying in bed listening to everything going on around us. When we finally have the strength to worry about missing work and all the rest of our worldly schedule, the realization hits us that nothing in life matters if we are unable to function physically or mentally. It doesn't matter how much money or education we have, how popular or famous or accomplished we might be. When we're not able to function, nothing really counts, and we can't do anything but be tended and sit there hoping that some pill, shot, or prayer will bring us around.

It's then all of our vows are made: "Man, when and if I get over this, I'll be the biggest sparkplug for health on the face of the earth!" How soon we forget and slide right back into our old habits of abusing our bodies and minds. Pretty dumb, isn't it? We can plan for and calculate and keep track of everything except the underpinnings of our whole existence.

"Managing" to have good health isn't just one of the keys to good personal management, it's the #1 key. **If you don't feel good all or most of the time, you won't do well, period.** If you're trying to run a homefront or any front with a weary, germ-ridden body or mind, you're on the loser's side of the line. We monitor and control our money, entertainment channels, stereo sound levels, carpet pile depth, and the fertilizer on the yard, but seldom spend a minute assessing our eating, exercise, and sleeping habits. Until we're in trouble, our system falters a little, and then we panic and send for the bottles of pills and the aerobics class schedules and start making that overdue appointment with the medical specialist. It's the old "when in trouble and not before, God and doctor we adore" mentality.

Bad health and the resulting lack of energy is a mighty big obstacle to good management. It means a lot of down time and expense, and it unfocuses us. When we're miserable or worried about dying, we sure aren't concentrating on the direction of other things!

It's just plain common sense—we need good health for good, comfortable, well managed, and effective living. Beating up your body with **any** bad habits is hooking a liability IV to your main vein. How often do we lose the whole next day to recuperating from a "night before" of doing bad things to our bodies? Punishing and destroying our long-range self for short-range pleasure and sensation is not good management of ourselves, and it prevents good management of all the other things we need to make and keep us happy. The homefront's health depends on your health. No one can manage without some muscle.

"You do need to find some time for yourself, too, to just be alone for a little while. Even if after an hour of it, you're ready to go back."

*"You can't find time, like a nickel in a parking lot. You must **make** time for yourself."*

"Just like making time for your family members, you have to schedule time for yourself. If you don't take care of yourself no one else will—and if you think you don't have time because you have to take care of your family, you won't be doing them a favor if you break down physically or mentally."

"Some self-recreation needs to be scheduled in, just like any other activity. So be sure to make time for some reading, concert going, short trips, walking, fishing, napping, or visiting—whatever it takes to relax and revitalize you. If possible, do something impetuously every so often. The world won't come to an end if you let something else go to do it. Gather the kids/partner up and take off for the zoo, the park, wherever. Or stop for a special treat during your errand expeditions."

Letting others assume that "home time" is worth nothing

There seems to be a sad set of values in operation here. "On the job," at work, we have a pay scale, an official amount our time is worth per hour, and because of this, time there is considered to be of value. But once we're home, because there is no salary or time clock, no perks, benefits, or golden parachutes for our coming retirement, we're free game. "Unpaid" rapidly evolves into "**unappreciated**" and this situation has caused much moaning, rebellion, protest marching, discouragement, marriage failure, and plenty of other negatives. The big difference between the value of time at work and home isn't merely unjust, it just plain doesn't make sense. Homefront management is more complicated and two or three times as hard, physically, mentally, and emotionally. And its outcome affects us, our family, the economy, and the world more than the workplace ever will. Yet, because it has no price tag or salary range, it gets no respect. This can be demoralizing at times for even the most masterful home manager.

My operations manager mentioned the other day that when the mothers of her community meet on a committee and come up with something that needs to be done during the day in the neighborhood, all but three of them have office or other outside work and jobs. So the three people at home are the victims: "Gee, you aren't working, why don't you deliver this/pass these out, etc., ...we work."

The stay-at-home mothers' time is no freer than the "working" moms, it just doesn't have a price tag on it. And these women who are "free" to go do the passing out, they have to use their car, gas, hire a babysitter, and put something off they need to do for themselves. So while others enjoy their paid immunity on the job, the homefront women are paying (with their time *and* money). These are the same women who (for a first-grade class of 21 children) are the ones who always chaperon the field trips, bring the treats—in short, do the work for the other 39 moms and dads.

The problem, again, is that we've stooped to measuring all worth with a monetary measuring stick.

The only salvation for this situation is to disabuse ourselves and others of the zero worth of the people at home. Home efforts aren't incidental, never let anyone think of or treat them that way. They're the invisible support system of the economy, and if they didn't operate, the paid section of society would never be able to, either.

What would a home manager be worth if we did try to put a price tag on it? The latest estimate by economists is $44,000 annually.

Bailing out

All of us set sail in life, prepared for a nice smooth cruise or journey. We know there are storms out there, but we convince ourselves we won't be the ones to encounter them. But often there's no way around stormy weather. Some pelts us briefly, or we may have to endure for years before we find calm water again. Sometimes our ship stops, or lists and starts sinking, and we're ready to panic. Who wants to go down with the ship? That's fine for hero novels and war stories, but knowing that you're failing, losing your grip on home, family, and relationships is the worst feeling around. What do you do? (You'll get plenty of advice, counsel, and newspaper clippings from family, friends, psychiatrists, and soap operas.) Our overall tendency is to want to bail out, get out, get away, escape.

In other words, declare bankruptcy, start drinking, sleep or eat all day, space out, get divorced, go on remote control, work more hours, have an affair, contemplate murder or suicide, Harlequinize yourself, retreat to a cabin in the wilderness, and more. A few of these might be worth considering if your ship is irreparably damaged. However, 90% of the time a better solution is to tie down the hatches and ride out the storm, repair the damage and sail on. The problem with ship jumping as a cure for stress is that when you jump, you have to land **somewhere**. We don't know where that is, and it might be worse, and for sure the thing(s) we left behind will follow us forever, crying to be fixed or punishing us.

We seldom really get away from things we run from, whether they're debts or bad deeds. Hanging on beats hanging out or hanging loose.

Lots of people live their lives with their bags packed, always looking and always ready to move to greener pastures. Greener pastures are worth moving to, but better yet is to green up the pasture you are grazing. In other words when you take on, own, possess, or bite off something, then unpack your bags and mentally burn some bridges and leave your one big choice as making it work. Remember **most** management is **making it work**, not managing something that's already working. Management isn't a genius of manipulation and inspiration, it's commitment and perspiration. Always looking for something better often blinds us to what we already have, that could be made better with a bit of committed application.

Managing behind

One of the teenagers in our community had just gotten his driver's license and was riding high indeed, leaving tire-spinning tread marks all over the place. He irritated many a bystander, but neither his parents nor any of the rest of us managed to quell his dangerous show-off driving habits. His final stomp on the gas pedal was a grand event indeed. One evening, we were all at a big community park project in the mountains and he'd borrowed his dad's favorite vehicle, a classy little '65 Chevy coupe, for the event. He turned in front of a group of cute girls, revved the motor, and screeched out unmercifully toward the blacktop, looking back to see how many people were impressed with the noise and ruts he'd left behind. What he didn't see was a 300-year-old, three-foot thick yellow pine tree, and he ran straight into it, instantly destroying not only the vehicle's ability to ever run again, but his driving privileges for the next year. A little kid standing on the side said to him later, "You should have been looking where you were going."

Talk about a profound management summary! It's pointless to manage behind you, the past is gone. You can't correct a course traveled, **only the course ahead**. Trying to manage what happened, what's over and done with, is a problem with lots of people. Twenty years later, I still see people wringing their hands over a high school tournament where one shot would have changed the destiny of the whole school district. It didn't happen and won't, but the person is playing it over and over and managing and re-managing it in his mind. Don't manage things that are past, like:

If there hadn't been that price drop,
 I would have...
If I'd just waited until...
If only I'd had that insured...
If we'd met sooner...
If they'd worn safety belts...
If I'd only taken Computer Science....

The past is to learn from, not live in.

"D-Day" management

Aren't we all, more than we ever will admit, dreamers, idealists? Always lurking somewhere in our mind is the hope or expectation that someday, some big day everything is going to come together for us. There will be a big "Do" day where we get everything done and everything worked out, when we will get caught up totally. Everyone who owes us and has borrowed from us will pay us back and return things, all those strained relationships will clear up and all sorts of "needful things" will be worked out.

I have great faith that eventually most of this can and will happen to us, but it's always slower and more subtle than we think. Haven't you had a long list of to-do's and coming up soon is a day, an entire day with nothing scheduled, so you can use the entire time to catch up and complete and do, do, do! As the day gets closer, you almost salivate for it, making lists and preparing to conquer all kinds of things that've been on your mind and list forever. And then the big day comes and at the close of that day, no matter how fantastic you did, you realize that not only didn't you get anywhere near all the things done, but you actually added more to the list. So the day ends a discouraging one, not the delight you had planned and predicted.

This is normal and to be expected, folks, it simply means you are alive. Catching up is a relative term and if it actually happened, you'd be so depressed that the night after the great "got it all done" day you'd get up out of bed and begin looking for "something to do." Those 1,000 things lined up are not a sentence for you, but something that will help keep you and others healthy and happy. Someone once said the recipe for happiness has only three ingredients:

1. a clear conscience
2. someone to love
3. something to do

When you think about it, this is pretty profound. So don't be condemning and persecuting yourself for not getting it all done. That's not nearly as important as having enough plans and obligations to keep yourself productive, needed, fresh, challenged, and charged up. That list of expectations–those 1,000 things you have to do–is really a blessing. Just quit dreaming of finishing it all in one big push.

Looking at the practical instead of the possible

Unquestionably, one of the most common management mistakes. When it's time to pull it off–do the deed, make the decision, cook the Cornish hen–we use or consider only the tools, information, or ingredients presently at hand. A lot of people are content to do things this way: If "X" and "Y" are here and they have "Z" available to add in, then they'll use the "XYZ" plan or process. That's a poor way to manage, yet most people do it–look at the need in one hand and the available resources in the other.

Real managers don't do this, they go first for **possibilities**, **not practicalities**. When a situation comes along, be it a career to change, a car to get unstuck, an article to write, a meal to make, news to break, a vacation to take, they don't say:

"Well, here's what we've got (the tools and supplies and time) and this is how we did it before."

Instead, they say, "What's new, better, wiser? What other help could I get? Are these my only choices?"

Practicality is accepting what's available, the familiar tools and re-sources. Possibility is tapping unseen and perhaps presently unknown resources.

Ask an adult (even a highly educated one), "How would you cut down this tree?" and you get a quick, practical answer: "**Saw it down or chop it down**." (Adults are practicality.)

Now ask a four-year-old, "How would you cut down this tree?" and you'll get a possibility answer like:

saw it down
flood it down
beaver it down
chop it down
termite it down
dig it down
burn it down
pull it down
blast it down
Karate kick it down
have the Big Bad Wolf blow it down
tickle it down
have a giant push it down
ask my Dad

Once you present yourself with more **possibilities**, you can be even more "practical" or efficient.

During the Idaho Bicentennial celebration in 1976, for example, the mayor of our little town called me not long before the big event and asked me to make a float to take to the parade in the nearby "big" city of Pocatello. The budget was only $200 for a huge float, so a couple of costumed people was about the only **practical** choice. Instead of laboring with the few obvious alternatives, I took a few minutes to jot possibilities, and then pondered them over the next several days. I walked through the storage shed on my ranch as I thought it out—and there was thirty-five feet of aluminum sprinkler pipe and some chicken wire and some old belts. Resources all over the place! We made a frame of wire and pipe, put some papier maché over it, added some furry material we found on sale… and had a forty-foot long dachshund float. Our parade entry, all told, cost $157.80, and it won first place! It was even on television!

And instantly we zero in on these practicalities, weighing what we did last time, how far away things are, how much time or money they will involve, what people will say or expect. All the logical, realistic, obvious pluses and minuses come to mind and are fed into our inner computer. Then we begin to plod away in the direction of the decision.

From now on, before you pare all the options in anything down to practicabilities, list everything you can think or dream up. Yes, shower yourself first with all the **possibilities**, no matter how wild. It costs nothing, it feels good, and it will expand and excite you.

For example, if you're planning the annual family trip or a wedding or reunion, instead of immediately saying, "Well, we can afford this much time and money, or this many rooms/guests," go into orbit a few minutes and consider even your wildest fantasies and dreams. Maybe holding the reunion in Europe or Hawaii, inviting the governor or president to the wedding, or giving new

When something comes up, or we decide to do it (because we want to or we have to) the usual questions and concerns come to mind about it:

WHAT we can do?
What can we AFFORD?
WHERE we can go for it?
Who can HELP?

watches or tools as gifts instead of the usual tacky $2.50 favors. If you're thinking of doing some remodeling, consider putting a cantilevered deck with glass doors on the top story of your house addition instead of just a double-hung window, because the view is so nice up there.

Even if they're a big "Maybe," the possibilities are alive and fun and stimulating. And often a good practical decision or solution to a problem can be extracted from them.

I've seen people eliminate some of the greatest chances of their lives (and good management) because they were gridlocked into just playing with the usual game pieces, looking at things in a practical, everyday way. Often, bigger and better costs little or no more, takes less time, will enthuse more people and end up compensating for the difference, if there is any. Next time "What shall we do?" "Where shall we go?" "What shall we buy?" "Who should we ask?" or "What will we serve?" pops up, before you immerse yourself in the mundane, write down all the possibilities. Then watch how much better things go, how much more help you get, and how much more motivated you are.

Management gets much more mileage per gallon on high octane excitement and enthusiasm than on plain old regular and practical.

Peeking at the soufflé too soon

Getting overanxious for results can really foul up a good management flow. We're so used to fast things today. Everything is right here and now—instant replay, quick drying paint, ten-minute oil change, one-hour developing, overnight delivery, etc.—that we have trouble waiting for a nice healthy plant to grow. We won't leave it alone, or keep the fertilizer off it and give it a chance to develop and mature naturally. It's kind of like asking someone an important question that you really need to know the

answer to and then not giving them time to answer it.

Don't interrupt your own management process. When you have something cooking, drying, working, growing, soaking, or ripening, be wise enough to let it alone while it is "rooting" itself. I see people jump in and snatch work away from kids, meddle with eggs in the process of hatching, handle varnish that's still drying, fiddle with glued pieces that haven't set yet, take what's still cooking off the stove, hover over children that were quietly getting acquainted with each other, oversell ideas that were slowly taking hold, etc. When things are on their way and developing, be sure to let them finish. Over anxious generally results in over management (see following).

Overmanaging

Once my wife and I went to a rock (mineral rock, not music rock) show in Quartzite, Arizona. It was a tiny town of 600 citizens, and at least 50,000 enthusiastic rockhounds had swarmed there in their cars, motor homes, and campers. At closing time, the **single** four-way stop intersection in the center of town was handling the influx perfectly. Each driver knew when to stop

and go and the huge throng was quickly emptying from the display area. Then, three police officers with white gloves and whistles showed up and within minutes the flow was practically at a standstill. Tempers flared and all was a mass of confusion. Finally the patrol left, proud of their great job of overmanagement. Maximum flow with minimum interference would have been a lot better.

On the home front we are by no means free of the problem of too much management. I see people with more ambition than a whole town mow their lawns and clean their houses to death. Nice is nice, but using a T-square to line up the placemats just to feed the family lunch is not the best way to spend those valuable hours of our lives. Doing department-store level decoration of our home for every holiday (from Christmas to Halloween to Groundhog Day)—unless you love every minute of it—is not knowing the difference between adding a little atmosphere and overgearing.

Somehow we gradually push over the line in many things, from neat to neatnik, from workable to overworked. We make minute things into month-long marathons, the end results of which just don't make much of a dent or difference in the overall scheme of things.

Taking time just because you have it is overmanagement. Reacting to a situation instead of responding to it is overmanagement. Puttering, fiddling, tinkering, and doodling for hours with something that could have been done in minutes is overmanagement. Doctors tell me that two-thirds of the trips to rush children to the hospital are unnecessary—overmanagement. Retyping or worrying about the appearance of your rough draft notes for something is overmanagement.

Most of us have friends or know people who do things like this… but not us, surely…. Or maybe us, too! I've started an off-the cuff list of "overkill" activities (things that go way beyond accomplishing the objective, that take a lot of time and management, but don't amount to much in the end). I've left some blanks at the end for you to continue the list of things you see or even do that are just a little "too much" for what you get in return. Writing them down will help you isolate them and put them on ice—permanently!

elaborate gift wrapping (a lot of expense and effort, for something whose main function is to be torn off).

cleaning for company (as someone said to me once, "We're coming to see you, not the house"). And these days, you can be fairly sure that their house is not much cleaner, so you needn't be ashamed.

folding napkins for company (there are entire books on this!).

yard manicuring (great for the exercise of it, and if you like being outside, otherwise a lot of effort on behalf of those driving by).

removing every imperfection from a surface before you paint/varnish it (the smoother and more magnificent you make it, the madder all those new scrapes, bumps, and holes are going to make you).

insisting on a smooth fancy finish on something (such as a fence or shelf board) where rough would do as well, or better.

elaborate recipes (in which everything is done from scratch, and there are three or four sub-recipes within the recipe). You can easily sink half a day or more into a single dish here, not to mention all those sequential sessions of dishwashing . Not worth it, unless you truly enjoy every minute of it, are cooking for a guest you want to really impress, or someone whose greatest joy in life is food. (Besides, simple food is often tastier, less fattening, and less expensive.)

clothes/curtain, etc., styles that involve a lot of ironing, starching, and frequent cleaning–including fancy clothes for kids!

overelaborate, expensive gifts that just make the giftee feel obligated/uncomfortable.

organizing your possessions (can be taken so far as to be an unsustainable nuisance, such as when all plastic containers are supposed to be kept arranged by shape and size).

spit polishing things/the whole house instead of just cleaning them/it.

cutting firewood into precise 18-inch lengths.

hand drying the whole car, after you've washed it.

research (going back to the original hand-written pioneer journals for how to make maple syrup, when you could have got a two-page pamphlet on it free from the Extension Agent).

raking up the lawn clippings, when leaving them would be fine (in fact better for the lawn).

planning and paying for an $8000 wedding, when the happy couple would be happier getting married in the backyard.

planning and paying for a $15,000 funeral, when your loved one would be better remembered by _____.

taking a sixteen-week course in computers, when you could have just read the book that came with your new computer, or spent a day with someone experienced in this particular kind.

getting/keeping the house hot/cold when it just needs to be warm/cool.

installing an elaborate, expensive fence or barrier where something simpler and cheaper would do the job.

draining the whole pool and re-chlorinating it, when simply fishing out the dead dragonfly would have done it.

making elaborate excuses (no one really listens to them, anyway).

telling someone the story of your life (or at least the last two weeks) when all they asked was "how are things?"

insisting on the entire battery of diagnostic tests when the doctor/mechanic is fairly sure you just have the flu/need a new muffler.

swatting a fly with a sledgehammer/sending a tiger to chase away a dog/going after the gopher with an elephant gun.

having your dog's hair set, styled, and festooned with ribbons instead of just combing him from time to time.

drawing someone a map to the airport that includes every billboard and point of interest along the way.

making up elaborate formal agreements full of technical-sounding wording where something short and simple would do.

writing lengthy, convoluted letters where a simple note would do.

elaborate entertaining where an informal get-together would be more relaxing and fun.

fastening something with fourteen knots where one good one of the right kind would do (better).

_____

_____

_____

_____

_____

_____

Giving the authority without the power

If you've asked someone to do something, before you criticize them for not doing it, ask yourself if they have all the rights, powers, and authority they need to act.

If we give them the right to the car, then they have to have the keys. If we want them to do purchasing, we can't cut them off from the checkbook. We have to give the helper the gun, dangerous or not, if we expect him to bring back any game for dinner. If we give someone the right to choose, we must honor the way they choose!

One telling phrase that makes me wonder right off the bat how well a home is managed is when the spouse will respond to even the smallest or simplest decision or request, "I'll have to ask my husband/wife." All members of a home must have access to the tools and resources of the responsibilities they have, or you get nowhere. Never tie any hands that have work to do. This means not just adults, but children, hired help, relatives, and others.

Blaming it on "them"

I do believe in ghosts! For sure we've all got one around the house. It's the "they" ghost. No one's ever seen it, but it's there, everywhere, all the time. It's that phantom who gets the blame for everything that's not right, or not done. Old "they" is responsible for everything wrong, forgotten, left out, or broken. And as long as you feed and stroke it, the "they" ghost will stick around to haunt you and hurt your managership! As long as there is a "they" to blame and heap accusations on, we may never

realize there is an I, me, you, us, and we around, to really get the answers from and the job done.

Getting rid of the "they" ghost can't be done by shrinks, seances, or ghost-busters, by waiting, bribing, or ignoring. Only by assuming of all of your home responsibilities. If it's your area, life, or job, then you take care of it and reap the gory or the glory of the result.

Worrying about what you can't do anything about

Keep out of others' problems that you can't do anything about. Managing your own affairs well is probably the best way you can help others.

There are platoons of people out there who will bend your ear and pocketbook for hours with all of their "problems" of running home and hearth. We spend about half of our conversation time with many people just listening to their management screwups. They don't want advice, they don't want help, they just want to talk about it. Kind of a live soap opera. Shed these, don't spend time listening to them unless they really want help and will take it (and you can give it).

Likewise, I don't even want to know about Liz Taylor's traumas, Pete Rose's debt, O.J.'s latest appeal, or the New Orleans weather. I can't help or change it. Why concern myself with it and carry it around in my head?

When someone brings up some media-inflated emergency like "Do you realize there might be no World Series?" or "There may soon be a shortage of aluminum for beer and pop cans!" I always reply, "In all my worries and needs that number about eight hundred and sixty, those two concerns are #1880 and 1881."

We need to set our 911 sensitivity level to fit what really matters to US. Then lots of "problems" will just roll off our backs, and never even twitch us.

Negotiation

You might have been taught (and convinced) that negotiation, bargaining for the best deal is an honorable, if not necessary, skill to be sure you get what you want, and for the price you have in mind. Many people believe it's a key part of reaching any agreement. I can see some adjusting of positions, some yielding of expectations and ideas on either side to be fair. But in general, I think negotiation is a waste of time and a great way to delay and confuse things.

I saw this clearly demonstrated in a department store one day, as a woman tried to get "a better deal." She'd found a dress on sale, 40% off, and had discovered a flaw in it (a tiny one in the hemline) and wanted an additional discount. I watched two clerks and her negotiate for twenty minutes over $4. Each clung to their side while haggling for a compromise position. One of the clerks lost three big commissions on a juicer that was on sale, and the woman dickering for the deal lost track of her husband (who wandered away and bought a $95 pair of running shoes). Plus she got a $15 parking ticket, and delayed herself into traffic jam time getting home. But she did finally browbeat the clerk to a quivering defeat, and strode away triumphantly with her $4 victory!

The end result of negotia-tion is something whittled down from where either party wanted it, and usually reduced strength and confidence in the final outcome. Where negotiation exists, the yielder (which often means both sides) is unhappy. If the result *is* just what someone wanted, then they were unfair or dishonest in their initial presentation. When you disagree and can't accept someone or their price, demand, or request, be careful about "compromising," from either direction.

True, often we're up against situations where things are too high, too low, wrong length, wrong color, unfair, or not the right schedule. Where is the real bottom line here? Maybe yelling your way through or demanding your price isn't the best deal. Even if it's overpriced, unjust, bad timing, maybe you should just pay the $4 and get on with it! Too often, the time and emotion expended to "get them down" or get your way—turning a transaction into a turmoil—**just isn't worth it.**

NEGotiating at home

We—parents and kids, old and young alike—use it almost as often as the TV knob. I'll bet you yourself have negotiated plenty:

"Okay, if you'll clean your room, you can use the car."

"Well, maybe when your grades are better we'll talk about a bigger allowance."

"That trip to Disneyland is looking a little doubtful because your chores are lagging."

"I did those dishes for you, the least you can do is let me _____."

Just to get things moving, or get them done in our time frame (exactly as in a business deal) we'll pull all kinds of angles. And we teach the little ones to negotiate like boardroom wizards– age 6 months to 21 years, they have negotiation down pat:

"If I practice my piano lesson for an hour, can I..."

"Hey, I went to church for two months, now I should be able to..."

"All the other kids are going, how come you have to be such a stick in the mud?"

"You treat me like a little kid, you know!"

"You don't trust me!"

Kids are natural, if not expert, negotiators with each other and their parents and other adults–the ol' wrap 'em around your little finger trick. Even at the dinner table, to get dessert they bargain over vegetables. Granted, a little exchange of ideas, some trade-off and compromise of positions or opinions has merit; but here's the biggie: when we allow lots of negotiation to go on in the home, we plant the seeds of doubting the rules and doubting our authority. If everything is open to negotiation, it undermines our attempts at order and control. It says no value or boundary is absolute! Then no one will do anything without striking a deal or pushing to get their own way.

This really muddies the water and delays getting anything done. The more something is bantered back and forth, the more complicated and arbitrative it becomes, the more time it takes, the more running in circles and burned up energy, the more irritation and animosity results. But worst of all, it teaches that a rule or law or request really isn't firm, it's possible that with enough leverage and whining, you can and will get your way instead. Cultivating this in your offspring isn't going to do anything positive for management anywhere.

Start today, to minimize your negotiation with folks on the homefront. And watch how much more peaceful things are, how much time is saved (and how much better people will like you, and work with you). We all like firm, clear, and fair rules and requests.

Letting yourself get sidetracked

One of the biggest risks in the world of management, personal or otherwise, is getting sidetracked. Remember the "side track" is where the slow or stopped trains are routed. It can easily be where our brain gets routed, too! When you're on track, even if your train stops, stay on the main track, hold your position and direction. That's good management.

I had a manager once who knew his goals and pursued his duties earnestly, but there was a sidetrack that always derailed him: "glory." He was forever taking his eyes off his objective to strut and stroll through the cheering section, and his operation would slip in his absence.

A limousine driver in Tampa gave another illustration of "sidetracked" in describing the difference between a first-class chauffeur and an average one. Chauffeurs are often engaged to drive important people to three- or four-hour dinners. Once they drop off the party and see that they've entered the restaurant, a driver can easily leave and take an hour or so break, and come back later. "But," he said, "the real pros stay right there, and park somewhere close, within sight, and keep an eye open because their party might get sick or have an emergency and need to leave, or the whole group might just hate the place. Zip! You see the party appear at the door and you're right there."

If, on the other hand, the driver is sidetracked with buddies over at Burger King or on some personal errand, and the high-paying hosts have to hunt him down... that's bad management!

Home has about a hundred times as many sidetracks as work, because remember, work operates within a structure and home is usually a free-for-all. Say you are heading out to pick some flowers for an important bouquet you agreed to furnish at a funeral. As you reach for the car door, you notice the handle is loose so you stop to find a screwdriver. Hunting for the screwdriver, you see some fruit jars are crowded on the shelf and will get broken, so you carry them down to the cellar. The minute you get back outdoors,

you notice a drip under the car, so you stop and call the garage or dealer about it. While on the phone, the mechanic asks how your Aunt Lilly is doing, and that triggers the urge to write to her, so you start a note and during it, hear a noise outside and it's the neighbor's cat after yours. Chasing the cat away you see a sprinkler you need to move... and the list can and often does go on all day.

The flowers were the no-delays-allowable #1, and nothing in all that time really got done toward them. That is pure sidetracking. True, all the sidetracking things needed attention. Let's call these the satellite jobs apart from the focus job, which was the flowers. You still could have worked on and gotten some of the other jobs done or at least on their way while keeping in pursuit of the flowers. That is the way to avoid sidetracking.

Keep the hundred or thousand things moving, but don't let the focus off the one or two. Never let the focus things just blend into the satellite things or you are lost!

187

**300%-the "too much"
we all have to handle**

50%	Lack of Direction
40%	Junk & Clutter
35%	Procrastination
30%	Unrealistic Standards
30%	Carelessness/Failure to Prevent Problems
25%	Not Doing Things Right the First Time
20%	Refusing to believe history
15%	Fighting
40%	Unavoidable Chores

Causing our own management problems

Sometimes we get so far behind we feel like shooting ourselves (so we say), but we may have already shot our-selves... in the foot. We often cause many of our own management problems, or bring them on ourselves. There is sure no glory in working out a problem that should never have been a problem in the first place.

No matter how brilliantly or successfully you handle any problem, at best you are still just even with where you were before the problem cropped up.

How much of your home management time is spent fixing and fighting and redoing something that got out of control, something you could have prevented? There always seems to be the time and money to fix something and pay for it and justify it all later, doesn't there? If we'd just practice the behavior necessary for the prevention, the need for control would be out the door.

Prevent others from causing problems, too

When it comes to prevention, it isn't enough to mind our own actions and those of our family. It doesn't matter who or what would be responsible if something unfortunate happened, you must look ahead, anticipate, and do all you can to PREVENT it, anyway. (Because you will be left with or dragged into the consequences.) For example:

• *Don't let yard toys or tools be left out anywhere they might possibly be run over, especially if you know guests or delivery vehicles are coming.*

• *Watch carefully when the tractor-trailer delivering the load of concrete blocks or whatever comes. Don't take a chance that he will decide to turn around in the soggy yard, and get stuck/need to be pulled out,* and leave giant ruts **you** will be stuck filling and reseeding (no matter how nicely he apologizes).

- If you've invited a bunch of kids to a summer party, don't just tell them to stay out of the rabbit pen. (Those "cute little bunnies.") Padlock it! Or no matter what you say, while you are busy greeting people and serving pop, at least six of those kids (and some of their parents) will be running through the pen, chasing the rabbits, catching them and manhandling them, etc.

- Stay aware of what the carpenter is doing as he constructs that "custom-made" cabinet or whatever. Otherwise, he may make decisions you don't like, and you will have to live with, and pay for the consequences. (Even if something you don't like **can** be fixed or redone, and even if you don't have to pay for any remakes that may be necessary, he'll be losing some or all of his profit over them, and the whole situation will sour).

- When the tree-trimmers come to "trim the trees away from the electric lines," don't trust that the discussion you had with them a week ago as to what you did or didn't want done, will be honored. Stay aware of what they're doing–trees take decades to regrow!

We don't want to be right ("I told you that would happen…"), we want to be trouble-free!

THE SIX BIGGEST MISTAKES OF MANAGEMENT

1. The illusion that someone else will take care of it for you. No matter who you are, what age or sex, no matter what your life circumstances, there is no "someone" who is going to take it all off your shoulders. You may get helpers, yes, but the *responsibility* is yours. You are that "they" ghost.

2. Believing that you are too valuable to do it yourself. Trying to be a "manager" ruins more good managers than any single thing.

3. Thinking that once something is planned, financed, and outlined, it's on its way. Intentions don't manage anything. Neither does hoping and praying and assigning. Only action and completion count.

4. Carrying unnecessary burdens like junk and clutter, luxury and formality, and other people's problems that you can do nothing about. Don't waste energy on these.

5. Considering the practical instead of the possible.

When you start ruling things out right off the bat, dwelling on and weighing all the practicalities, few possibilities are considered. (See page 179.)

6. Getting sidetracked. Losing sight of your main goal, or altering your course and actions to fit the mood of the hour or the popular views of the day!

12

Staying out of Problems

Somewhere in grade school I came across the word "handicap" and never did understand it. In high school I was hearing it more and still didn't quite grasp its meaning. I finally asked my coach what handicap meant. "Like in golf, well, it's an extra burden put on the extra good players to keep them even with the average player." That didn't make a whole lot of sense to me. Why in a game where people are competing to outperform each other, would you hold someone back just because they're superior in ability? I thought being best was the name of the game, not limiting the best so others can keep up. Then I learned that even in horse racing a horse who ran faster and rated higher had to carry extra weight to slow him down and make a fair race out of it.

More than forty years later now, I still don't understand the value of handicapping anything, especially **ourselves** when we're managing our activities.

We have a life to run, and it seems the better, more easily and skillfully we can do it, the better off we are. Management of plain old ordinary everyday life is complicated and heavy enough without adding any handicap weights.

Let's look at some of the more common home management handicaps now.

Plural piloting

Here's a little glitch in home management that can become a canyon—deciding who is in charge overall. Co-managers, partners, associates, mutual agreement, and all of those nice "fair" systems of running things at home are great when and if you can make them work. But pride, greed, the power drive, tradition, and about a hundred other emotions, hangups, and prejudices we humans have make joint management a tough, tough method of running things. In sixty years of home life and forty-five years of managing businesses and numerous community and church organizations, I've learned that committee leadership and co-responsibility works poorly. Sounds good on paper and in Sunday school, social science classes, and on the picket lines, but in the actual working situation, almost never. Every operation (war, peace, hunting and fishing trips, playing in the yard, the bowling team, club, union, etc.) needs a leader, some**one** in charge with the ultimate responsibility to answer and decide. A home without a head will likewise be a mass of disorder and dissension.

I'm not talking about a ruler or king, just a leader to keep things unconfused. It doesn't matter if it's he or she or it that runs the home, but it better be one of them and not all. Equality is the stalemate of management. If you want to see instant chaos, then put a group or a team in charge of something and you'll see it. When parents send children out to rake the lawn as a group they've created instant bureaucracy and inefficiency, if not war and revolution. Mankind learned quickly (nearly 10,000 years ago) that someone has to be the head, the general, the captain, the leader, the stopping place.

191

"Leader" doesn't mean they give everyone orders or direct every move. It means they preside, have the final responsibility and power of decision. If a husband and wife or grandparent can't decide who the leader should be, then trade off each year, one agreeing to let the other have the final responsibility for direction and arbitration. My wife runs more than I do around home and is free to do anything any way she wants, but I preside as the patriarch of the family to anchor the whole thing, and see that the facilities and finances are squared away. She doesn't have to ask my permission or answer to me, but she allows me to do the final dealing on major things and consults me when she feels uncertain or in need of direction. In your home you may be the matriarch, or leader.

If you are having trouble with things like money, discipline, or priorities, decide on a leader at home and watch how much better things work afterward, once you have a pivot point. It doesn't mean someone is lesser or better, it just means one is a copilot, the other is the pilot. Switch if you have to, but don't both command at the same time or you'll crash.

Getting along with others

In the workplace, in business and on the job, when some uncomfortable situation develops we have lots of options for relief. We can quit, get fired or transferred, go start our own business, or go dump the whole mess on the boss. But our escape options for tight squeezes on the homefront are not so plentiful. When we get in a bind around the house, **we are it**. Once in a while, there is a friend or family member who can help from the sidelines, but often our only real choice is managing to live with what's there or what we can't change. The more dramatic ways of relieving difficulties at home (like divorce, bankruptcy, beating up on someone, or just plain RUNNING) usually generate even more management problems in the long haul, so here we are!

Some of us find out after our happy home is set up that kids aren't easy, taxes never quit, no job is permanent, and our spouse has disabilities like not putting the cap on the toothpaste, acute laziness, unceasing criticism, a roving eye, alcoholism, shopaholism, sports addiction, or any of hundreds of other big and little habits that just plain drive us crazy. Homemaking always involves bringing more than one family and culture together and that also makes for interesting stew. Most of these habits and traditions are ingrained into each of us so deep that change just isn't likely. So all of this calls for some adapting and handling, some good management—you **can** manage these things. I'm not saying if you can't lick them, join them; if you can't lick them then at least position them so that they're easier on everyone. A second TV in another room is sure cheaper and less stressful than arguing for an hour a day, practicing and priming for a divorce.

You can manage shouting and dissension out of your place, or at least minimize them. A constant need to lecture and correct kids who refuse to put their toys away, for example, might be remedied by better, brighter toy boxes and maybe less toys or restricted hours for using some of them. Those more intolerable homefront heartaches (like infidelity, which always destroys everything in its wake) are even a matter of management in the end. Even the most extreme or stressful situation can be dealt with and taken care of in some way.

It is simply more productive to spend your time finding alternatives than arguing or being irritated. Something is going to happen, have to give in the situation, so you might as well use your energy to think up and list and choose from alternatives. Something will have to solve the situation in the end, and you might as well be the solver rather than the victim of whatever will happen if things are left to fate or the future.

What you can't change

Many people live a frustrated life, unhappy because they can't change something or someone. They spend a lifetime moaning and groaning about the weather, the economy, the morals of the world, an illness, an injustice, a relationship, or someone they detest, but there's nothing they can do about it. If it goes 30° below zero for two weeks in a row, walking around the house wringing our hands and cursing old man winter is pretty futile. Grinding your teeth for two hours every night after updating yourself on the situation of the world in the evening paper is a waste of good time and tooth enamel.

Good management isn't just controlling your own things. There are outside forces like those impersonal, impartial elements, and other people's problems to deal with, too. Lots of people can handle their own personal property and affairs well in life, keep their room, desk, diet, automobile, and everything else in good order and working well. But when they're dropped into the chaos of a social world and have other people's diets, rooms, traffic, lateness, and failures dropped on them, they can't handle it and go to pieces.

Management is basically twofold: you and them, and you have to deal with both. You can change yourself pretty easily, but them, their way of life or of putting away their clothes or handling their affairs... just try and change any of that. You can't and won't. But you can manage it. It doesn't take us long to figure out (after getting acquainted with an Idaho winter, an aggressive weed, or an obnoxious person), that they're not going to go away just because we don't happen to like them very much. Good management is finding a way to deal with all of this: dressing warmly, heat taping your pipes, applying some Roundup, and avoiding or learning to love the obnoxious one. **What you can't change, you manage.** You can manage to be away when the winter or a weirdo comes around, you can manage to insulate yourself or give them something to distract them. There are all sorts of things you can do to handle and control a situation.

Management by manipulation

Some time or other we've all found a shortcut that seems to get things done quicker or better, and often with less effort. Its short-term rewards lead us into its clutch. It's called "manipulating." You can manage, which is a proper, solid structure, or you can manipulate, which is skipping some rules and times, sweet talking and smoothing and jockeying the process through the application of some "con." Throwing our weight around, flimflamming, playing politics, hoodwinking, smoke screening, and more–manipulation has all kinds of ways and means for easy victimiz-

ing. We all do it. We started doing it when we were infants, to get attention, food, changed, or a toy. Some of us used it later in faking sick, whimpering, whining, bullying–anything to get things done our way. Waitresses learn to get better tips by wearing black lace bloomers and bending just right; vacuum salesmen learn how to exaggerate dirt and pickup power and the ease of payments. Others use charm, payoffs, gifts, etc., to swing or manage a situation to their advantage.

Manipulation often works well at first, but it's always short-lived and the bank account it builds never offsets the character it robs from you and others.

I remember when I thought I was Mr. Star of the baseball team at the age of sixteen, and my two younger brothers were seven and eight. Somehow I found out they had visited a neighbor's house, found his shotgun, and while playing with it blew a ten-inch hole in the ceiling. Then they ran. With this knowledge, I blackmailed and manipulated those two little kids for a year into chasing my batting practice balls in deep pasture. One day they'd had it and went on strike. They decided the neighbor's punishment for the hole would be better than mine. I still feel bad about it, thinking back. How often do we do

things like this? It's not management.

Manipulation may seem easier than cooperation or coordination, but folks, don't press your luck. People hate to be manipulated. Sure, they're fooled for a while, but they'll see the truth someday and it will be a bad day for you when someone, a close friend or a loved one, finds out you were playing them along for some kind of gain. Flattery and faked affections all read clearly in the end, and manipulation management (and its operators) are doomed.

Aren't we all sick of politics in the world and in business? So by all means, let's not bring it into our home, yard, and playground, our interactions with our neighbors and friends. Manipulation is an art, and doing it well consumes a great deal of time and energy, whereas doing things in the open and honestly, up front, is a hundred times easier in the end. Plus our kids, spouses, neighbors, and friends won't find out later that they've been manipulated, and hate us.

Fighting

I don't mean sword or fist fighting, but the more subtle kinds of battle we resort to to accomplish our ends. We push, seize, force, lean, negotiate hard, demand, pressure–use all of the techniques of **force**. There are those of us who, no matter what we are involved in, end up in a big fight or struggle– legal, political, verbal, or emotional. I watch enormous numbers of home managers operate on the defensive, as if they were "after" someone, or someone was after them. So often we wait until it's too late or we are threatened, irritated, or served notice and then try to administrate our affairs. At this point, we're just as burdened as the golfer or the race horse.

Any aggression or negativism you allow to enter your management process will just dampen, if not dissolve it! If you want to succeed and take full advantage of any opportunities that come your way, you can't manage mad or fighting anything or anyone. The reason is obvious. Your will and wits all go into the brawl, leaving you little to overcome the actual obstacle.

I've seen city and state governments, organizations, school boards, teams, and families who really don't get anything done but fighting. I think they get so addicted to bickering, that feuds and tiffs and power plays become the real focus. If you find yourself forever yelling and snipping and fighting and poking and jabbing and growling, you're using up all your "do" time skirmishing instead of living. No matter what you

fight—ex-spouses, your kids, health worries, finances, creditors, that sticking drawer or door, even hair that falls in your eyes every other second—you lose! Not only time, but the presence of mind and mood to do anything constructive.

When we were kids, when something we were working on wouldn't fit or open or move, we lesser experienced would always run for a bigger pry bar or turn the blowtorch up. Dad would warn us, **"If you force it**, it'll break." And it did! So it is with anything you're trying to manage.

When a situation we're trying to control flares up, there isn't one of us who doesn't have impulses and feelings that rise up inside us and say, **"Charge!"** As babies we learn to hit back right after how to hold onto the bottle, and then we spend years learning to control the tendency to fight and inflict pain and get even, and many of us never do master it.

Carrying this with you into your maturity is a real management liability.

Fighting of any kind is war, and in war you lose lives as well as time, feelings, and dignity, plus you carry the wounds and battle scars forever. **All for what?** Our battle issues on the homefront are often things like some city ordinance or trash pickup policy that we decide to make a matter of right or wrong, and we'll stand by our proclaimed principles to the death, losing sight in the end of what is good for the trash or the lawn. Likewise, little differences of opinion with our husband or wife, neighbor nuisances, and many other relationships and things are managed poorly, simply because we choose to fight instead of figure it out. We get focused on the irritations, instead of the mate or neighbor.

I've seen farmers who are not just friends but members of the same church, their wives are sisters, their kids cousins, attack each other with shovels over a share of irrigation water thought to have been misdirected. A lifetime of misery thereafter from one measly trickle of water.

This is poor management. Good managers focus on the problem and the dilemma, and then only to get it taken care of or get rid of it, not to dwell on downing or casting out the causers.

Peace and calmness (before, during, and after) will help any management. Peace is like oil to a motor—it lubricates the whole process and makes it work better. Managing while at war, with ill feelings against anyone or anything will absolutely thwart your progress. You cannot "manage mad." So, especially prior to any big moves or changes in your personal or homefront agenda, make peace with everyone and everything you can before you start. Otherwise you'll have a load of misery along with every management maneuver.

Being a peacemaker, refusing to fight or be antagonistic regarding whatever isn't going your way, will gradually give you the advantage. So step back and consider other approaches and resources. You can fight city hall, the system, the IRS, the administration, the establishment or whoever you want, but **peacemaking** is ultimately the best management.

I'll hold my ground on a moral issue I believe in, but for the 99.9% of other conflicts that come up every day on the homefront (and always will), I've learned to back off. Moving out of the way and even giving ground to those fuming with unhappiness is the quick-est way to cool things down. I always feel good about backing off from an unnecessary fight. Almost always, the person I yield to thinks it over and comes back a friend, giving back anything they might have taken in the fray. I've never surrendered any ground to avoid a confrontation that I didn't get back, with interest. Plus I kept a friend. Try it yourself and see. Bite back that acid remark and instead say something like "OK, if you feel that strongly about it, we can do it your way."

When you accomplish your ends by friendly, even loving logical persuasion instead of pressure and threats of punishment, you give people "want to's," rather than "have to's." Which do you think they're going to get around to first?

Don't fight injustices, either

This is even true of things you might consider an issue of "justice" (or injustice). I remember once renting uniforms from a laundry for one of my maintenance crews. When the uniforms showed up there was a bill for $600 "for cleaning" with them. They were new, we hadn't even worn them, so I called about the unjustified $600 and they assured me this was for the final turn-in day of the uniforms (like a rental deposit) it was company policy. I accepted that and paid up. Two years later, when we turned in the uniforms at the end of the contract, I got another bill for $600. I called and reminded them of the agreement (sending copies of it), they billed me again, and again I refused to pay. They sued me for the $600 plus collection. This was injustice, and as they say, I had it in "black and white." I called my lawyer, he looked the contract over, and shook his head. "Yes, they are screwing you over. But they have a couple of fine print terminologies in there that mean if you fight them you might lose." I was really bent and came up with the position we all reach sometimes: "It's not a matter of money, it's a matter of principle. Go after them."

My attorney (a quiet, wise, gentle, and fair guy–rare attorney) took off his glasses and tapped them on the desk pad thoughtfully, "Okay, Don, but let me give you some free advice. If we go after this, even if all goes well and we win, it's going to cost you at least $1200 just to file, etc., plus your own and your secretary's time and preparations. If I were you, I'd pay the $600 even if they are rats or crooks. Take the other $600 of my fee and your time, and buy your wife a dress, take a trip, and forget about it. Because if you're up against a big company that's pulled this before, injustice can rule and you can lose. You'll be out the $600, collection costs, my $1200 and all the time, probably over $3000 or more." I was infuriated and only said through gritted teeth. "Do it." He did, and we lost.

This was one of many such life and business lessons I've learned. As a VP of a home loan association once told me, "Don, the first lesson of management is: There isn't always justice in the law." I've had notes and agreements go sour, with big companies, too, who just went bankrupt on me, when my wife and I were almost penniless, struggling to not only start up a business but raise a large family. There were thousands of dollars of my money and hundreds of hours of my life and sweat involved, and I lost it all through someone else's stupidity and poor management. Then thanks to a tiny piece of paper they walked away from it all, untouched. Months later, when I was still struggling from the loss and trying to get a loan, they were driving new cars and got loans easily.

For a while, I really let this grate on me, went on and on about it, fighting and somehow trying to get them legally. In the end, it generally only benefited accountants and lawyers. So one day (like giving up a bad habit) I quit. I decided my only recourse was to be real selective who I did business with, in my personal life and in my company.

Justice is simply being fair. So I seek out and support people who are fair. The unfair ones, I ignore. I love them as fellow humans but won't deal with them. You have to do your own determining in this area. When you do what's right and get slapped in the face, turn the other cheek (but get out of arm's reach of the slapper as quick as you can after that).

What about those inevitable differences?

Always, even in the most compatible marriage, family, community, committee, crew, team, neighborhood, there will crop up differences. People in perfect harmony have differences. That is natural, fine, and healthy. The key of management is what you **do** about the differences.

Good, smart managers don't expand them. They resolve them.

You will have, even leading the most exemplary life…

<u>DIFFERENCES!</u>

Poor Management = **React**	Good Management = **Respond**
Argue	*Stop-Look-Listen*
Dispute	*Reconsider*
Bicker	*Apply logic*
Quarrel	*Try to see the other side*
Yell	*Yield*
Stomp off	*Agree*
Sue	*Decide not to make an*
Try to get revenge	*issue of it*
Give them the silent treatment	*Decide not to worry about it*
Tempers flare	
Everyone upset	
Everyone hardens their positions	*END RESULTS:*
	Softening on both sides
	Cooperation
END RESULTS:	*Compromise*
Emotional upset	*LOVE*
Physical and mental damage	*RESPECT*
Extra expense	
Stress	
Health risks	
Withdrawal of spirit	
Disharmony	
Leads to more of the same	

Some of the prime sources of contention

money
who is right
whose job it is
selfishness (it's mine!)
junk
jealousy/envy
boundary crossing
kids
religion

loss or injury of something or someone
lateness
faultfinding
sarcasm/rudeness
driving/vehicles
remodeling and redecorating

Ever notice how we put on our best face for the public, put our best foot forward on the job or at school? Our friends and associates always see us at our best. At home, we let our hair down, we're our slouchier selves. There isn't much energy left over for kindness and understanding at home, either. We've been so nice and friendly and obeyed all the rules of civility all day, so when we get home we're just too darn tired for courtesies and pleasantries, pleases and thank-yous.

Who really deserves our best side? Do we benefit more from a happy home or an impressive everywhere else?

Beware of professional strugglers

Don't we all have friends and loved ones, associates and neighbors who are "professional strugglers," for whom everything seems to go wrong every day of their lives? They may be good and nice people, too. They try hard, but it seems they catch every sickness, are always out of money, their cars are forever breaking down, they lose their jobs and get all the bad breaks. Bad luck follows, if not stalks them (or do they make their own bad luck?) They seem to always be on the brink of some disaster, from a nervous breakdown to their family or finances falling apart any minute. They're always late and behind and always comparing themselves with you or others and sniffling and complaining about their misfortunes.

We all have such people in our lives and they don't go away. They need constant help and supplementation—they're always borrowing or asking for loans, always needing advice, inspiration, morale boosts. Half the time they're living with you or eating off you, or sending some member of their family for you to shape up. Helping is our duty as fellow humans. We all want to and will help the physically or emotionally needy, any way we can, even "seventy times seven" as the scripture counsels us to do for others.

But in the case of these "professional strugglers," at some point we really aren't helping them, we're just feeding and strengthening their dependency and weakness. Then talk about a difficult situation to manage—we've created, developed, and cultivated a leech or deadbeat that can and will drain us. Generosity and love have to be tempered with wisdom and caution when it comes to any professional struggler you know. Eight out of ten of us who have helped the professional strugglers at length have enough horror stories to fill a small library. I've seldom had a co-signed note work out well, for instance. Of the last thirteen people I've given money and other help to (loans, etc.) I've had 100% disappointment. It didn't help them either, and they only disliked me in the long run.

This is a big management question you'll have to face all of your life. The better you manage, the more of these folks you will attract. What are your choices in dealing with them?

- *Just say no! (A selfish, unrewarding thing to do.)*
- *Avoid or ignore them completely. (Gets rid of them eventually, but does nothing for your character or reputation.)*
- *Steer them to someone else. (That's chicken.)*
- *Accept, tolerate, and preach to them. (You'll be one of hundreds doing it.)*
- *Love and help them. (The right thing to do, but a huge management challenge.)*

How do you handle this? Carefully! After six years of managing assistance programs for "those down and out on their luck," I discovered that many have made a real profession, or at least a part-time job, out of being down and out. The rules I've learned for dealing with pro strugglers not only at home but in church and the community are:

1. Be the perfect example of and teach them constantly, things that will help them get along better in life. Show, not tell, them what to do. People **can** learn and change, when they see things in action and see the results.
2. If they've promised to do something or pay something back, don't cave in and let them off the hook. Accountability brings out the best in people, having to answer for their promises.
3. When you spend something, time or money, on them, take them with you or have them there to see it done. Amazing what this will do for education... and appreciation.
4. Leave all responsibility for their needs and requests with them—make it clear that you are their supplement, not their sustenance.

5. Your overall goal is to gradually convince them that the definition of luck is self-reliance, gut hard work, and perseverance—things most "bad luck" people think they practice, but don't.

How to deal with overload panic

"I'm behind, I mean really behind and so tired my butt's dragging. And more is coming–Gasp!"

For a long time in my life, I thought I was the only one over-bombarded with responsibilities, demands, short-comings, guilt, not enough time, and 500 other "better get it done now, buddy" anxieties. But about 98% of people, when they hear the statement above, think that I'm quoting them!

There is nothing wrong with having your bucket brimming full, as long as it doesn't lose some. When I feel a little (or big) panic over my load:

1. I type up all my "to-do's" on one page, single-spaced, if possible—it's less intimidating.
2. Then I reason with myself. What if I do or don't do these things—the consequences. When you think it through this way, there may be some you don't really need to do at all, that can just be eliminated.
3. I pass around the rest or post them to solicit help (volunteers).
4. That big, long load makes little short items look easy so I knock off ten little ones I've been stalling on. This shortens the list and makes the big load seem more attainable.
5. I stay up later, get up earlier.
6. I cut out TV and entertainment—projects and accomplishment are more entertaining in the end, anyway.
7. I hire some of it done.
8. When there is no light at the end of the tunnel, step or turn back and reread your

life's compass. Reaffirm your purpose and direction and surge ahead. Dark or not, you'll know you're on the path.

9. If you seem to be bogged down with one of your big objectives, see if you can reschedule it. Don't keep trying to walk uphill on a sidewalk that's as slippery as glass. Go do something else until the ice melts or spring comes, or until you get some ice gripper shoes. Many people think determination is the essence of management, but often wise repositioning is more like it.

"When there's too much to do, you've got to get things in perspective. There are some things that HAVE to be done, and you know what those are. All the other stuff is 'would like to,' 'could do,' or 'if have time' things, and you sort and treat them accordingly."

When you think your circuits are full

We're so overloaded we seem to have lost our sense of purpose and direction. We feel disoriented, confused, in conflict.

If you haven't been gripped by this circuit overload strain yet, have pa-tience because if you amount to anything in life, it will hit you every so often.

Fear not, human circuits are never full. Our capacity to handle "life's calls" is beyond our comprehension, so forget all those claims we make to ourselves:

I can't take another step.
This is the end.
This is the last time.
It's over for sure.

We've all said things like this and then gone on to extend ourselves double beyond where we were then, and often the reach of the doubling did nothing but revitalize us.

It isn't the capacity of the circuits, it's our assessment of their capacity that is the problem (and our will and motivation). Admit it–if you were in the middle of one of these circuit overloads right now and someone offered you the "big thing" you've always wanted as soon as you've cleaned up your backlog, you'd have it done in hours or a day or so, even those most dreaded items.

Readying yourself for those inevitable reversals

We can plan and work so hard to make sure all goes well in life–build a savings account, a good relationship with our wife or husband, and a nice home just where we want it. We have good friends, kids enrolled in not only good schools but tap and toe classes, too, a good standing in the community and church, a good job, fun pets, and then... those reversals we're **all** so vulnerable to occur.

Our new neighbor plays the trumpet for a hobby and he has a pack of dogs that poop on our lawn, there are two robberies in the community and we're one of the victims, a cranky old relative moves in with us, the interest rate goes up right before we decide on the new house. And then those biggies no one wants and yet they happen to the very best of us: divorce, serious illness or injury, fire or flood, war ships our child overseas, a tragic death in the family. Or we want kids but our fertility specialist says forget it.

Even the strongest of us will stagger under some of these happenings. They can damage our souls and spirits so much, we want to slump over and give up on life, just coast the rest of the way through.

Those setbacks will come, sure as the sun comes up in the morning, and seemingly always at a bad time. Most of these things aren't even our fault, they aren't due to bad management or bad planning, either. Our only choice is to roll with them and manage to manage well anyway. It's my old Scouting motto again, "Be prepared." And I don't mean stand beside your grave with a lily in your hand just waiting for the big day.

Because there's no way we can anticipate many of the misfortunes that surprise our lives, there's no choice but to spend some time NOW getting ready, before any of this occurs. It's a lot tougher to do during or after a tragedy. You can't think or act rationally in a setback situation, so you have to do it **before**. If something is looming or sooner or later inevitable, think about it and educate yourself in it. Rehearse and learn your reaction to it. Find out what you need to know and do about it. Just what is involved in handling a funeral, for instance, if you've never had anything to do with one. Or how **would** you make ends meet if Herbie or Helen decided to leave?

The official word for this is contingency planning, mentally anticipating what could or might happen and then mapping out some plans. In other words, facing the situation and the adjustments in your mind and on paper before you have to in reality.

Get your priorities and commitments and direction straight before that aged parent suddenly needs round-the-clock care, or that car accident happens. Then if something bad hits you, you'll have the strength to get through the grief and struggle and know where to go from there. Lots of people say, "Oh, I don't want to think about things like that, I'll handle that when it comes." That's like ignoring being prepared for winter. It will come, and having some warmth stockpiled can fight off the bitter cold misfortune brings.

Two different friends of mine had house fires, both lost everything except their lives. One of them, thirty years later now, still talks and wails about it and blames and whines about "the fire." My other friends, a couple in their mid-twenties at the time with four kids, had lots of nice irreplaceable things too—furnishings, books, photos, art, clothes, collectibles, handmade treasures worth a lot. At three o'clock one Saturday we were all at work when a panic call came from the wife, "Our house is on fire!" We sprinted out of the office, leaped in the company truck, and sped the five miles to their house which was indeed aflame. All the family was safe but the home didn't have a chance. The gas furnace had ruptured, and the house was reduced to a charred heap in less than an hour. (There was no fire department in that rural area even though they paid fire taxes.) Everything from a lifetime of investment was gone, they had nothing left but the clothes on their backs.

Friends put them up for the night and the next morning in church there they were, in work clothes, but clean and fresh. The father taught the adult Sunday School class as usual, in a red plaid shirt and mountain boots and unshaven, and never said a word about it. That was twenty-four years ago and I've never heard any of them utter a single word about all that was lost (except for a joke or two about how no one had the presence of mind to grab the Christmas present bicycles leaning against the burning house when we arrived). They were gracious to all who gave them coats and shoes, but never asked or begged for anything, nor even mentioned a word about their misfortune. They went on to raise six wonderful, well-adjusted kids and become leaders in the community, business, and church. Within a few years they seemed to have accumulated as much as before.

No one ever promised us that life would be fair. It may be just in the end, but it sure isn't fair as we go along. The only real choice we have is to handle what comes our way as well as we can and get on with what is good. Hashing and rehashing our background and battles really dulls any management edge. We have the right to cry when our dog is hit by a car, or feel bad because we lost our job (deserving or undeservingly), but laying down and dying over it emotionally is a real stumbling block and a luxury most of us can't afford. It won't change anything, either, except the number of wrinkles on your brow.

To manage setbacks well, rehearse and practice ahead, and keep yourself physically and financially healthy. Be kind to others and get rid of grudges and the like, too. If you do this, then when the bad times roll in and try to smother you, you'll have cultivated lots of resources to lean on and pull you out—and they will. So good management for misfortune is:

1. Mental preparation and education
2. Keeping yourself physically and emotionally healthy
3. Cultivating some spiritual strength (such as trust in God)
4. Close family
5. Good friends
6. Some set-aside resources and savings
7. Looking forward, not backward

What to do when you're walking wounded

A neighbor who works professionally with the homeless, victimized, and abused referred to them once as the "walking wounded." Doesn't that describe us all at times? Young or old, we have aches and pains of the body, and even worse of the heart and mind, that follow us around like a shadow that we cannot, may not ever be able to dismiss. To one extent or another occasionally we find ourselves "doing in a daze."

We've all had and will have yet some blows and losses that if we knew now what they were we couldn't comprehend a way through them, let alone doing anything else while we suffer. I don't like to feel sorry for myself, or to feel overwhelmed, so when things like these reach the "wonder" point, I jot down the option/solution list:

❑ Pray
❑ Bawl
❑ Quit
❑ Run
❑ Yell for help
❑ Roll up in a ball
❑ All of the above

No matter which of these we consider or use, however, the worry is still there to work out, heal, or overcome. Prayer may give comfort, direction, and assistance, but even here **we** are ultimately the agent of action. So this is part of the reality in which we have to do our 1,000 things at once. Sometimes we have to carry 100 worries at the same time. Most of us have done it and will keep on doing it. You can't always take a break when your heart is breaking, or stop things until "I'm well!" Especially if you are active, charitable, and ambitious.

But what about when that "big one" hits—the biopsy results, the divorce, a tragic untimely death—something you cannot fix ever. Even after your best effort and strongest correction measures you are limp and 1,000 things (or for that matter, even one) has no appeal or purpose, what then? There is no place you want to go and nothing you want to do, the brakes are on and you seem stopped. You are stopped. You're so sad you can't even find feeling to be sad with anymore.

We've all lived or are living through this. Of the many things we lean on and grasp for to get out, back, up, on with life again—our faith, our friends, the sheer passage of time—the thing that works faster than anything to stabilize you, to return sanity and a sense of purpose is the things in your 1,000 that are done to serve and fill needs beyond yourself. No matter how you feel, you can still be a strand in the cable of support for others. If you are doing much then you are changing and affecting many other lives. And no matter what your own condition is, **theirs** is still important and you can still contribute to their goals and purposes. If you can't feel good, at least you can make others feel good—that is the best medicine you can take. Keeping ourselves busy in itself isn't the help, it is being busy doing worthwhile things for others who may be walking around with worse wounds than ours.

Tired of getting no respect or recognition?

Acutely weary from forty-four straight days on the road, and often three or four performances a day on TV or in person, I was moaning and whimpering (and I hate whimperers) to Matt Crawford, the professional chauffeur and escort who was driving me to my appointments. Matt had toured with some of the biggest name performers, over the years–Frank Sinatra, Barbra Streisand, Neil Diamond.

Matt told me he toured with Johnny Cash for a long time and that often after a long concert they'd drive all night. They'd get to bed at 2 a.m. and then be up again at 5 a.m., day after day, traveling and then a concert every night. He saw Johnny so tired, so incoherent from strain and exhaustion that "We'd almost have to prop him up before a performance. In fact once we had two doctors standing by backstage, anticipating a collapse before he even got on there. Yet when the time came and the audience was chanting and screaming and yelling in chorus, 'Johnny, we love you!' he'd go out on that stage and for two and a half solid hours put on the most tremendous performance you've ever seen–alert, awake, sensitive. And then afterward go to a hotel or local lounge with the fans and sing and dance and play and drink until dawn, then do it all again! He was truly amazing."

That in a nutshell, folks, is what respect and recognition can do for you. Gadfrey, Evel Knievel jumped the Snake River Canyon just a few miles from where I live. It scares me just to drive over the four-lane bridge where he went off. Yet bravery, inspiration, visions of glory and endorsement money–or whatever–made him want to do it, and indeed he did it. At work, it's that promotion, paycheck, or raise. At war, it's the objective or the medal, and at the county fair when I was young that blue ribbon was worth even risking your life for.

The power of acknowledgment for achievement is so phenomenal, it never ceases to amaze us all. What any of us will do for public credit! And then there is… the homefront. Where we really live and do and develop and spend most of our lives. A place where almost none of this glory exists, that is seldom in the news, and where even a pat on the back every so often is rare! Not only are our own accomplishments neglected, but home is where we bring all our work and business and outside problems. We save up unpleasantness for our home time. It gets all the nagging, bills, and blame; it's the cushion for the bumps and bangs from everywhere else. And no matter how many days, weeks,

months, or years our household performs well, there are no cheering, whistling, and paying crowds yelling, "Hank Homemaker and Connie Cleaner–WE LOVE YOU! More, more!"

At work we get bonuses, wood-grained plaques, promotions, and other perks for managing well. At home, church, on the playing field, in Rotary or Kiwanis, or the library club we get people drawing back and giving us more work and less thanks. Good home and personal management is just not as publicly prestigious as business management. I guess that's why so many good mother managers want and like to get back into the work force. It isn't the money or the musclemen around, it is getting some notice at last for doing something well.

Even the most dedicated of us will wither away without some praise and credit, but I doubt we'll see the day when there are curtain calls for a well-prepared breakfast or a triumphal march for the first ripe tomato from the garden. Attention is usually only focused on the homefront when there is a negative. Mere worthiness isn't newsworthy, so why manage well and break your butt to do something that will never earn you medals or pay or cheers? Because good management is its own reward!

Doing more better enhances the lives of others and your own. And I'm talking about tangible enrichment, not the vain praise of other people. We reap the results of our management skills directly, so we don't need to look for any trophies or certificates, when we do manage to do lots at home or in the community. We grow in experience, character, and stature, and that blesses our lives forever.

Sure, the stadiums and coliseums collect the credit up front, but seldom in the long run. Real heroism is personal, not public. Real credit is for right, an inner comfort for its achiever, not a spectacle for some spectators.

We have to make a decision in our lives as to whose praise are we going to react or respond to. The public's, or our closest family's? We don't have to guess which is the most rewarding.

It is interesting to interview those who have made it to the top, the "successful" and constantly applauded. They have all they could ever want by way of recognition, but their deepest desire and regret is often to savor the success of being wanted and loved on the homefront. Have them tell you about their real fulfillment and they will tell you they want and need their "roots" rooting section above all–family and close friends–not the public. The public will believe anything and clap and cheer for it, even dogs racing and cocks fighting. There are plenty of silent sighs of acclamation at home, if we just listen for them.

Rut relief

"Getting in a rut" may occasionally be a problem in the business culture, but at home, every one of the many lines and roads on the map of making things work, is a potential rut–with little pay or praise, and no relief programs or even pity for the hours and conditions we have to work under. At home, we can and often do find ourselves in "ruts" (and a rut is a lot like a grave, only longer!).

I remember one afternoon, my mother knocked on the door of a neighbor woman who had six little kids, and when the woman appeared, my mother handed her some homemade cookies and bread. Totally ignoring the nice gifts, the woman hugged my mother and said, "Oh Opal, you were heaven sent, an adult voice, a real live grownup!" The woman, who for two weeks solid had communicated only with the little ones, was ecstatic. "Just talk to me!" When I heard this story I was first amused, and then impressed with the seriousness of it. Even doing good things for good reasons, and doing them well, can sometimes put us in such a deep rut that we can't climb out or even see what's on the road ahead. Yes indeed, **routine**, a great management principle, will rut you so quickly and silently you'll never even know you slid in. When something gets old, we feel ourselves oozing away and bogging down, but dedicated to duty we trudge on, ever slower and slower. The biggest trouble with ruts is that no one notices us down there. Others are in ruts too, but they can't see us and we can't see them. If we could, we probably wouldn't be so discouraged, because at least we'd know there were plenty of others in the same position.

Here are the best de-rutters I've come across.

• **Dose of best friend:**

When you're in a rut, a best friend transcends kids, spouses, movies, trips to Australia, and winning the lottery. Always cultivate and manage to keep a close relationship with your best, best friend (who may even be a relative). In just a call or visit, they can be your financial analyst, shrink, doctor, counselor, and minister all rolled into one!

• **Visit a grade school playground for fifteen minutes:**

This will refocus you quickly, remind you of the meaning and purpose and worth and goodness and spark of life. Even the deepest rut will suddenly be a pleasant canyon.

• **Go donate your service–to anything or anyone:**

The only way a human being is ever really satisfied and released is in giving unselfish service to others. Service will not only tow you out of the deepest ruts, but be like a healing balm for any emotional or psychic injury you may have incurred while in there.

"How do I get out of the dumps? Keep busy, accomplish something, set goals, and take steps to get there."

"Every person on earth needs to have one or two close friends to share their thoughts with. If a so-called friend turns out not to be such a good friend, make them an acquaintance and find another friend. On rare occasions, your mate can be your friend, but even then he or she sees a situations through a different gender. An outside point of view is usually just what you need."

"I have a couple of favorite movies that always cheer me up.

Also songs or tapes. I've even made my own 'feelgood' tape, my own personal collection of songs that invariably cheer me up.

I dance twice a week too and that helps a lot. Playing the piano does sometimes too. Or taking a bath. We are lucky enough to have a hot tub and I like to sit in there in the morning when the sun comes up. It's awesome and quiet, soothing.

Reading a good book can help, too. Or calling someone you haven't talked to in a long time."

If all else fails, contemplate this elderly woman's comments:

*"Do you know how I start my day? I get a cup of coffee, sit in front of the TV, and wonder what I'm going to do today. Often I have to look in the paper, or invite someone over, to find something to do. So enjoy your busy times–because someday you won't have them. Kids grow up fast and move away. It's just as bad **not** to have responsibilities, not to have people depending on you."*

Check out your intelligence sources

Remember all the times you reacted or made a decision on what you thought was sound information and it ended up to be just rumor, hearsay, gossip? Your management moves can't be brilliant if they're based on bad data. The best decision made with bad intelligence is doomed. Battles and wars have been lost because a decision was based on an inaccurate "fact." Lives have been lost, marriages ripped apart, hearts broken, health ruined, planes crashed, all

by undependable information. Someone yells "Fire!" "Recession!" "Rain!" "The sky is falling!" or "Buy!" and ten million people fall over each other in the rush to buy, sell, get out, or get under cover. A brother or sister telling a lie got many of us undeserved spankings; many an investor has lost his shirt moving on a hunch or premature piece of "news." I've seen office managers make gross blunders basing their decisions to hire or fire, buy or sell, on some hearsay or salesperson's opinion. I've seen whole states and countries pulled into some bad program because of a legislature swayed by a committee, or a few people's opinions somewhere.

Don't run your life on rumors or manage from murmurs!

How good, how accurate, how complete, how up-to-date are the facts you're using to make a decision? Long before the saying "garbage in, garbage out" came along about the computer, this was true in managing our lives or anything. Look at the dumb things our forefathers did when "**gold**" stories came from California and Alaska. Only a fraction of the people who sought, got, because the stories were just that. Do you believe and base your life, family, business, and management moves on TV, radio, newspapers? "Don't believe everything you hear and only half of what you see" is truer than ever now, because we live in a marketing world. We all survive by selling each other something, anyway we can, using any line of reasoning we can come up with, and creative packaging or convincing.

Uneducated jocks, or someone only smart enough to wax skis, or dumb enough to get a heavy tan, will pose on the cover of a publication and tell us what gas to use, what car to buy, who we should donate to, how to run our sex lives, adjust our furnaces, and spend our money.

Let me give you just a few home-front examples of misfires as a result of misinformation, from our jumping to conclusions or gullibility.

1. We get one of those "best guess" medical diagnoses (from the first doctor we go to, or often just a friend who thinks she had the same thing). For weeks and months we pine and worry and make out wills and tell everyone about it, when we really aren't sure if and when. Almost one-half of the original "diagnoses" we hear that sent people into spending sprees and depression, turn out to be something else in the end.

2. "Do it right from home" pyramid sales schemes, or "get in on the ground floor" investment opportunities. I've met hundreds of people just among my own friends and associates who bit on the basis of that first demonstration or introductory seminar. They bought in, paid out their hard-earned money, then spent more money and lots of time on it, and it fizzled out in the end, costing them self-esteem as well as cash.

3. Selling the house and moving to a different school district on the word and tales of your kids, only to finally find out it wasn't the school or those twelve teachers who were incompetent, it was your kids feeding you some mighty biased information.

4. Panicking and rushing into a job change as a result of things you hear around, see on TV, read in the paper, or learn during a coffee break. I've seen people charge in and tell off a boss of five years, as a result of something some idiot said "he heard from a friend who heard it...."

5. Unfounded neighbor snubbing or bashing. You've avoided or ignored a neighbor for years because another neighbor or two told you those folks were screwballs or what-ever. Only to eventually find out the avoided ones were the real good guys and you've been hooked up with the losers all this time.

6. Picking slow or shifty contractors. Always double check, find out for yourself, start looking early and really look around. Then qualify the information you get. You'll save time, money, and aggravation (if not your mind).

If there's anyplace you need the straight scoop or the nitty gritty on things, it's around the house. There are a few courses in high school, such as Home Ec, and maybe a couple in college that give you a glimpse of what'll go on on your homefront someday, but for the six thousand different happenings that occur every month in running a home, there's nothing out there to bone up on. So you have the option of either working blind, the trial and error method, or studying the materials at hand (magazine articles by the hint and tippers, learning a lesson from others' mistakes on the news, or lapping up those old wives' and husbands' tales). However, there's far more restorative than preventative advice around.

Always check it out. Statistics might be accurate but aren't always pertinent. Avoid reading rubbish; there are racks of not only media-made heroes, but media-made opinions and values. I'd bet you half of the dissatisfaction of spouses with each other's appearance and sexual performance is caused by us believing exaggerated exploits and touched-up pictures of glamorized actors and actresses, athletes and models—more opinions, gossip, and hearsay.

Careful—careful—check your sources and don't buy all the grapevine information sold or given freely to you. Don't join associations or clubs thinking they're your connection to pure intelligence–they aren't.

So where do you get your intelligence reports to keep up with the competition and demands of survival at home? How to raise kids, handle finances, stay healthy, remember birthdays, relax, buy wisely, and clean well? (You knew I'd get cleaning in there.)

There are four areas you can rely and depend on for homefront intelligence:

1. *Observation: Not to copy, but to learn from those who have their house in order. There are families and homes and couples and singles and households that run smoother and happier than others, and that manage to help and serve others, too. Don't be afraid to hang around, become friends with and associate with them, and ask them how they do it. It's amazing what you'll learn.*

You can learn more from a few hours of watching an expert (fencebuilder, housepainter, or experienced mother) than from years of reading.

2. *Yield to your instincts: Someone said, "Success is responding positively to the first impulse you have to do good." Your brain and spirit have gathered material for years and years and sorted and stored it on those hard and soft disks in our head. So we do have 90% of the right answers and all the management power we need right in our mind. Learn to follow your instinct to do what seems right to you. Most of the time, you'll choose right and the best management path. When you hesitate, however, and think and listen to others and fudge and strain too long, you shift yourself into social instead of self thinking and that's never as good as what you come up with yourself. We have a wonderful built-in intelligence source, but it doesn't beg us to follow it. It flashes ideas on the screen and prompts us to act on our feelings of compassion, service and love. When we wait and let our practical and political mentality take over, we often err.*

3. *Believe history: Let me remind you again here that history is a record of wrongs and rights and how things came out under different circumstances with different people. Someone, somewhere, sometime, has done the very thing you want or intend to do, and when history shows whether it was a success or disaster, you have a pretty good foundation of fact to base your thinking and decisions on. People, organizations, and land and weather patterns (like where it floods, or frosts) have all left a great legacy of intelligence to learn from. Look back at it, believe it, and then make your judgment calls. You will be close on most of the time.*

4. *Scripture: God continues to outsmart man, and following just a few pages here like the Commandments, the Sermon on the Mount, the parables, or proverbs will*

give you better results than all the counseling sessions offered and articles and books written. It's so simple, so proven, and so workable, anyone–3 to 103–can understand and apply it.

Good management is self-perpetuating. It nourishes and multiplies itself. As you get better and more skillful at directing the traffic through your life, it sharpens your value system. You spend less and less time on lost causes, and more on the things that really count, which saves wear and tear on you, the environment, and your pocketbook. At last, you have that "control" of things you've been seeking and reaching for.

Sound management with no real effort gradually becomes second nature to you.

Remember all of this... is to HELP YOU LIVE LIBERATED

Good home management–in fact any skillful management–in the end is meant to allow you to **live liberated**, free from the burdens and bondage of circumstances and habit. It will keep you from waiting, wanting, wishing, weighing all the time of your life away. You'll be someone who makes things happen instead of someone things just happen to.

Nobody else has the system or the secret of being a good manager for you... only you do... and only you can. And believe me, you can! Maybe not in one big turnover of a new leaf, but slowly and gradually incorporating some of these principles of good management. No one is in official charge of them, no one doles them out or licenses them, or even keeps track of them. Those principles aren't an enemy or taskmaster either–good management is loving and kind and so will be the end results of your adopting and using it. Don't be afraid or too stubborn or prejudiced to use even some of the suggestions or ideas that previously you have disagreed with (or never even tried), just because other people are doing it. Nobody owns any of the principles of good management! They are all yours, if you want them!

Remember, anything you learn and incorporate at home to help you run things more smoothly and happily will carry over into your job, community activities, and other parts of life to reward and bless you many times over.... What a deal!

DON ASLETT, "America's Cleaning Expert," has written an amazing string of bestsellers. The most popular of all are his guides to dejunking. *Clutter's Last Stand* has sold more than a quarter of a million copies and become the bible of dejunkers everywhere. Its successors, *Not for Packrats Only* and *The Office Clutter Cure*, have just as passionate a following. These books have changed so many lives, helped and influenced so many people, emptied so many attics and closets, that readers just won't let Don stop writing about clutter! They've called, written, e-mailed, faxed, and asked—pleaded—with him for more. So here it is:

Clutter Free! Finally & Forever plus *Clutter's Last Stand*

BOTH books only $20 + $3 shipping.

Is There Life After Housework?

If you've tried the miracle formulas, quick tips, and super systems but still find yourself fighting a losing battle with grit, grime, and grubbies... then this book is for you!

America's #1 Cleaning Expert shares his revolutionary approach that will free you from the drudgery of housework. You can spend 75% less time on housework! Step-by-step instructions on how to clean every area of your home.

216 pages; illustrated; $10.99.

How to Have a 48-Hour Day

The man who helps Americans do their housework 75% faster and more effectively, now shows how to apply that magic to every aspect of our lives! Discover how to get more done and have more fun.

"I just completed this book and it WORKS!"

How to Have a 48-Hour Day is an entertaining, common sense page-turner of a book on productivity by a very productive person. It is not a compilation of research written in a stuffy, academic way, nor is it a hook to buy an elaborate and expensive calendar or software. It is, quite simply, a highly-readable, powerfully motivating book you'll find difficult to put down.

160 pages; illustrated; $12.99.

INDEX

Quantity Discount for your group:

SAVE • SAVE • SAVE • SAVE
How to Handle 1,000 Things At Once

Quantity	Discount	Price
7 to 49 copies	30% Off	Only $9.09 ea
50 to 999	40% Off	Only $7.79 ea
1000+	50% Off	Only $6.50 ea

Please call for more info:
208-232-3535

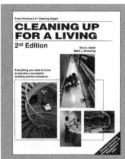

TITLE	Retail	Qty	Amt
Clean In A Minute	$5.00		
Cleaning Up For a Living	$16.99		
Clutter Free! Finally & Forever	$12.99	①	12.99
Clutter's Last Stand	$11.99		
Both of the two books above _(Only)_	$20.00		
Construction Cleanup	$19.95		
Everything I Needed to Know About Business I Learned in the Barnyard	$9.95	①	9.95
How to Have a 48-Hour Day	$12.99		
How to Upgrade & Motivate Your Cleaning Crews	$19.95		
Is There Life After Housework?	$10.99		
Make Your House Do the Housework	$14.99		
Not For Packrats Only	$11.95		
Pet Clean-Up Made Easy	$12.99		
Professional Cleaner's Clip Art	$19.95		
Speak Up	$12.99	①	12.99
The Office Clutter Cure	$9.99	①	9.99
The Professional Cleaner's Personal Handbook	$10.00	1	
			45.92

Shipping: $3 for first item plus 75¢ for each additional item.	Subtotal	
	Idaho res. add 5% Sales Tax	2.25
	Shipping	3.00
	TOTAL	51.17

☑ Check Enclosed
☐ Visa ☐ MasterCard ☐ Discover ☐ American Express

Card No. _____

Exp Date _____

Signature X _____

Ship to:
Your Name _____

Street Address _____

_____

City ST Zip _____

Phone _____

Mail your order to:
Don Aslett
PO Box 700
Pocatello ID 83204

Phone orders call:
208-232-3535

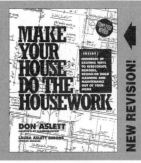

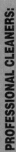

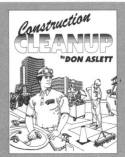
❑ Don, please put my name and the following friends of mine on your mailing list for the **Clean Report** bulletin and catalog.

Name _____

Street Address _____

_____

City ST Zip _____

Name _____

Street Address _____

_____

City ST Zip _____

Name _____

Street Address _____

_____

City ST Zip _____

Name _____

Street Address _____

_____

City ST Zip _____